Conscious Discipline

by
Dr. Becky A. Bailey

7 Basic Skills for
BRAIN SMART CLASSROOM MANAGEMENT

1-800-842-2846
P.O. Box 622407 / Oviedo, Florida 32762
www.beckybailey.com

Loving Guidance

Published by: Loving Guidance, Inc.
P.O. Box 622407
Oviedo, FL. 32762

Printed in the United States of America

Cover Illustration: Cornwell Enterprises
Cover Design: Aardvark Productions
Illustrations: Jeff Jones
Editor: Julie Ruffo Waller, Words of Winter Park, Inc.
Layout: Julie Ruffo Waller, Words of Winter Park, Inc.

Library of Congress Catalog Card Number: 99-066610
ISBN 13: 978-1-88960-911-9
ISBN 10: 1-88960-911-0

The author of this book may be contacted through Loving Guidance, Inc.
Phone: 1-800-842-2846
Fax: 1-407-366-4293
Online at www.ConsciousDiscipline.com

This book is dedicated to
your peace of mind.
It is from your peace of mind
that a peaceful world is created.

Acknowledgements

Every effort is the result of a synergy of experiences and people. This book is no exception. It represents a culmination of over 25 years of work with children and families. For all the teachers I have had the privilege of teaching, I thank you. For all the children who wisely reminded me to be humble, I am indebted. They continually taught me that "one size does not fit all." They also graciously allowed me to learn over and over that there is no right or wrong way to offer guidance. There is only a loving intent or a fearful intent and each gives different results.

The following people have shaped my thinking and I would like to acknowledge them. First and foremost are my Mom and Dad. They are steadfastly encouraging of me. My Aunt Ellen further showed me how it felt to be loved and treasured. Dr. Mary Thelma Brainard opened my eyes to seeing within myself. Dr. Kay Streeter opened my heart to work with others. Kate O'Neil continually sees me as worthy, allowing me to see myself differently. Linda Harris Dragnich supports me by being a wonderful mirror, as well as a dear friend. Donna Bardell and Jan Hrkach give me technical support and loving thoughts, helping me to continually expand on many levels. Finally, thank you to my wonderful staff, Cathy Beverly and Michelle Buckley, who hold me up and hold the fort down.

This book would not be possible without the talents of the following people: Jeff Jones who drew the delightful cartoons. Julie Ruffo Waller of Words of Winter Park, Inc. for her talented editing and layout skills. Gwen Mugmon, Patricia Peadon, Cindy Larrabee, Sarah Simpson, Carolyn Brookes and the faculty of Orlo Vista Elementary School in Orlando, Florida who offered suggestions and feedback for improvements. We all need loving guidance, I am grateful for mine.

If we don't change our direction,
we are likely to end up where we are headed.
—Ancient Chinese Proverb

Table of Contents

Foreword 7
An introduction to *Conscious Discipline* 11
   The *Conscious Discipline* program 14
   Getting started 17
Summary of Conscious Discipline 22

Chapter 1: Composure 23
   Principle 1: Composure is self control in action 25
   Principle 2: No one can make you angry 28
   Skill 1: Changing trigger thoughts to calming thoughts ... 31
   Principle 3: Implement stress reduction activities 34
   Skill 2: Reduce stress 35
   Becoming brain smart 42
   Principle 4: Your job is safety 51
   No time like the present! 52
   Look for these teaching moments 54

Chapter 2: Encouragement 55
   Principle 1: We are all in this together 57
   Principle 2: Contributing builds self worth 68
   Skill 1: Meaningful jobs for all 68
   Skill 2: Service jobs 71
   Skill 3: Noticing children's contributions 71
   Principle 3: How you see others 74
   Skill 4: The "call for help" perceptual frame 76
   Principle 4: We are unique, not special 78
   Principle 5: Some kinds of praise can be discouraging ... 79
   Principle 6: Children need encouragement 84
   Becoming brain smart 85
   No time like the present! 86
   Look for these teaching moments 87

Chapter 3: Assertiveness 89
   Principle 1: What you focus on, you get more of 91
   Becoming brain smart 92
   Principle 2: When upset, you focus on what you don't want ... 95
   Skill 1: Pivoting 95
   Skill 2: Assertiveness 97
   Principle 3: Passivity invites aggression 103
   Skill 3a: Assertive commands to individuals 112
   Skill 3b: Assertive commands to groups 113
   Skill 4: Tell and show 115
   Skill 5: I-messages 117
   Principle 4: Children teach others how to treat them 120
   Skill 6: Tattling as a teaching tool 121
   No time like the present! 128
   Look for these teaching moments 128

Chapter 4: Choices 131
    Principle 1: The only person you can make change is yourself 133
    Principle 2: Giving your power away sets you up to blame 136
    Principle 3: How do I help children be more likely to choose 138
    Becoming brain smart 139
    Skill 1: Two positive choices 141
    Principle 4: Choices build will power and self esteem 144
    Skill 2: Think aloud 146
    Skill 3: Parroting technique 148
    No time like the present! 154
    Look for these teaching moments 155

Chapter 5: Positive Intent 157
    Principle 1: See the best in others 159
    Principle 2: What you offer to others, you strengthen in yourself 160
    Principle 3: Children either extend love or call for help 163
    Skill 1: Reframing 163
    Principle 4: Transforming resistance into cooperation 165
    Becoming brain smart 169
    Principle 5: Negative intent promotes "gang readiness" 172
    Principle 6: See children differently so they can behave better 174
    Skill 2: Positive intent, hurtful actions 176
    Skill 3: Positive intent, hurtful words 180
    No time like the present! 184
    Look for these teaching moments 185

Chapter 6: Empathy 187
    Principle 1: The moment is as it is 189
    Principle 2: Resisting creates upset, upset stops empathy 191
    Principle 3: Empathy is the heart of emotional intelligence 192
    Principle 4: Empathy is not taking on the pain of others 193
    Principle 5: Feel your feelings 202
    Becoming brain smart 205
    Skill 1: Reflecting back what you see 214
    Skill 2: Reflecting back what you feel 214
    Skill 3: Reflecting back what you hear 215
    No time like the present 220
    Look for these teaching moments 221

Chapter 7: Consequences 223
    Principle 1: Mistakes are opportunities to learn 225
    Principle 2: Consequences rely on reflection 227
    Becoming brain smart 228
    Principle 3: Intention determines effectiveness 231
    Principle 4: Deliver consequences with empathy 235
    Skill 1: Natural consequences 236
    Skill 2: Imposed consequences 239
    Skill 3: Class meetings 243
    Skill 4: Problem solving 244
    Principle 5: School-wide discipline programs 247
    No time like the present 251
    Look for these teaching moments 251

Foreword

Many years ago, I was working as a volunteer aide with mentally challenged youth in Tallahassee, Florida. We were on a field trip, swimming at a nearby park. The plan was to swim from ten in the morning until noon, have lunch and return to the school. I had never been on a field trip before, and I was looking forward to helping and enjoying the students. Most of the students adored the water. They delighted in every splash and squealed with awe as they watched me blow bubbles. I felt like I was *some-body*. I thought maybe I would like to be a teacher. At noon the whistle blew, signaling lunch was over. Everyone hurried out of the water, hungry and ready to eat—everyone except Marcus. Marcus stood in the water. He would not budge. A teacher came to the edge of the water saying, "Marcus, come out of the water." He squatted down so the water would roll gently over his shoulders to cool off the top part of his body. The teacher became very upset. She shouted, "Marcus, you know the rules. Marcus, don't make matters worse. Marcus, do you want a candy bar? Marcus, don't make me have to come in there after you! Marcus, we are going to get on the bus and leave you. Marcus, you are being a bad boy." She continued shouting bribes, threats and condemnations to Marcus. Marcus continued to bob in the water.

Finally, the supervisor of the program intervened. He took over and said, "Marcus, you get out of the water this minute or you will not get any lunch!" The supervisor held up Marcus's lunch over the top of a trash can for him to observe. This got Marcus's attention. At this point, I couldn't take it anymore.

I walked over to the supervisor and said, "Stop! There has got to be a better way!"

The supervisor looked at me and responded, "Who are you?"

I answered, "I'm Becky Bailey." Then I continued, "There must be a better way to deal with Marcus."

He said, "Are you a behavioral specialist?"

I said, "No."

He said, "Do you have any degrees in working with the mentally retarded?"

I said, "No."

"Do you have any degrees in education?"

Again, I responded, "No."

With that, the supervisor looked at Marcus and said, "You have until the count of three to come out, or I'm throwing away your lunch. He counted, "One two, ..."

Then I boldly shouted, "Wait! Please, just give me a chance. I think I can get him to come out of the water."

The supervisor looked at me and said, "Okay. You have three minutes."

I walked into the water toward Marcus with no skills and no idea what to do. All I knew was what didn't work, what didn't feel good in my heart. Something in me knew there had to be a better way to reach people. I spent three very unsuccessful, frustrating minutes in the water with Marcus. As I walked out of the lake leaving Marcus blowing bubbles in the water, I passed the supervisor and said, "Take his doggone lunch and throw it away." Heaped in humiliation, I decided I would get the degrees, become a teacher, and find a better way.

That was almost thirty years ago. This workbook, *Conscious Discipline*, is the core of my life's work. I sought to develop the positive skills necessary to deal with any and all discipline situations. As I visit classrooms and schools around the country, I am saddened by the struggles teachers face. We are using old strategies to deal with a different child in a different, high-tech, high-paced, materialistic time. Children and families are faced with enormous obstacles to happiness and success.

I listen to the stories of teachers and their struggles to find joy and meaning in their chosen field. I listen to the children's stories and wonder how on earth they survive with the stressors they face. I ask myself, "If I were living in a violent neighborhood, staying with a friend because my closest family members were in jail, wondering where and when I might get my next meal and watching my loved ones destroy themselves with alcohol or drugs, how many books would I read? How much delight would I find in learning? How much compassion would I have for others?" I know many teachers throughout the world live in conflict. On one hand, they know the hardships many of their children face. On the other hand, they know the hardships these children create in their classrooms. This conflict, unresolved in teachers, hardens the soul. I hear the unspoken cry of teachers—they are shouting as loud as the children. We *all* need help. We need new skills, not quick fixes. We need a way to resolve our internal conflicts and be the person we want children to become. We need to be compassionate without being permissive. We need to be firm without being disrespectful. We need changes that start from within us--changes that heal our souls, strengthen our character and improve our willpower--so we are strong enough to do the same for the children who walk through our doors and in our halls.

Conscious Discipline is this program of new skills. It is for those who know inside them there *is* a better way. It is for those who feel punishing children for their wrong doings will not create change—just a need for more punishment. It is a program for teachers who are ready to teach the whole child through a whole curriculum. It is for teachers who are ready to transform competitive environments into caring school families, troubled children into caring class members and curious children into compassionate, happy learners.

Two prisoners recently escaped from a local jail in my town. Years ago, one of these young men attended an elementary school I now consult with on a regular basis. A third grade teacher had taught this boy and now has his sister in her class. The children came to school after the breakout, discussing the escaped convict. The sister sat hunched over in shame and guilt as she quietly endured harassment by other students. Finally, one boy allowed his comments to be heard, giving the teacher the opportunity to address them. To the children's surprise, the teacher said, "I know Bobby. I was his teacher. He sat right over there." She pointed to a group of desks by the window. She continued, "He was a bright boy. He loved to sing. He also was an excellent artist and would illustrate many of the class books we wrote." The children's eyes were as big as saucers as she continued to talk about the convict in a different light. His sister, Sarah, began to raise her head. The smile that had been missing from her face for days began to form. The teacher then said, "Many beautiful people make poor choices. I have made poor choices in my life. I now think: *Is this choice I am going to make helpful for me and others?*" The teacher was able to take this uncomfortable situation and turn it into a brilliant teaching moment.

This is my hope for you. Each of us are placed in uncomfortable situations. A child may refuse to complete an assignment, call another child names, be aggressive or strike out at you. How do we handle these uncomfortable situations? Are we able to model our highest values or do we resort to threats, lectures and removal from the classroom? Do you find yourself continually removing the most hurting children—the ones already abandoned by their families? There is a better way. Work with this program. The changes you experience will not only help you at school, but with your own parenting and relationship skills with other adults.

We no longer need to walk into our classroom like I walked into the water almost thirty years ago. The skills in this workbook will empower you to handle conflicts with integrity. They work for all children. They will teach your children to be respectful, responsible members of your classroom. Equally as important, you will feel in control of yourself and in charge of your classroom.

I am grateful to Marcus and I am grateful to you. Each person who is willing to make changes becomes the map-maker for others to follow. One of my favorite songs is "Let there be peace on earth and let it begin with me." I know that change starts with me and extends outward. The willingness to make these positive changes is my hope for you. I wish you well.

An Introduction to Conscious Discipline

Believe nothing merely because you have been told it.
Do not believe what your teacher tells you merely out of respect for the teacher.
But whatsoever, after due examination and analysis,
you find to be kind, conducive to the good, the benefit, and welfare of all beings -
that doctrine believe, cling to and take it as your guide.
— Buddhist aphorism

During the past decades, schools have been inundated with social and emotional programs for children. Many schools have adopted information-oriented, single-issue programs. Programs such as Character Education, Values Development, Multicultural Education, Conflict Resolution, Peer Mediation, Violence Prevention, Social Skills Training and Drug Education are utilized. Sadly, many of these programs are implemented in current school climates of individualism and competition, as well as in school-wide discipline systems based on control and compliance. Teachers reprimand and punish disruptive students for infractions of rules, yet teach conflict resolution or "build character" in class meetings. In other words, the programs can end up promoting the "do what I say, not what I do" syndrome so prevalent in our conflicted world.

All teachers demonstrate a code of conduct and a value system. This is done through daily interactions with others. Until we become conscious of these patterns of interaction, we will not be able to guide the morality of the next generation. Most of us model respect when we are calm and life is going our way. However, what happens to our values when we are stressed and life becomes complicated? How do we behave when traffic is backed up, our own children forget their permission slips, our spouse fails to mail a package, the children in our classroom aren't lining up or our school test scores are falling instead of rising to meet legislative standards? What happens to treating each other with respect during these times? Each classroom and school is a culture. It is time to become conscious of behavioral patterns among staff members and among children.

Conscious Discipline is a comprehensive social and emotional intelligence classroom management program that empowers *both* teachers and students. Based on current brain research, child development information and developmentally appropriate practices, the goal of the program is to provide systematic changes in schools by fostering the emotional intelligence of teachers first and children second. Teachers have been put in the impossible situation of teaching students without the necessary discipline skills to address the emotional and social issues of today's children. Teachers must be empowered. They need to know what to do and when. They need answers, new skills and a greater understanding of the behaviors they are seeing and being asked to deal with. A prescriptive "one size fits all" approach to discipline has not and will not work.

Conscious Discipline leads teachers, providers, schools and programs through a process that promotes permanent behavior changes in both teachers and children. The change is from a traditional compliance model of discipline to a relationship-based, community model. The traditional model of discipline is founded on rules. The rules are upheld through consequences. The goal of the consequence is to obtain obedience. Those who are compliant are rewarded. Those who aren't are punished. If disobedience persists, the child is removed from the program or the school. This approach is based in rejection and removal. Fear is the tool used to empower the system as teachers attempt to control children. This system is built on three major premises **1)** it is possible to control others through environmental manipulations, **2)** rules govern behavior and **3)** conflict is a disruption to the learning process.

It is time to become conscious of our beliefs about children, ourselves, discipline and change. Is controlling others possible? If so, what values does it teach? Do rules govern behavior? Or does our connection with others foster our respect for rules? Is conflict an attempt by children to sabotage their own education? Or does conflict reflect children who lack appropriate social skills for getting their needs met? Attempts to control others create a classroom culture and climate that teaches the following values:

Belief	Value it Teaches Children
It is possible to make others change. Failure to make others change equals failure on the teacher's part.	When others don't do what you want, you must try to coerce them.
When we succeed in making others behave, we demonstrate power and authority.	Power comes from overruling people.
When we fail to make someone obey, it's their fault. We are entitled to blame them and others.	If others do not do things your way, they are bad, lazy and deserving of hardship.
If others would change (do as we say), we could be happy and peaceful.	Blaming others for your upset is justifiable. Others are responsible for your behavior.
Children must feel bad to learn how to behave better in the future.	Revenge is the answer to life's upsets.
Conflict is bad, disruptive and must be eliminated.	If you are good enough, conflict will never trouble you.
Fear is the best motivator for learning.	Fear is more powerful than love.

Current brain research indicates fear is detrimental to optimal learning and brain development. No one would think of relying on fear or threats to teach reading, writing or math. Yet we persist on relying on fear when it comes to teaching discipline and guiding children into becoming socially competent members of a group. There is another way. *Conscious Discipline* offers a relationship-based community model of classroom management. The key is a sense of community. The "school family" is the core of the program. The school family is held together through communication skills. These skills are taught during conflict moments in the classroom and through active learning lessons. The goal of the school family is to create problem solvers. If the school family fails to promote pro-social behavior, rules and consequences are implemented to motivate children to use the socially acceptable communication skills being taught. Love, expressed through safety, cooperation and respect, is the tool used to imbue the system with power. Both teachers and students are empowered to control themselves and to relate to others. The system is built on three major premises:

☑ Controlling and changing ourselves is possible and has profound impact on others.
☑ Connectedness governs behavior.
☑ Conflict is an opportunity to teach.

Believing we must *first* change ourselves and model our expectations for others through self-control, creates a classroom climate and culture that teaches the following values:

Belief	Value it Teaches Children
Changing ourselves is possible. As teachers, it is our choice to decide whether or not to change.	You are in charge. You can become the person you want to be.
By choosing to control ourselves instead of others, we feel empowered.	Power comes from within.
When things don't go our way, we will seek solutions.	You are responsibile for your feelings and actions. Your choices impact others.
In order for children to learn to behave properly, they must be taught.	You must teach others how to treat you. You cannot expect them to magically "know."
Conflict is an essential part of life. It presents us with the opportunity to learn a missing skill or let go of a limiting belief.	Conflict is a part of life. Mistakes offer opportunities to learn.
Love is the best motivator for learning and growth.	Love is more powerful than fear. Cooperation is more effective than coercion.

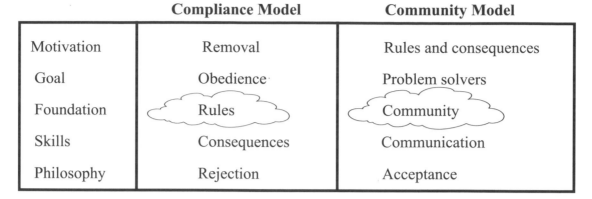

	Compliance Model	Community Model
Motivation	Removal	Rules and consequences
Goal	Obedience	Problem solvers
Foundation	Rules	Community
Skills	Consequences	Communication
Philosophy	Rejection	Acceptance

Times have changed

"Times have changed" is probably an understatement. There have been many shifts in our society, yet none so profound as the shift from roles to relationships. Building steam in the late fifties, society began to enter bold new territory. Collectively, we decided that the roles of the past were too limiting. The roles of husband and wife were explicitly defined. The role of the child (seen and not heard) and the role of the parent (boss) were clearly articulated. Relationships were based on these prescribed roles. As long as everyone performed their ordained duties, all was well. Yet in the comfort and safety of these roles, we felt something missing, especially for those relegated to subservient roles. The powerless groups rebelled. Consciousness expanded in regard to women, minorities, people with disabilities and ultimately with children. People boldly demanded more. We wanted relationships, companions and closeness based on equal worth instead of hierarchically prescribed roles dictating "powerful" and "powerless." Sadly, we did not have the skills or social competence to make these new relationships work. Divorce rates skyrocketed to 50%. Children grew demanding and parents felt at a loss for appropriate action. We placed ourselves on new ground.

We must obtain new tools for new times. As we seek meaningful relationships with one another, we must also learn skills of interaction that promote respect. *Conscious Discipline* is a skill-based program to help teachers build respectful relationships with themselves, other staff members and children.

The *Conscious Discipline* program

Conscious Discipline empowers teachers with the **Seven Powers for Self Control**. These powers allow teachers to draw from within themselves to become proactive instead of reactive in conflict moments. They create a peaceful inner state. From this state, the lens of perception is changed. This perceptual change then promotes behavioral changes. These powers allow teachers to stay in control of themselves and in charge of children. Consciously increasing the emotional intelligence of teachers, child caregivers and parents is the missing piece in efforts to improve schooling in the United States. Self-control must be the first priority of all teachers. Self control is not pretending to be calm in difficult moments. It is the ability to reach out and empathize with others, to accept and celebrate differences, to communicate feelings directly, to resolve conflicts in constructive ways and to enjoy being contributing members of a community. It is the ability to embrace conflict as a teaching opportunity instead of viewing it as a disruption to learning. Each of the seven powers has a slogan to help you remember to use it in conflict situations. The slogans to support each chapter follow:

1. **Power of Perception:** No one can *make* you mad without your permission
2. **Power of Unity:** We are all in this together
3. **Power of Attention:** What you focus on, you get more of
4. **Power of Free Will:** The only person you can *make* change is yourself
5. **Power of Love:** See the best in others
6. **Power of Acceptance:** The moment is as it is
7. **Power of Intention:** Conflict is an opportunity to teach

From the Seven Powers for Self Control emerge the **Seven Basic Skills of Discipline**. These are the *only* skills a teacher needs to constructively respond to any conflict in the classroom. These skills promote a peaceful inner state in children. From this state, children are free to learn, cooperate and help each other to be successful. Each of the seven skills has a slogan to help remind teachers the purpose of each skill. The Seven Powers for Self Control, along with The Seven Basic Skills of Discipline, define the chapters in *Conscious Discipline*. The Seven Basic Skills of Discipline and the slogans that support them are as follows:

1. **Composure:** Becoming the person you want children to be
2. **Encouragement:** Building a school family
3. **Assertiveness:** Saying "no" and being heard
4. **Choices:** Building self esteem and willpower
5. **Positive Intent:** Creating teaching moments
6. **Empathy:** Handling the fussing and the fits
7. **Consequences:** Helping children learn from their mistakes

Teachers who draw upon the Seven Powers for Self Control and use the Seven Basic Skills of Discipline create a classroom climate that models the **Seven Essential**

Life Values and teaches children **Seven Basic Social Skills**. This will happen *automatically*. As teachers change their attitudes and behaviors, so will the children. No separate artificial lessons are needed. This program creates change from the inside out. The Seven Essential Life Values and the Seven Basic Social Skills that become a living component of the classroom culture are listed below:

Seven essential life values
1. Integrity
2. Interdependence
3. Respect
4. Empowerment
5. Diversity
6. Compassion
7. Responsibility

Seven basic social skills
1. Anger management
2. Helpfulness (kindness, sharing)
3. Assertiveness
4. Impulse control
5. Cooperation
6. Empathy
7. Problem solving

The complete *Conscious Discipline* program is displayed in a chart on page 22. *Conscious Discipline* is a reflective self-study workbook that helps teachers discover and use their Powers for Self Control as well as instructs teachers on how to use the Seven Basic Skills of Discipline. Activities, assessments and guiding principles make this a concrete, practical guide. According to brain research, it takes twenty-one days of stimulation to create a new neural network. In other words, it takes twenty-one days to develop new habits. *Conscious Discipline* is a self-study, reflective training program designed to successfully change adult habits in order to change the lives of children. One power and skill is studied per month. The total program lasts seven months. It is designed to be self-directed instead of consultant driven. At the core of *Conscious Discipline* are "teaching moments." Teaching moments are the daily conflicts that occur regularly in schools. Developing a systematic means for socialization of children poses quite a challenge. However, shifting the emphasis of instruction from a solely academic curriculum to a combination of academic and social behaviors does not mean lengthening the school day, eliminating required course work or sacrificing academic achievement. Rather, it requires the dedication of school personnel to seize the opportunities children regularly offer in the classroom, corridors and school playground and to view conflict as a teaching opportunity. When classroom conflict becomes the core of the social-emotional curriculum, children learn valuable social skills, develop self-discipline and self-control, and are able to focus on schoolwork more effectively.

Violence Prevention, Safe Schools, Character Education and Conflict Resolution are not separate curriculums, they are a mind set. They are skills related to social and emotional competence. They are a set of beliefs about human nature and getting along with one another. They rely on the ability to trust, establish relationships, set limits, offer and ask for help in socially appropriate ways, and solve everyday problems in a constructive way. *Conscious Discipline* offers programs for violence prevention, character education, conflict resolution and social skills all in one place. It integrates all these programs into your existing academic curriculum. It's better than happy hour because you get more than just two for one; you get it all!

Getting started

Understanding the demanding nature of teachers', administrators' and providers' jobs, the program is designed with the utmost flexibility. You can proceed through the self-study manual alone, with a colleague, in teams or as an entire staff. If you choose to proceed individually, you will not be able to complete some of the activities in the manual. If you find yourself in this situation, seek assistance for those exercises from your spouse, children, siblings and friends. They will enjoy being part of your life and your growth.

The ideal journey would involve reading the Power of Perception and the Power of Unity before the school year begins. The Power of Perception teaches the skill of composure, a prerequisite for success of any kind. The Power of Unity teaches you how to physically design the classroom to build your school family. The first six weeks of school focuses on these two powers to structure your classroom. Then begin with the Power of Attention and the Skill of Assertiveness. Focus on this power and skill for one month. Continue with a new power and skill each month until you complete *Conscious Discipline*.

As you progress through the manual, you will feel deep changes. These changes will manifest themselves in your life outside the school. You will begin to respond differently to yourself and to others. You will begin to treat yourself with respect. It is a wonderful, empowering feeling. Change does not come without some anxiety. As you learn new skills, old skills die kicking and screaming. Breathe deeply and continue your journey. As you work on one skill, continue to run other facets of your class as you always have. Each month you will be making small but significant changes. By the end of the seventh month, you will be prepared to reflect on how you want to structure your classroom for the upcoming year. Once you complete the program one year, do it again the next year and you will be surprised at your continued growth. Be patient with yourself and enjoy the process. You cannot have an unhappy ending to a happy journey!

A key to using the icons

Golfer = "Skills to learn"

Conscious Discipline is a program about acquiring new skills. Every activity we undertake consists of learning new skills. When we first learned to read or drive a car, skills had to be acquired for success. Each skill to be learned in *Conscious Discipline* is marked with the icon of a golf player. It could just as easily be a tennis racket, basketball, piano keyboard or knitting needle. I want to represent the learning process in this program as that of learning a motor skill. No one thinks they could read a golf manual, then go play like Tiger Woods. No one attends an hour clinic or a week-long golf workshop, expecting to leave at a professional level. At best you would become motivated to want to practice swinging the club and attempting to play the game. Through practice and the willingness to swing and miss more times than you can imagine, you will ultimately become proficient at the game. The same is true of playing a musical instrument or learning a new computer program. These skills are not innate. Neither are the social and emotional skills taught in this program. Often we believe that they *should* be innate. Somehow children should magically know how to behave in certain situations and adults should have all the answers. The fact is our relationship skills, reflecting our social and emotional intelligence, need assistance.

Look for the golf icon and practice the skills. I suggest you make a banner of the skill you are working on for the month and post it in your classroom. Use it as a reference. When I was learning the skill of choices, I had a two foot by six foot banner posted high on the wall above the children's work that read, "You have a choice! You may ___ or ___. What is your choice?" When a situation that lent itself to the skill of choices arose, I would look up and read the words on my banner. It was funny at first. The children would look up at the banner also. Soon many of the children who were reading began using the poster to help their friends make helpful choices. The point is, I didn't need to know everything or have it perfect. I just needed to find a way to practice the skills until they became part of me, just like with reading or driving a car. With practice, persistence and forgiveness, you will make changes. Without practice, persistence and the ability to forgive yourself for not learning fast enough, you will not make changes. The choice is yours.

Lightbulbs = "Activities to do"

The lightbulb icon denotes activities. They signal to you it is time to practice, discover or reflect. The goal of the activities is to synthesize, apply and integrate the information into practice. If you skip the activities, you miss the application of the program into your life, classroom or school. When you avoid doing the activities, you are saying, "I want the information presented to stay on the intellectual level, not on the practical level." In other words, "I am not willing to change at this time." There is nothing wrong with resisting change. The important point is to realize that's what you are doing.

Be conscious of your tendency to skip the activities. Ask yourself, "What am I afraid of?" If you are reading the book and working the program alone, *do the activities*. If you are working with a partner, team or school, *do the activities*. By doing the activities, I hope the lightbulb goes on in your head with insight, clarity and increased confidence.

Brain = "Information to help you become brain smart"

The brain icon represents the brain research that supports the principles presented in the chapter. It is not required that you know this information or even read this section. It is helpful, however, to understand why you are asked to change how you relate to others. Change is difficult. The more information we have to assist the process, generally the more successful we will be. Understanding "why children act as they do" or "why we act as we do," may motivate some people, yet overwhelm others, with unnecessary information. How much energy you direct to learning the workings of the brain and the research that supports this program is up to you. As always, the choice is yours.

Clock = "It is time to start practicing"

The clock icon signifies the end of the chapter and the beginning of your 21-day commitment to the principles and skills presented. "There is no time like the present" is a good phrase to jump-start your mind into taking action. The "action" is to start practicing the items listed in each chapter. The action is to be taken this very moment, not tomorrow or on Monday. The program is about change. Putting off change represents anxiety from within, usually originating from some sense of guilt (I should have known all this before) or fear (I might fail, make a mistake or not be perfect). After the icon there is a list summarizing the chapter and the efforts required of you. Review the list and begin working the program immediately. You may decide to remove the list and post it on your refrigerator at home or in your lesson plan book for work. The way you remind yourself is not important. What matters is that you remind yourself of your task over the next 21 days.

Eyeball = "Look for these teaching moments in your classroom"

Conscious Discipline is a social and emotional program that derives its curriculum from the daily conflicts that occur in the classroom. These day-to-day conflicts are referred to as "teaching moments." Most of us are used to seeing these conflict moments as irritations and disruptions to the learning process. The children who create these moments have historically been looked upon as disruptive, bad, unmotivated and/or mean. We have been trained to ignore or punish these behaviors, hoping they would go away. *Conscious Discipline* takes a different approach to the problem. The program trains teachers to the see conflict in a positive light. Conflicts represent, for the most part, children who are lacking some essential social skill or emotional foundation to be successful. Therefore, the conflict must be seen as a teaching moment. These moments will occur in the classrooms, in the corridors, on the school bus, in the cafeteria and on the playground. They also occur between adults in faculty meetings, in team teaching, and between teachers and paraprofessionals. All conflicts are teaching opportunities if we choose to seize the moment. The eyeball icon is a reminder to look for these behaviors and use them as the core of your social and emotional curriculum.

Eyeglasses = "Look for the ways children present teaching moments to you"

Under the eyeball icon you will see some eyeglasses. The behaviors you are looking for show up in many forms. For example, some children explode in the classroom and become aggressive when upset, while some children implode and become withdrawn. Both the aggressive and the withdrawn children are upset and require our empathy before we can expect further compliance from them. The eyeglasses indicate the various forms these behaviors may take in your classroom. Regardless of form, these are still teaching moments and the skill you are studying will be effective in transforming the moment from resistance into cooperation.

Pen and paper = "Assessments and reflections"

The pen and paper icon signals an assessment. This assessment will help you look within yourself to become conscious of your own upbringing and its impact on your current choices. The assessments will also help you become aware of your current school practices. Awareness is the first step to change. Skipping over the assessment exercises would block your ability to successfully change. Assessments are all placed in shaded boxes for ease in locating them.

Outlined shaded boxes = "Committments"

The shaded boxes hold *Conscious Discipline* commitments. These commitments are designed to help you stay focused and motivated to achieve your goals. If a commitment does not reflect your current thoughts and feelings, simply do not sign it. If it speaks to your heart and you are ready to take a stand, sign the commitment and date it. It will add direction and impetus to your change process.

Did You Know?

☑ Social and emotional skills are essential for the successful development of thinking and learning activities that are traditionally considered cognitive (Perry, 1996).

☑ It is impossible to attain true academic and personal success without addressing social and emotional skills (Langdon, 1996).

☑ Emotion is very important to the educative process because it drives attention, which drives learning and memory (Sylvester, 1995).

☑ Effectively promoting social and emotional competence is the key to helping young people become more resistant to the lure of drugs, teen pregnancy, violent gangs and dropping out of school (Elias et al, 1997).

☑ Competence in recognizing and managing emotions and social relationships is seen as a key ability for success in the workplace and for effective leadership (Goleman, 1995).

☑ Until we acknowledge we are emotional beings and learn to deal constructively with that reality, we will continue to have problems. Emotional illiteracy can ruin families, finances and health (Jensen, 1997).

☑ When the emotional brain is driving the body with anger, there can be little empathy. Empathy requires calmness (Goleman, 1995).

☑ Hope, a positive emotional feeling, was a better prediction of college freshmen first semester grades than were the scores on the SAT test (Snyder, 1991).

Discipline is a lifelong journey, not a technique. Enjoy it!

If you diligently apply the concepts of *Conscious Discipline*, you will be astonished at the results. To reach your destination, you mustn't obsess about the outcome. Instead, enjoy the process of personal growth. Ironically, the less you focus on the desired result (happy, respectful, responsible children), the more easily it will come.

A fable demonstrates this point. A young boy journeyed far from home to study with a sage. When the boy met the teacher he asked, "How long will it take before I am as wise as you?" The sage answered, "Five years." Stunned, the boy said, "That is a long time. What if I work twice as hard?" The teacher then responded, "Ten years." "That is crazy," shouted the boy, "What if I study all day and all night?" Calmly the sage replied, "Then it would take you fifteen years." "I don't understand," said the young boy, "Every time I promise to work harder to reach my goal, you say it will take longer to achieve. Why?" "The answer is simple," replied the sage, "With one eye fixed on the goal, you have only one eye left to guide you on your journey."

Relax. Enjoy this workbook and the process of change. Be willing to let your old beliefs go and let new ideas enter. Do the exercises. Practice using the skills.

Good journey and I wish you well!
— *Becky Bailey*

Summary of Conscious Discipline

Chapter / Skill	Power	Classroom Structures	Value	Purpose	Brain Smart Tips	Emotional Development	Key Phrases
1 Composure Being the person you want children to become	**Perception** No one can make you angry	Safe place, circle time and morning meetings	Integrity	Remain calm and teach children how to behave.	The brain functions optimally in a safe environment.	Anger management is integral for social competence.	**S** - Smile **T** - Take a Breath **A** - And **R** - Relax
2 Encouragement Building the school family	**Unity** We are all in this together	Meaningful jobs, friends & family and ways to be helpful boards	Interdependence	Create a sense of belonging.	Social successes prime the brain for academic successes.	Relationshipss are the motivation for learning.	You did it! You ___ so ___. That was helpful.
3 Assertiveness Setting limits respectfully	**Attention** What you focus on, you get more of	Time machine and instant replay	Respect	Set limits and expectations.	Telling children what to do aligns their bodies with their willpower.	Healthy boundaries are essential for all relationships.	Did you like it?
4 Choices Building self esteem and willpower	**Free Will** The only person you can make change is yourself	Picture rule cards	Empowerment	Empowers children while setting limits.	Choice changes brain chemistry.	Building self esteem and willpower reduces impulsivity.	You may ___ or ___. What is your choice?
5 Positive Intent Creating teaching moments	**Love** See the best in others	Celebration center	Diversity	Create teachable moments especially for difficult children.	Thoughts physically alter cells in the body.	Positive intent improves self image and builds trust.	You wanted ___. You may not ___. When you want ___, say ___.
6 Empathy Handling fussing and fits	**Acceptance** This moment is as it is	We care center	Compassion	Help children accept & process feelings.	Empathy wires the brain for self-control and higher cognition.	Empathy is the heart of emotional intelligence.	You seem ___. Something ___ must have happened.
7 Consequences Helping children learn from their mistakes	**Intention** Mistakes are opportunities to learn	Class meetings	Responsibility	Help children reflect on their choices and change.	The brain thrives on feedback.	Consequences help children learn cause & effect relationships.	If you choose to ___, then you ___, will ___.

Chapter 1

Composure

Being the person you want others to become

Power of Perception

No one can make you angry without your permission

Composure
Being The Person You Want Others To Become

Power: Power of Perception
   No one can *make* you angry without your permission

Value: Integrity

Purpose: To remain calm enough to teach children how to behave by example

Brain Smart: The brain functions optimally in safe environments

Emotional Development: Anger management is integral to social competence

Composure Principles:
1. Composure is self control in action. It is the prerequisite skill adults need to discipline children.
2. Healthy, secure relationships require that we control our own upset. No one can *make* us angry without our permission.
3. Start each day the brain smart way and implement stress reduction activities.
4. Your job in the classroom is to keep the classroom safe so children can learn. The children's job is to help keep the classroom safe.

Principle #1: Composure is self control in action. It is a prerequisite skill adults need before disciplining children.

Begin the *Conscious Discipline* program with a focus on self control. Take a moment to reflect on the Power of Perception. This is the power you will be drawing upon to strengthen your composure. Breathe in and say to yourself, "No one can *make* me angry," then exhale and say to yourself, "without my permission." Do this one more time. The way we choose to perceive a situation dictates our level of upset or composure. The Power of Perception reminds us composure is a choice we can make, regardless of how crazy the outside world appears to be. The icon for the Power of Perception is a star. In any situation, we can choose to be a **S.T.A.R.** This star represents <u>S</u>mile <u>T</u>ake a deep breath <u>A</u>nd <u>R</u>elax.

Self control is mind control. It is being aware of your *own* thoughts and feelings. By having this awareness, you become the director of your behavior. Without self control you may turn your life over to people, events and things. You may go through life on remote control, either unconscious of yourself or focusing solely on what other people think and feel.

Becoming aware of your own thoughts and feelings is a major accomplishment. Most people don't have a clue what they are thinking. Ask them. Usually the answer is, "Nothing." Yet psychologists know and your own observations can confirm that self-talk and inner speech runs continually in our heads. Experts estimate that each of us has more than 77,000 thoughts a day. Where are your thoughts right now? My mind wanders so much that sometimes while reading I realize all I am thinking about is my to-do list. The irony is that I don't know what I have read *and* I don't finish any of my tasks. In effect, my cluttered mind leaves me mindless.

> ## Becoming aware of your own thoughts and feelings is a major accomplishment.

It is time to retrain our minds. We are slaves to our impulses and our insecurities. Building willpower over impulse and insecurity is self control. With self control you are self disciplined. Self discipline will allow you to teach composure by example. It is an essential prerequisite to disciplining children. You cannot teach skills you do not possess.

As I began making the shift from being an unconscious teacher relying on controlling others to a conscious teacher who relied on self control, I was often discouraged by how often I would slip back into discipline strategies that used fear tactics. I became a reactive, screaming nut (as I swore I never would) more often than I care to admit. I had always heard to discipline children you must "be firm but fair, more positive than negative, treat children with respect, hold them responsible for their own behavior, be consistent and predictable, and model self control." Yet I had never learned *how* to do all these fine things. How do you exhibit these shining qualities with children who may act wild, disrespectful and irresponsible? How is an adult supposed to remain calm when a child is screaming, "F___ you!" or shouting, "You can't make me."

Teachers who have mastered self control and model the Skill of Composure, do the following:

- ☑ Focus on what they want the child to accomplish.
- ☑ Celebrate the child's successes and choices.
- ☑ See situations from the child's perspective as well as their own.
- ☑ Creatively teach the child how to communicate her wishes and frustrations with words, and in an acceptable manner.
- ☑ Hold the child accountable to those teachings.

An out-of-control adult cannot do any of these things. Out-of-control adults focus on what they don't want to happen. ("Stop that this minute!") They see only from their own point of view. ("You are driving me nuts!") They also punish rather than teach. ("Go to the office!")

©1999 Loving Guidance, Inc.

When teachers lose control, no one wins.

When you lose self control, you lose your ability to discipline yourself or your children. For this reason self control—the awareness of your own thoughts and feelings—must be your first priority as a teacher. No longer can we have teachers who scream at children to be quiet. No longer can we attribute negative intent to children's behavior yet expect children to respect each other. We can no longer bicker with other faculty members while demanding children use problem solving strategies. It's time that adults begin leading the way instead of simply demanding better ways from others.

The Skill of Composure requires we control our own upset and establish a relationship with our thoughts and our feelings. To touch others, we must be in touch with ourselves.

> **Self control must be your first priority as a teacher.**

Principle # 2: Healthy, secure relationships require that we control our own upset. No one can make us angry without our permission.

"Look what you *made me* do. Don't *force me to* send you to time out. *You are driving me nuts.*" Have you said anything similar? When you resort to these angry exclamations, you send a message to the children that they are responsible for your upset. When you place someone in charge of your emotions, you place that person in charge of you. If you believe long lines drive you nuts, then you have given your power away to a line. If you believe your spouse is driving you to drink, then you have given your power to your partner. If you believe the children are *making you* scream at them, you have placed them in charge of you.

> Whomever you have placed in charge
> of your feelings,
> you have placed in control of you.

Wouldn't you prefer to be in control of your own life? To do so, you must be prepared to control your own upset. Your perception of an experience creates your feelings about that event. Pretend you and I were dating and I brought you roses. As I arrived at the door, you might marvel at how thoughtful I was. If you had this perception, you would probably experience joy at receiving the bouquet. What if I brought flowers again the next night? This time you might think, "What are these for? It's not my birthday." With these kinds of thoughts, you would no longer feel happy but suspicious. Did the flowers make you happy or suspicious? Did I make you happy or suspicious? Or did your thoughts about me and the flowers create the emotions? It wasn't me or the flowers. Your thoughts created your emotions.

Each of us carries an image of how we think the world should work. We are conscious of some aspects of this image and unconscious of others. Do you have an expectation about what constitutes a *good* school? Do you have an ideal for a *good* marriage? Can you picture what a *good* morning would be? You probably have images for all of these, but you don't often think about them. You also have an image of how "*good* children" ought to behave.

We see the world not as it is, but through the lens of our judgments about what is desirable. This lens alters everything. When children or your spouse fail to meet your expectations, you become upset because the world didn't work as you thought it should.

Amazing though it may seem, this is the same reason a toddler throws a fit when you take away the markers she is using to color the living room walls. To the toddler, coloring is what should happen. To you, drawing on walls is not the way things should be done. You both become upset, overcome by the feeling of being powerless to run the world by your own plan. The upset is not *caused* by the other person. It is *triggered* by the other person. Upset is an inside job. You are never upset for the reason you think you are.

You are never upset for the reason you think you are.

Commitment # 1: I acknowledge that when I feel upset it is because the world is not going my way. I am willing to spend some time working on owning my own upset. I no longer want to give my power away to others, then blame them for taking it. I want more control in my life.

Signature _____ Date _____

Anger management is an inside job

Anger is difficult for everyone. Many teachers have felt out-of-control with anger. The first step to learning to control your anger is to find out where it comes from and how it works. Stress and trigger thoughts are two specific elements that always precede an angry reaction. Stress is the gasoline and trigger thoughts are the match that creates the explosion. There is an important reason why stress and anger are so closely related. Except when you are being physically threatened, the main function of anger is to alleviate stress. The stress response in the body emits chemicals (glucocorticosteroids) such as adrenaline and cortisol. At high levels these chemicals are uncomfortable and sometimes painful as the body becomes tense and rigid. Anger can momentarily block the awareness of painful levels of stress. As stress increases, the body feels like it wants to blow. Anger outbursts can act as a quick release valve for overstressed systems.

Think back to a very stressful time in your life. Remember how edgy you felt. If you had noticed your body, it would have felt tight, uncomfortable and maybe even achy. Think also back to a time when you "lost it" with an angry outburst, maybe toward someone you love deeply. Did you feel moments of release, followed later with feelings of guilt and remorse? A child's relationship with stress is the same. Teachers often comment that some children blow up violently and seem to enjoy it. That is the release part of the equation. The next question to ask is, "How was the child thirty minutes or an hour later?" Did she feel remorse, demonstrated by withdrawing behaviors, or did she seem unaffected? The children who appear unaffected are the more troubled children experiencing high levels of chronic stress. Any anger management program *must* include effective strategies for identifying and changing trigger thoughts as well as reducing or coping with stress.

> **Children who seem to enjoy hurting others are extremely stressed.**

Trigger thoughts

Trigger thoughts transform high levels of stress into attacking outbursts. Trigger thoughts distort the situation by making it seem bigger than it is, making children's behaviors seem deliberate and bad. An essential step in anger management is to learn the trigger thoughts most likely to make you mad. Trigger thoughts can leave you feeling helpless and powerless. When you feel powerless, you are likely to blame someone else. Through blame you try to make others suffer for what they have done to you. This is a form of attack. It does not create security in the classroom. You create danger anytime you try to make someone else feel responsible for your upset. Trigger thoughts prevent you from seeing the underlying causes of behavior. As headlines tell of more children killing children, we also read about all the adults who missed the signs that the child was so troubled. The signs are there. Our trigger thoughts keep us blind to them. The research (1996) by Matthew McKay, Patrick Fanning, Kim Paleg and Dana Landis discovered that trigger thoughts could be grouped into three main categories. The categories are as follows:

1. **Assumed Intent:** The teacher thinks the child is misbehaving deliberately to upset her, the classroom or another student.

2. **Magnification:** In the teacher's mind, the situation is much worse than in reality.

3. **Labeling:** The teacher uses negative or derogatory words to describe the child or her behavior.

> **Trigger thoughts blind adults to the real problems of children.**

Assessment: Read the following trigger thoughts. Put a check mark beside the ones that sound familiar to you and may contribute to your anger response. The list is adapted from the research cited previously. If your particular trigger thoughts are not listed, add them at the bottom of the list.

Assumed intent

_____ You are just doing this to annoy me.

_____ You are deliberately defying me.

_____ You are trying to drive me crazy.

_____ You are trying see how far you can push me today.

_____ You are tuning me out intentionally.

_____ You are doing this deliberately to get back at me, hurt me, embarrass me, spite me, etc.

Magnification

_____ I can't stand this one minute longer.

_____ This behavior is intolerable.

_____ You have gone too far this time.

_____ You never listen, pay attention, stay on task, etc.

_____ How dare you speak to me like that, look at me like that, etc.

_____ You turn everything into a power struggle, lousy time, nightmare, chaos, etc.

Labeling

_____ You are getting out of control.

_____ This is just plain manipulation.

_____ You're lazy, malicious, stubborn, disrespectful, ungrateful, willful, selfish, cruel, etc.

_____ You don't care about anyone but yourself.

_____ You're deliberately being mean, cruel, hurtful, a jerk, a smartmouth, etc.

_____

_____

Skill #1: Changing trigger thoughts to calming thoughts

Trigger thoughts can be changed in one of two ways. You can use generic calming self-talk to override them or you can refute them. To calm yourself, you could say, "I am safe. I am calm. I can handle this." I do this for a number of reasons. By saying, "I am safe," I send a message to my brain to turn off the stress alarm system. When I say, "I am calm," I assist my body in relaxing. By saying, "I can handle this," I affirm to myself that I am capable. This allows me to to stay calm so the child knows that the current problem belongs to her and not to me. My job is to help the child come up with solutions to her problem. When the solutions come, the child will feel confidence and success in solving her own problem. This builds character and responsibility.

Refuting trigger thoughts requires you to talk back to the trigger thoughts and perceive the situation differently. You must see beyond the child's behavior and assign a positive intent to the child's actions. For example instead of saying, "She is deliberately doing this to me," you can choose to refute this by saying, "She is just trying to cope with a lot of frustration and disappointment. It is not about me."

> **Commitment # 2:** I understand people or situations do not make me angry, but can trigger my anger. These trigger buttons stem from my own sense of inadequacy and wounds from the past. By choosing to breathe deeply and calm myself, I am able to heal old wounds and be proactive with children. I am ready to own my own upset.
> Signature _____ Date _____

Activity to remove your "buttons" children push

1. I seem to be upset because my trigger _____ (write in the child's name or the event) is _____
_____ (write what has happened).

2. This triggers my feelings of _____(use feeling words).

3. My trigger thoughts that cause this feeling are _____
_____.

4. While upset my inclination is to punish by _____ or get the child to feel bad by _____or to blame_____.

5. I want to feel better. I accept and let go of my feelings _____ (write in the feelings from question 2 above), my thoughts that cause them_____
_____ (write in trigger thoughts from question 2 above) and my need to be right and punish by _____ (write answer from #4).

6. I want to be responsible, happy, and peaceful.

7. What I really want to happen is (use positive words only) _____.

> **Commitment # 3:** I understand that punishment, getting children to feel bad and blame are not solutions but part of the problem. I am now ready to let go of the need to punish, get revenge and blame others for how I choose to feel inside.
> Signature _____ Date _____

8. I am not really upset at this child or situation, but at my own thinking and ultimately at myself, for not knowing what to do and how to help.

9. I take responsibility, not blame, for all my actions, thoughts and feelings in regard to _____ (write child's name and/or situation).

10. I forgive myself and now choose to connect with love instead of my upset. One loving thought I can think about the child is _____.
One loving thought I can think about myself is_____.

11. Thank you _____ (child's name) for teaching me
_____.

*This exercise is modified from the work of Dr. Michael Ryce, Rt. 3 Box 3280, Theodosia, MO 65761.

Below is a sample response to this activity:

1. I seem to be upset because my trigger *Jim* is *continually hitting other children.*

2. This triggers my feelings of *anger and fear.*

3. My trigger thoughts that cause this feeling are: *he doesn't listen, he's seeing how far he can push me, he's acting mean, someone's going to get hurt, he should know better.*

4. While upset, my inclination is to punish by *chastising the child* or get the child to feel bad by *removing him from the group to pay for his crime* or to blame *parents for not teaching him to behave in the first place.*

5. I want to feel better. I accept and let go of my feelings *of anger and fear*, my thoughts that cause them: *He is just acting mean, etc.* and my need to be right and punish by *chastising or removing him so he'll feel bad for what he has done.*

6. I want to be responsible, happy and peaceful.

7. What I really want to happen is *for Jim and all the other children to feel safe and be able to use their words to solve problems.*

8. I am not really upset at this child or situation, but at my own thinking and ultimately at myself, for not knowing what to do or how to help.

9. I take responsibility not blame, for my actions, thoughts and feelings in regard to *Jim*.

10. I forgive myself and now choose to connect with love instead of my upset. One loving thought I can think about the child is *he is really calling for help and doesn't know any other way to interact or connect with others.* One loving thought I can think about myself is *I am not responsible for how he acts, but how I act. I can do this differently. I can stay calm and teach him different ways of behaving.*

11. Thank you, *Jim*, for teaching me *to be more patient and forgiving.*

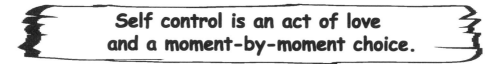

**Self control is an act of love
and a moment-by-moment choice.**

Principle #3: Start the day the brain smart way and implement stress reduction activities.

Start the day the brain smart way. Many children come to school stressed. The transition from child to student is a tremendous one. They have had a busy morning. Some wake up early and attend a before school program. Some prepare their own breakfast and aren't sent off with a hug and a kiss. The same is true for teachers. Teachers transition from being a mother, father, husband or wife, to being a teacher. Some days the transition can be difficult. The following routine to start your day is designed based on current brain research to turn off the stress response, create a favorable emotional climate and help children focus during the transition from home to school. The components of the routine are as follows:

1.   Activity to **unite**
2.   Activity to **disengage** the stress response
3.   Activity to **connect** the children to the teacher and each other
4.   Activity to **commit** oneself to learning

Uniting activities bring everyone together. The pledge of allegiance is a uniting activity. Singing would be uniting. Activities to disengage the stress response involve deep breathing and stretching. Students can be asked to be a **S.T.A.R.** which means **S**mile **T**ake a deep breathe **A**nd **R**elax. Activities to connect pull people together usually through touch or eye contact. Creating a school family song can help children connect. Children may sing the following school family song to the tune of *D'em Bones*:

This is our school family
This is our school family
This is our school family
Wave to a friend (shake hands, pinky hug, etc)

Affirmations have been used with great success in tapping the power of positive thinking. Affirming, "I commit to focus today on smiling to everyone I see," gives the brain a goal. The brain is a goal-directed, problem solving organ. It can be directed from the inside out through commitments or from the outside in through sensory impulsiveness.

Commitment to remember my worth

I

dedicate this time to becoming a more conscious, compassionate person.
WILLingly,
I provide safety, support, and structure for the children in my care.
REMEMBERing always,
that what I offer to others I strengthen in myself.
May I never forget that **MY** worth depends on seeing
the **WORTH** in others.

Assessment: How do you start the day?

In the space below write how you begin your school day. After listing the activities, decide if you are using brain smart strategies. Do you have an activity to unite, disengage stress, connect or affirm? If not, how might you begin to make changes. List one change you are willing to make.

Current beginning of the day: _____
_____
_____

Changes I am willing to make: _____
_____
_____

Skill #2: Reduce stress

Anger management requires teachers to implement stress reduction activities in the classroom. The three skills of stress reduction essential to successful anger management programs are:

1. Being able to *relax*. This must be done on a regular schedule to block the accumulative nature of stress.

2. Being able to *focus*. Tuning into the body to recognize early warning signs of anger is a prerequisite to anger management.

3. Being able to *breathe*. The first thing that happens when you experience a stressful situation is that you hold your breath or start taking short, shallow breaths. Breathing is an antidote to stress.

Activities to relax

☑ **Draining:** Extend both arms out in front of your body parallel to the floor. Have the fists closed palms facing down. Pretend your arms are faucets on a sink. Your closed fists are acting as drains. To open the drain relax your fingers by opening them and making a swishing noise (sssshhh). The noise represents water flowing out of a faucet. Close the drain by tightening your fist. Tighten them so that your arms, neck and face are constricted. Then, open the drain and release with the sound.

☑ **Ballooning:** Show children how you blow up a balloon, then demonstrate what happens when you hold the lips of the balloon and allow the air to escape. Explain this is what we can do with our lungs. Have the children inhale a number of times sucking in air and holding it as if to blow up their lungs like balloons. Then have the children purse their lips and allow the air to escape.

☑ **Pretzel:** Sit or stand crossing the left ankle over the right ankle. Extend the arms out in front and cross the left wrist over the right wrist. Interlace the fingers and draw the hands up toward the chest. Close your eyes and breath with your tongue pushing flat against the roof of the mouth when inhaling and releasing when exhaling. The pretzel shifts the electrical energy from the survival centers of the brain to the reasoning centers. This creates hemispheric integration. The tongue pressing against the roof of the mouth stimulates the limbic system to work with the frontal lobes. Dr. Dennison (1989) discovered this posture releases emotional stress and can help with learning disabilities.

☑ **Stretching:** Stretching helps release tension from muscles and preoccupations from our minds. Stretching can improve circulation, strengthen breathing, relieve fatigue, release nervousness, improve flexibility, promote mental clarity and energize the system. The following activity is based on Martha Belknap's (1997) work and book called *Mind Body Magic: Creative Activities For Any Audience*. It is called **A-B-C Stretching**. It uses the letters of the alphabet to lead children in stretching their bodies.

A = Arching (link your thumbs and raise your arms overhead and arch back)
B = Bending (reach forward toward the floor)

C = Climbing (with both hands, pretend to climb up a wall high onto your tip toes)

D = Dancing (sway your body side to side and spin around)

E = Energize (five jumping jacks)

F = Flip (flip hands from palm up to palm down)

G = Growing (lengthen different body parts - neck, shoulders, arms, fingers)

H = Hugging (give themselves or each other a hug)

I = Inline skating (pretend to skate around the room)

J = Jumping (jump forward, backward and side to side)

K = Kicking (do a Charleston kick)

L = Leap (leap over a pretend stream and leap back)

M = Moving (stretch your fingers wide apart pull them together)

N = Nodding (move the head up and down slowly)

O = Opening (open your mouth and close it, open your arms wide and close them)

P = Patting (pat your knees twice and then your toes twice)

Q = Quivering (shake your whole body)

R = Running (run in place)

S = Swimming (pretend to swim with different strokes)

T = Twisting (keep the feet still and twist your back to look behind you)

U = Up (slowing raise one leg up and put in down, repeat with the other leg)

V = Vibrating (have different body parts shake and relax)

W = Waking up (stretch up high and pretend to yawn)

X = X-ray (take a deep breath, hold still and release it)

Y = Yawning (pretend to yawn)

Z = Zipping (pretend your shoes have zippers, bend over and zip them on)

*Reproduced with permission from *Mind-Body Magic*, © Martha Belknap, $21.95, Whole Person Associates, 1-800-247-6789.

☑ **Extensions to A-B-C stretching:** Have the children create their own stretch alphabet. Have children who have pets watch how they stretch when they wake up. Use animal or pet names in the alphabet as children teach others how their dog stretches. Have children use the alphabet to spell their own names. Have children spell with stretching and guess each other's words. Words such as joy, smile, play, etc., are fun. Post the words on your word wall. Do the stretches to a rap beat.

☑ **Taking a trip:** Brainstorm with the children where they might like to go on a trip. Using guided imagery lead the children on the trip. In the story emphasize actions that require stretching, moving and breathing. If the children decide to go to the zoo, have them stretch like animals, look up to the see the tall giraffes, look down to see the small frogs. If they decide to go to the beach, have them sway like palm trees, reach up to grab coconuts or move their hips like hula dancers. Let your imagination run wild. Ask the children what they would see next, how it would move and how they might move to see it, touch it or taste it.

☑ **Poems for peace of mind:** Some poems lend themselves to the addition of stretching movements. Children also can write their own poems that promote the stretching of the body and encompass deep breathing. Here is one that is modified from Martha Belknap's work.

<u>Poem</u>	<u>Stretching Actions</u>
I bow to mother nature	Do a forward bend
I lift to father sky	Reach up with both arms straight over head
I open to the sun	Open both arms to parallel with the ground
And the clouds going by	Have arms sway overhead
I welcome the rain	Lower your arms to the side with fingers moving
That flows to the sea	Roll your shoulders forward and backwards
I honor the kindness	Tun to a partner and bend to take a small bow
In you and in me	Point to your partner andthen to yourself.

*Reproduced with permission from *Mind-Body Magic*, © Martha Belknap, $21.95, Whole Person Associates, 800-247-6789.

☑ **Extensions to poems for peace of mind:** Children can do this poem with partners facing each other. When children bend to take a small bow encourage them to make eye contact with each other and give a smile. During the last line of the poem the children can give each other a handshake, hug, pinky hug, smile or some other gesture of courtesy and affection.

☑ **Human protractor:** Show the children what a protractor looks like. Tell them they are going to make their bodies into a protractor. Have them touch their toes. This will be 1 on the protractor. Have them reach to the ceiling. This will be 10 (or 20, depending on the grade level of children). Have the children show you the one position. Then have them raise slightly for the 2 position. Each body position represents a number. When they are bent at the waist with their arms horizontal to the floor that would be the position number 5 (if the top number was 10, number 10 if the top was 20). Once children understand the positions you can then give them simple math problems to compute in their heads. For example you might say, "Show me 1+ 2," or "3-1." Older children can do more difficult math problems.

Activities to focus

Focusing is a way of listening to your body with compassion. When we become stressed, overwhelmed, frustrated and anxious the body sends us signals. These signals indicate a change is needed. If we are not aware of the warning signals, we may lose control of ourselves and not be able to make the necessary changes in our behaviors. This is similar to boiling water. When we boil a tea kettle, it whistles to indicate the water is ready. If we ignore the signal, the boiling water can overflow and cause damage.

☑ **Saying hello:** Every relationship begins with, "Hello." Have the children take some deep breaths and say hello to parts of their body. You might start the process this way, "It's time to say hello to our bodies this morning. Reach down to your feet and say: *Hello feet.* Touch your knees and say: *Good morning knees.*" Continue through different body parts. Older children (grades 3-5) can just bring their awareness to their feet and say hello in their minds. They may not need to actually touch the body part mentioned.

☑ **Extensions to saying hello:** Have the children concentrate on relaxing the part of the body they are touching or have them touch their foot to another child's foot to say, "hello." There is no talking. The touch itself represents the "hello" process.

☑ **The body tune-up:** Have the children close their eyes and take a few deep breaths. Help them focus on their own bodies and breathing by guiding them in the following way: "Listen to your breathing. Listen to the air as it goes in through the nose and out through the mouth. See if you can slow your breathing. Breathe in while I count to five. Hold your breath for five, then exhale as I count to seven. Notice the parts of you that are touching the floor, touching the seat. Can you feel your back against the chair? Notice how your hands feel, how your shoulders feel and how your ears feel. Check over your body like you are a mechanic making sure a car is ready to run. If you find any tight parts that hurt, talk to the part by saying: *Hello, it is okay to relax.* If you find a part that feels sad, you can say: *Hello, it is okay to feel sad.*" End this exercise by saying, "Hello brain, get ready to learn!"

☑ **Feel the heartbeat:** Teach children how to feel their heartbeat. This is best done in the neck. Older children can learn to take their own pulse. Have the children discern between their heartbeat when they are calm and when they have exercised. Teach them to breathe to slow down their heartbeat. Do experiments with heartbeat counts while laying quietly, shouting, exercising, listening to calm music and listening to loud, fast music. Have the children chart the results.

☑ **Frustration charts:** Tape a "frustration barometer" on the desk of each student. Select an activity and tell the children to color a bar on the frustration barometer each time they feel frustrated. Bar number one is the least frustrated level. At the end of the activity or lesson have the children tally their frustration number by counting the number of bars colored.

Frustration Barometer

10
9
8
7
6
5
4
3
2
1

Over a period of several weeks, take a frustration barometer for each subject. Young children can have pictures of feelings on their desks instead of barometers. Periodically throughout the day, ask these young children to get quiet inside, to decide what they are feeling and to mark the picture that applies. Ask them questions like, "Can you feel your heartbeat? Can you hear your breathing? Does your chest feel tight? What could we do to feel more peaceful and relaxed right now?"

Activities to breathe

Our mental and emotional states are reflected in the way we breathe. Our breath tends to become rapid and shallow when we feel confused, tense, scared or angry. We tend to hold our breath, downshifting our brain from the cortex (the thinking and learning system) to the brain stem (the fight or flight system), when we first become upset. Conscious slow, deep breathing brings more oxygen to our lungs and our brains for greater clarity, calmness and energy. Breathing is one of the few physiological functions that is automatic, but also under conscious control. It can upshift your brain!

☑ **Belly breathing:** Place both hands on your belly. Practice inflating your abdomen when you breathe in and deflating your abdomen when you breathe out. Breathe in—have your belly go up. Breathe out—have your belly go down. Have children use their hands as a guide to see their bellies rise and fall with each breath. For programs with a rest time, belly breathing is an excellent transition from high activity to a resting state.

☑ **Be a S.T.A.R.:** This activity uses a mnemonic device to remind yourself to release tension from your body and focus your attention inside. Mnemonic devices are memory tools that trigger the recall of information or remind us to do something. Sit comfortably with your eyes closed. Become aware of your breathing. Breathe slow and deep. Listen to the sound of your breathing. Picture the word **S.T.A.R.** Use the letters to remind you to:

S **S**mile
T **T**ake a deep breath (inhale)
A **A**nd
R **R**elax your eyes (exhale)

With relaxed eyes, begin to focus inside on your body and feel yourself radiating *energy*.

S **S**mile
T **T**ake a deep breath
A **A**nd
R **R**elax your jaw

With relaxed jaw, feel yourself radiating *joy.*

   S **S**mile

   T **T**ake a deep breath

   A **A**nd

   R **R**elax your shoulders

With relaxed shoulders, expand your heart, and feel yourself radiating *safety.*

   S **S**mile

   T **T**ake a deep breath

   A **A**nd

   R **R**elax your belly

With relaxed belly, find your center and feel yourself radiating *peace.*

Reproduced with permission from *Mind-Body Magic,* © Martha Belknap, $21.95, Whole Person Associates, 800-247-6789.

☑ **Extensions to be a S.T.A.R.:** With your students, brainstorm situations in which reminding ourselves to be a S.T.A.R. (**S**mile, **T**ake a deep breath **A**nd **R**elax) would be helpful. Compose additional mnemonic devices to stimulate the relaxation sequence. Make up stories in which a person became tense and was ready to be hurtful, but decided to change his or her mind and relax before acting, ultimately choosing to be helpful. Create a book from the stories and illustrate them. Create teams in the classroom to come up with code words to help each other relax. Design signals children can send each other when they see a friend getting "uptight." Research the relaxation sequence by having students take their pulse before and after being a S.T.A.R. and recording the results on paper.

☑ **Inhale, exhale:** Sit in a comfortable position with your feet flat on the floor. Press the top of your head up toward the ceiling as if a string were pulling your head up, stretching and straightening your spine. Tell the children that "inhale" means to breathe in and "exhale" means to breathe out. Have the children inhale and exhale as you read the words below.

Inhale	**Exhale**
Breathe in and	**B** elieve in yourself
Breathe in and	**R** elease your tension
Breathe in and	**E** xpand your vision
Breathe in and	**A** cknowledge your strengths
Breathe in and	**T** rust your intuition
Breathe in and	**H** onor your uniqueness
Breathe in and	**E** njoy your day

☑ **Extensions to inhale, exhale:** Using the same mnemonic breathing format, choose different words to affirm qualities you hope to share with children. You can change the structure of the breathing as demonstrated with the word "friends" below. Have the children think of words they would like to breathe into their classroom. You can change the acronym to anything—family, friends, spelling words or a child's name.

<u>Inhale</u>	<u>Exhale</u>
I breathe in	**F** un
I breathe in	**R** elaxation
I breathe in	**I** ntelligence
I breathe in	**E** nergy
I breathe in	**N** iceness
I breathe in	**D** etermination
I breathe in	**S** trength

☑ **Breathing to the beat:** As you listen to the following words, breathe in on one line and out on the next. Follow each line with two even claps. In this way each line will have four counts—two syllables and two claps.

(Inhale)	**Breathe in**	(clap, clap)
(Exhale)	**The skills**	(clap, clap)
(Inhale)	**That help**	(clap, clap)
(Exhale)	**You learn**	(clap, clap)
(Inhale)	**Be filled**	(clap, clap)
(Exhale)	**With kindness**	(clap, clap)
(Inhale)	**Help others**	(clap, clap)
(Exhale)	**To learn**	(clap, clap)
(Inhale)	**And grow**	(clap, clap)
(Exhale)	**The end**	(clap, clap)

☑ **Extensions to breathing to the beat:** Have the children select or write a poem.

Becoming brain smart

Composure is a reflection of a balanced nervous system. Unbalanced nervous systems demand children strike out, struggling to control stimulation. The stimulation may feel like too much or too little for the child. Some children may tend to be aggressive and some children may tend to withdraw. Regardless, the underlying internal state is one of struggle and conflict. Without the skill of composure, violence is inevitable because a lack of composure leads to either irritability or lethargy. Irritability manifests itself in an attack on others and lethargy indicates an attack on oneself.

Many teachers deal with aggressive behaviors in children. Pushing, shoving, name calling and hostile acts of violence are becoming more common. Controlling aggression requires a nervous system that is correctly attuned to the demands of the outside world. In other words, a balanced nervous system responds appropriately, whereby a hypersensitive nervous system may overreact. A person with an unbalanced stress response system may find themselves experiencing road rage in traffic jams while a person with a balanced nervous system may get upset, but can quickly calm themselves and redirect their frustration.

The first three years of life are the most critical period in human neural development. At this time the child learns whether the world is safe and dependable, learns to speak and recognize familiar faces, and learns how to use behavior to interact with others. The newborn immune system uses early experiences to create a repertoire of antibodies that determine the child's future vulnerabilities to infections. Similarly, during the early childhood years the brain and body use experiences to "educate" the child's naive stress response nervous system. Exposure to stressors during this time may be detrimental to the future sensitivity of the child's nervous system, preventing the ability to delay gratification, overcome impulsiveness, feel remorse, establish closeness, demonstrate empathy for others, establish friendships and maintain composure. A nervous system that is stressed can develop an over-reactive alarm system, undermine a child's motivation to behave in the future, sabotage the child's ability to form bonds with others and prevent the child from being able to focus. How does all this happen?

We used to believe that our biology effected our behavior in a one-way communication pattern. For example, we tended to think that biological events (a stomach ache) lead to certain kinds of behavior (vomiting). We now know that experiences (talking in front of a group) can create biological changes (vomiting). There is a reciprocity between biology and social behavior. Social stress literally has the power to turn genes on and off. Therefore, the quality of our early social experiences will ultimately determine our academic successes.

The brain carefully records and documents our social history. It records our social successes and our failures in the language of neurochemistry. The characters of the language of neurochemistry are neurotransmitters. They are the chemical molecules that allow nerve cells to have a dialogue with each other.

Winning a conflict creates one pattern of neurochemical changes, just as feeling victimized creates another pattern. Being a chronic bully, being a victim or feeling left out, shapes children's perceptions of themselves and others over time. This world view becomes hard-wired into the brain.

Imagine coming home from a two-week vacation to find your mail. Your neighbor has graciously dumped piles of bills, junk mail, letters and magazines into overflowing heaps on your kitchen counter. You are overwhelmed. The first thing you do is sort the mail, a form of triage, separating the junk mail from the priority mail. This is the role neurotransmitters play in our brains in regard to environmental stimulation. These chemical gatekeepers prioritize and categorize incoming sensory data as they hit the neural delivery network. Over time, the neurotransmitters analyze the pattern of our experiences and create a perceptual bias to "see" things a certain way. Using the example above, if all you ever received in the mail was bills, you may feel anxious as you walk towards the mailbox. This anxiety over the mail could increase as the bills increase and your salary decreases. Based on past experiences, we develop perceptions of what is threatening, what is rewarding and what we believe we can successfully achieve. All these perceptions are hard-wired into the brain.

Building a balanced alarm system: Is it safe?

The neurotransmitter that is activated under threat is called norepinephrine. It sounds the alarm system in the brain preparing a child for a flight or fight response. A cadre of neurons based deep in the brain stem (locus ceruleus) sounds the alarm for the entire brain. The alarm signal travels via neurotransmitters to all parts of the brain, especially the cerebral cortex. Once in the cortex,  the messages shoot up through the six layers of the cortex like seedlings grasping for sunlight. Near the outer surface, the fibers split at right angles of each other forming branches across the cortex. This is like a neurochemical internet linking neuron to neuron. Thanks to the elaborate fiber network, a perceptually threatening event is capable of ringing up the entire brain. This is just what you would want in an alarm system.

It is important to have a balanced, well-functioning alarm system. The most sensitive period for the development of a healthy alarm system is the first three years of life. If a child experiences persistent threats and stressors, the alarm system becomes out of balance. It can become oversensitive or undersensitive. Both create tremendous problems to overcome. An oversensitive alarm system sets the child up to perceive threats where there are none. Imagine having an alarm system in your home that went off all the time for no apparent reason. Children with over-reactive alarm systemstend to respond to everyday events in defensive or attacking ways. They tend to fly off the handle when they don't get their way. Impulsive violence is common in these children. They can be set off by other children just "looking" at them. They do not handle disappointment or frustration well and usually act out their feelings.

A nervous system that is chronically stressed may also shut down and become sluggish. An under-functioning alarm system would create a child who struggles to feel. They seem out of control, exhibiting bizarre acts of violence. They ignore real peril and substitute contempt for empathy. It's like having an alarm system in your house that doesn't work. Bizarre crimes occur without warning or signal. You don't even perceive the crimes as bizarre. They seem to be part of living in this particular house.

Norepinephrine Alarm System Pathways

*Reprinted with permission from L. Heimer, *The Human Brain and Spinal Cord* (New York: Springer-Verlag, 1983). NA = norepinephrine.

The motto of the alarm system is "better safe than sorry." A classroom that dedicates itself to safety will help reduce the triggering of the brain's alarm system in *all* children. Psychological safety for children can only exist when adults learn to manage their own anger and learn the Skill of Composure.

Building a reward and motivation system: Does it feel good?

The ability to decide what feels good and is rewarding versus what does not feel good, is wired into the brain. The neurotransmitter that is helpful in developing a reward center in the brain is dopamine. Dopamine is responsible for linking events and actions to positive outcomes, and assigning a value to certain behaviors. Infants and toddlers who receive positive attention learn that listening, looking and interacting with others is of value and produces pleasure. Children who are left alone, experience poor quality daycare or who are only spoken to harshly, learn that ignoring, shouting and disrupting are valued. Their body comes to learn that biochemically, these are pleasurable acts. Every teacher knows one child who seems to delight in disrupting others.

Dopamine sensitizes cells to look for patterns. Strong dopamine levels are reflected in sharper thinking and focused behavior. Children from chaotic, bickering, tension-filled and stressful homes have brains that lower the levels of dopamine in order to survive. Survival in this situation is dependent upon *not* paying attention to the fighting or problems threatening the family.

Dopamine assigns value to behaviors that pay off by promoting survival and enjoyment of social engagement. Such behaviors as fending off intruders are assigned high value in the dopamine system. These behaviors could be fighting back, giving in and running away or they could be assertively dealing with intrusion, helping others and building networks of support and friends. Behaviors assigned a high value by dopamine are the behaviors more likely to be repeated. Some children seem to find pleasure in irritating others while some children enjoy getting along and cooperating.

The dopamine system is jump-started in infancy through social games such as patty cake and peek-a-boo. Children learn to discern the patterns in faces and to extract information. Gentle touch and eye contact become a way of relaying information and creating connections. The bond that is created teaches children that feeling connected feels good and disconnecting from others feels uncomfortable. In doing this, children become motivated to please adults. Children without the motivation to stay engaged with adults are defiant and resist attempts we offer to teach them better ways of behaving. It is as if they just don't care what happens to them.

An unbalanced dopamine system creates problems in life. Like the norepinephrine in the alarm system, dopamine is sensitized through stress and is manufactured in the brain stem. Stress can raise or lower dopamine levels. Stress that produces anxiety raises the level of dopamine. Critically high levels of dopamine create over-vigilant children who are constantly on edge, afraid of making mistakes and seek perfection from themselves and others. An oversensitized reward system such as this results in children who may perceive constructive suggestions as criticisms. Mild suggestions such as, "Why don't you start with problems four and five, they might be easier," can throw a child into a defensive, aggressive, hostile position. They are hyper-focused and vigilant in attending to anything negative. Stress can also lower dopamine levels. Low dopamine produces a sense of hopelessness. This undersensitized dopamine system removes children's ability to focus and attend, leaving them without the motivation to accomplish tasks.

Chronic victimization and bullying have a profound effect on the dopamine system. Bullying raises dopamine levels just as a cup of coffee or other stimulant might. Victimization lowers dopamine, ultimately creating learned helplessness.

A classroom built on respect for one another, that spends time empowering both victims and bullies, will gain academic success by allowing a balanced reward center to mature in children. With a balanced dopamine system children pay attention, are motivated to achieve and treat each other with respect. It all depends on the values demonstrated in the classroom.

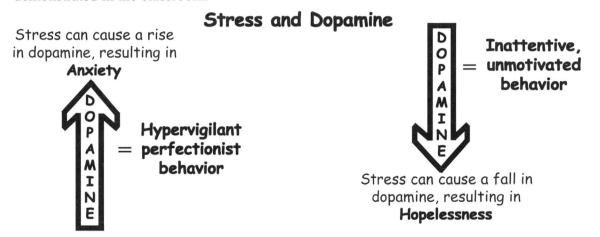

Stress and Dopamine

Stress can cause a rise in dopamine, resulting in **Anxiety**

Hypervigilant = perfectionist behavior

D O P A M I N E = Inattentive, unmotivated behavior

Stress can cause a fall in dopamine, resulting in **Hopelessness**

Building social bonds: Do I belong?

Everyone feels a need to belong, to have positive social interactions and to feel at peace. The neurotransmitter integral to these processes is serotonin. Serotonin works hand in hand with dopamine. The dopamine system works to help us focus, while the serotonin system keeps us from being overwhelmed with too much incoming stimuli. Serotonin is like calming music in the doctor's office. It modulates information. Part of the function in this modulation is to heighten the need for social contact and to reduce the urge to withdraw. Serotonin bonds us with each other. Inescapable stress lowers serotonin. Low levels of serotonin are linked to aggression, obsessive compulsive behavior and depression. Low serotonin leaves a person overwhelmed with life until ultimately the system shuts down with depression or explodes with aggression. About one in every six depressed patients ultimately commits suicide (Hamilton, 1989).

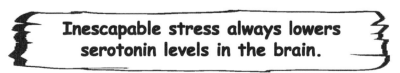

Inescapable stress always lowers serotonin levels in the brain.

A classroom that creates bonds and forms a school family focused on social success supports the serotonin system of all its members. A classroom that is built on children experiencing mastery and feeling a sense of "I can do this, I can be successful" will strengthen the serotonin system. Classrooms based on competition, reward and punishment will lower the brain function of the children who are unsuccessful.

Serotonin

Risks at low levels

- Depression
- Suicide
- Impulsive aggression
- Alcoholism
- Sexual deviance
- Explosive rage

Risks at high levels

- Shyness
- Obsessive compulsion
- Fearfulness
- Lack of self-confidence
- Unduly dampened aggression

*Reprinted with permission from *Chicago Tribune*/ Stephen Ravenscraft, Terry Volpp

Activity to take time to synthesize the brain information

Working with others, hypothesize the answers to the following questions. There are no correct answers, just educated guesses. The purpose of the exercise is for you to interact with the information presented about the brain and the nervous system.

1. Describe behaviors you might see in your classroom from a hypothetical child who possessed the following nervous system characteristics:
    a. Oversensitive alarm system, undersensitve dopamine and motivation system, low levels of serotonin
    b. Undersenstivie alarm system, oversensitive dopamine and motivation system, low levels of serotonin

2. Why might certain children respond differently to classroom teasing?

3. From your current knowledge, brainstorm the messages, types of activities and kinds of class climates children need to be successful. Focus on what would benefit *all* children.

4. Discuss how current policies/practices may destine some children for failure.

The role of temperament and environmental stressors

Some children are born with challenging temperaments. They are more susceptible to stressors. These children are more challenging for parents and teachers. Many parents who have more than one child can attest to the fact they interact differently with each child. Each child and parent create a dance of interactions. This dance to some degree represents the "fit" between the child's temperament and the parent's temperament. Some parents report they are constantly in power struggles with one child while the other child seems more cooperative. The same is true for teachers. The "goodness of fit" is important for the children and the teacher to feel successful during the year.

Understanding temperament

Temperament is the built-in wiring each child has at birth. Temperament is not reflected in occasional behavior. It is a pattern that's consistent over time. A child's temperament can be thought of as a constellation of nine characteristics. Each child will have each of the nine traits in different proportions. The nine traits are listed below. They are adapted from the work of Turecki and Tonner (1985).

☑ **Activity level**: How much activity or restlessness does the child demonstrate? How much spontaneous movement is shown? A child with this trait at a difficult level would be very active, restless and fidgety. The child would rarely slow down and hates to be confined.

☑ **Quality of mood:** How would you describe the child's basic disposition? Positive and happy or negative and fussy? A child with this trait at the difficult level would be cranky or serious. The child would appear to get little pleasure from life.

☑ **Approach/withdrawal:** How does the child respond to new experiences? Does she approach them with enthusiasm or withdraw in fear? A child with a difficult level in this area would be shy and clingy. The child would stubbornly refuse to go forward into new situations.

☑ **Rhythmicity:** How regular are the child's eating, sleeping and bowel habits? A child with this trait at the difficult level would get hungry and tired at unpredictable times, making regular mealtimes and bedtimes a source of conflict.

☑ **Adaptability:** How does the child adapt to transition and change? A child with this trait at the difficult level would be anxious and resistant to changes in activity, routine, food or clothing. These children are inflexible and very particular.

☑ **Sensory threshold:** How does the child react to sensory stimuli such as noise, light, smells, tastes, pain, weather, touch, wet diapers? Does she get over stimulated easily? A child with a trait at the difficult level would be easily bothered by the way food smells, the way clothes feel, the brightness of lights or the loudness of noise.

☑ **Intensity of reaction:** How intense (loud) is the child's reaction to both positive and negative stimuli? A child with this trait at the difficult level would be loud and forceful with all her emotions.

☑ **Distractibility:** How distracted is the child, particularly when upset? Can she pay attention? A child with this trait at the difficult level has trouble concentrating and paying attention, daydreams instead of listening and tends to forget instructions.

☑ **Persistence:** How long can the child remain focused on one thing? When happily engaged in an activity, does she stay with it for a long time? When unhappy, does she persist stubbornly with attempts to get his or her needs met? A child with this trait at the difficult level would be extremely stubborn, wouldn't give up, and might persevere with a tantrum for an hour.

Activity to discern your temperament

The traits above can be loosely divided into easy, moderate and difficult levels. The difficult descriptions have been given. You must estimate from this description what easy and moderate would look like. Rate yourself as easy, moderate or difficult. Also pick a child who you find challenging and rate them as well. Write **E** for easy, **M** for moderate, or **D** for difficult.

Trait	Your temperament	Child's temperament
Activity level	_____	_____
Quality of mood	_____	_____
Approach/withdrawal	_____	_____
Rhythmicity	_____	_____
Adaptability	_____	_____
Sensory threshold	_____	_____
Intensity of reaction	_____	_____
Distractibility	_____	_____
Persistence	_____	_____

Activity to find the goodness of "fit"

When children have one or more traits described as difficult they can be a challenge. This challenge becomes exacerbated if the adult's temperament does not provide a good "fit." For example, a child who reacts intensely in all situations would be difficult for an adult who has a low sensory threshold. Using the data collected in the activity above, reflect upon areas where your temperament would collide with the temperament of the child. Discuss your insights and discoveries with a friend. What plans can you make to increase the "fit?"

Principle # 4: Your job is to keep the classroom safe so children can learn. The child's job is to help keep it safe.

You might be thinking, "What on earth can I do?" There are solutions that are helpful for typically developing children, children with difficult temperaments, children with special needs (ADHD, etc.) and children who have received stressors early in their lives. First, social stress is reduced through aggression (bullying) or through affiliation (a sense of belonging). The choice is ours. We can consciously design classrooms that build a sense of connectedness or we can focus totally on academics and hope that the class "clicks" and connections are found. Second, the critical factor for governing stress levels is safety. We must build our classrooms on safety to help *all* children.

Start the school year off telling children your job description. Repeat over and over, "My job is to keep the classroom safe." Use conflict moments to repeat your job descriptions. You might say, "Michael, pushing Jamey in hurtful. My job is to keep the classroom safe. What could you do now that would be helpful instead of hurtful?" Relate everything you do to safety. You might say, "Leaving materials on the floor is not safe. Someone could trip or that might get lost." These techniques are wonderful but they will mean nothing unless the classroom is psychologically safe for the children. For psychological safety you must control your own upset. Remember, we create danger every time we attempt to make others bad, wrong or responsible for our upset.

Physical structures that support the Skill of Composure

The "safe place" is a center to develop in your classroom as a way to support the Skill of Composure. The safe place provides the opportunity for children to remove themselves from the group in order to become calm, regain composure and maintain control when upset, angry or frustrated. Children come to the safe place in order to be helpful and not hurtful to themselves and others. The choice to be helpful instead of hurtful can only be made when the child is calm. The safe place becomes the classroom center from which your anger management curriculum emerges. For younger children, I like to use a bean bag chair as a safe place. When a child sits in the chair, it's as if the chair is hugging or holding the child. The bean

©1999 Loving Guidance, Inc.

bag is also portable and can be moved around the room. With the bean bag, you might choose to have a small blanket, stuffed animal and lotion. Older students may use their creativity to design their own safe place.

Circle time/morning meeting

Circle time (preschool and kindergarten term) and morning meetings (first through fifth grade term) also support the Skill of Composure. Circle time or morning meetings can be equated to town meetings. They are each a central place where people gather together. Circle time and morning meetings allow teachers and students to start the day the brain smart way (first thing in the morning). The goal is to unite as one group, connect with each other through various greeting activities, disengage the stress response as children and teachers transition from home to school, and commit to a wonderful day of learning and caring for each other.

The morning routine sets the tone for the entire day. It is the first step in the process of developing the school family (described in detail in chapter 2). The circle is the single most important element in room arrangement. It is the focus of the room. It is the heart of the room which contains and loves all who enter. It is the "home" of the classroom. The shape of the circle is chosen because in a circle every child has the same visibility. No one is in front and no one is in back. It sends the message that each and every child is a valued member.

No time like the present!

This month focus on asking yourself, "Do I want to own my own upset and maintain self-control or do I want to give my power away and blame others for taking it?" The choice is yours and the choice never goes away, so you can draw on this power at any moment. To own your feelings, say, "I feel upset (angry, sad, etc.) and it's okay. I am safe and I can handle this." Some of us have sensitive alarm systems or possibly difficult temperaments ourselves. We must retrain our brains to "see" situations differently. We must draw on the power of perception to stay in control of our upset. The power of perception reminds us that no one can make us angry without our permission. When you exercise the power of perception you will demonstrate the skill of composure for children. As you live a composed life, you live your highest values and model for the children the true meaning of the value of integrity. Start practicing the power of perception right now by taking the following steps:

☑   Notice how your thinking creates your feelings. If you are feeling angry, sad or anxious, check to see what you are thinking and where your mind is directed. You can change your internal state by changing your perception.

☑   Listen to how often you blame others. Carefully note any "make me" language. Notice how often you disempower yourself by saying, "Don't make me." Replace "don't make me" statements with "I'm going to." Instead of saying, "Don't make me have to speak to you again," say, "I'm going to have you move to another chair if you continue talking."

☑   When you are upset say, "I feel angry and it's okay." You can also say, "I feel anxious and it's okay," etc.

☑   Affirm to yourself, "When I put another person in charge of my feelings, I put them in charge of me," and take back your power. Ask yourself frequently, "Where is my power?"

☑   Start your day the brain smart way with circle time or in morning meetings. Do stress reduction exercises for yourself and for your classroom throughout the day.

☑   Be willing to see things differently and refute or change your trigger thoughts. say to yourself, "I'm safe. I am calm. I can handle this," during upset times.

☑   Teach children about the classroom job descriptions. "My job is to keep the classroom safe. Your job is to help keep it safe."

☑   Create a safe place in your classroom.

Look for these teaching moments

Students become agitated before they lose control of themselves. This agitation is demonstrated by increases in certain behaviors and decreases in others. Usually when teachers see these types of behaviors they demand children focus and get back on task, instead of doing a stress reduction activity. Children with unbalanced nervous systems respond to these demands by becoming more antagonistic. Watch for the following verbal and nonverbal signals from your students indicating it is time for both you and the child to be a **S.T.A.R.** (**S**mile, **T**ake a deep breath, **A**nd, **R**elax). You might say to the child, "You're safe. Breathe wih me. You can handle this." When you miss these warning signs, send the child to the safe place so they can calm themselves using the strategies you have taught.

Increased behaviors

☑ **Darting eyes** - Children will look here and there with a level of intensity, but with little focus.

☑ **Non-conversational language** - Trying to have a conversation feels like "pulling teeth."   They respond with short answers such as "fine" or "nothing."

☑ **Busy hands and feet** - Students may drum their fingers, rub their thighs, open and close books, tug at clothes, kick the floor and swing or tap their feet.

☑ **Moving in and out of groups -** Children will want to play with others and then leave the group. They may join a group then pull away.

☑ **Off and on task -** Children will start a task, do something else, then return to the task. You will usually see very little sustained attention.

Decreased behaviors

☑ **Staring into -** Watch for all forms of daydreaming.

☑ **Subdued language -** This is similar to the non-conversational language above, plus it is soft and weak. You may have to get close to hear what the child says.

☑ **Contained hands -** Children will take action to "contain" their hands. They put them in pockets, sit on them or put them under their armpits, appearing to sulk.

☑ **Withdrawal from activities -** They pull away from groups, lag behind when walking and choose to withdraw instead of engage in activities and people.

*The above behaviors representing an agitated child were first conceptualized by Colvin (1993) and further developed by Walker, Colvin, and Ramsey (1995).

Chapter 2

Encouragement

Building the school family

We are all in this together

Encouragement
Building the School Family

Power: Power of Unity
We are *all* in this together

Value: Interdependence (caring, sharing, kindness and helpfulness)

Purpose: To create a sense of belonging for all children

Brain Development: Social successes prime the brain for academic achievement

Emotional Development: Relationships, embedded in a school family, are the motivation and cradle of all learning

Encouragement Principles:
1. We are all in this together.
2. Contributing to the welfare of others builds self-worth.
3. How you "see" others defines who *you* are.
4. We are all unique, not special.
5. Some forms of praise can be discouraging. Effective praise relies on describing, not judging.
6. Children need encouragement, especially when they have made "poor" choices.

Principle # 1: We are all in this together.

The Power of Unity reminds us we are *all* on this journey together. The icon for the Power of Unity is children holding hands circling the planet. This icon represents unity. Have you ever sensed that the phone was going to ring and it did? Have you ever been at a traffic light and somehow knew the person in the car next to you was looking your way? Haven't you thought, "I knew you were going to say that." Have you ever wondered how all this happens?

We once excused the phenomena described above as flukes and denied there was anything "real" to them. Now, modern physics has valid explanations for each of them. Modern physics, in its discovery of our unity with all things, has turned our view of the universe, each other, nature and ourselves upside down. Classical physics under Newtonian laws viewed the universe mechanistically. The universe was a series of separate objects moving in empty space. We were separate from each other and from nature. The basic building blocks of the universe were atoms. They were conceptualized as tiny "billiard balls." These billiard balls acted in prescribed ways, operating under fundamental laws. Change was created by friction, collision and force. One "ball" bumped another to take its place or to start a linear sequence of predictable chain reactions. Our job was to learn the fundamental laws of nature and manipulate them to our advantage. Control and domination were the keys to success and survival. Francis Bacon, a pioneer of the scientific method in the seventeenth century, phrased it this way: "Nature has to be hounded in her wonderings, put in constraint, bound into service and made a slave." (Capra, 1991)

The Newtonian view of the world has governed all aspects of society for centuries. Even classroom management reflects this perspective. Each person is viewed as a separate entity, and individualism and competition among these entities is promoted. Children who do not adhere to the rules can be removed without damage to the whole. "They made their bed and now they must lie in it," is justification for removal. Out of sight, out of mind is the answer. Problem students are placed elsewhere so as not to disturb the others. Fundamental laws of controlling human behavior are advocated. Rewards are taught as ways to reinforce behavior and consequences are espoused as ways to eliminate inappropriate conduct. Each person is treated with the same rules and consequences because it is assumed these fundamental principles work for all students. Student behavior is seen as something that must be controlled by the school. Change occurs through *getting* others to comply. Compliance is usually achieved through manipulation, force, domination and attack. Society attacks the accountability of the schools. Schools attack the accountability of parents. Parents attack the effectiveness of the teachers. Teachers attack the wisdom of children who make "poor" choices. Unity is viewed as something that results from competition and/or out of desperation.

Years ago, Miami experienced the awful devastation of Hurricane Andrew. The entire state rallied to support those needing help. During the recovery period, traffic patterns in Miami shifted as populations redistributed themselves. Yet the traffic jams were pleasant. Drivers kindly let others change lanes. Everyone took care of each other. However, as the crisis passed, horns began honking and merging again became impossible. Everyone drove normally—thinking basically of themselves.

Around the same time, the Orlando Magic basketball team made it to the national finals. Unity reigned in Orlando as people joined forces to destroy the Chicago Bulls. Magic bumper stickers plastered buildings and vehicles. Clerks were pleasant and strangers chatted as bonding occurred through the common goal of beating the Bulls. In both these cases, it seems that the stimulus of a common threat (a hurricane in Miami, the Bulls vs. the Magic) prompted unity. If threats were the only effective unifiers, families and schools would need constant crises or "black sheep" to work together. Is this our basic nature? Do we need to rely on threats to build a sense of community?

Modern physics, starting with Einstein, redefined unity not as something that must be contrived, but as our basic nature that needs to be supported. The universe is a vast sea of interconnectedness (Bohr, 1958). There is no separate self, no tiny billiard balls. Einstein hypothesized that we are all made of energy. Later, Faraday and Maxwell replaced the concept of force (billiard balls colliding) with the force field. With brilliant experiments they proved that one packet of energy (quantum) creates a "condition" in the space around it so that other quantum, when present, feels a force. Thus one quantum can influence and create change in another quantum (Capra, 1991). In human behavior this means if you want others to change, you must change first. You must be the person you want others to become. Quantum physics states all things inhabit one giant interconnected force field. The force field is dynamic and in a constant state of change. There are no fundamental laws that govern the field, just possibilities, potential and principles to guide our thinking.

Scientists, frustrated with not having specific answers, have tried to pinpoint nature through various experiments. Repeatedly, nature responds with unanswerable paradoxes. Most of the profound discoveries of the twentieth century have not come from logical thinking, but from intuition. Einstein resolved the paradoxes created by his experiments in his dreams. Quantum physics challenges us to go beyond our five senses to draw on intuition, insight and wisdom. There is no objective reality that we can describe, order, categorize and label. Reality is organized on the inside through our perception of events. How we choose to perceive an event dictates our reponse to the situation. Perception is a chioce, not a fact.

This new (1915 to present) view of the universe requires we let go of false images about human nature. Classroom management must shift drastically. Cooperation, not competition, is the cornerstone of evolution. Classrooms and schools need to embrace community, not as a strategy, but as an ideology that reflects the heart of humanity. Schools must think of themselves as school families, as extensions of the home family. All cultures and all people are simply part of a huge extended family—yours and mine.

Commitment # 1: I am willing to acknowledge that on some level we are all interconnected to each other. This oneness cannot be seen, but is sensed and felt on a deeper level. I am willing to embrace everyone as part of my extended family, thinking of and treating each person as I wish to be treated.

Signature _____ Date _____

School climate

School climate is the heart and soul of the school. It is the essence of the school that motivates children, teachers, administrators and staff members to love the school and look forward to being there each day. The school climate is the mood or feel of the school. If the climate is positive, it helps each person feel self-worth, dignity and importance, while simultaneously generating a sense of belonging to something bigger than themselves. During the last twenty years there has been extensive research to identify factors that make a high-quality school (Rogers and Freiberg, 1994; Fashola and Slavin, 1998). A meta-analysis conducted by Wang, Haertel and Walberg (1998), using 11,000 statistical findings, concluded that the top factors influencing learning include classroom management, school climate, home environment, metacognitive and cognitive processes. It's critical that schools focus on school climate and build a culture of caring. To build a school family you must focus on the following:

1. Physical environment (What the school looks, smells and feels like)

2. Social environment (The health of relationships and interactions)

3. School routines, rituals and rules (What creates "order" in the school)

4. Expectations (The beliefs we carry, both conscious and subconscious about how people learn and change)

Conscious Discipline is a program that is based on building a school family. This positive school climate supports the learning of *all* children, including those termed "at-risk" or "low-achieving." The Seven Powers and Seven Skills will change the school's social environment and uncover the beliefs of school personnel that create inconsistencies between the school's mission and the school's practices. The Power of Unity specifically focuses on changing the physical environment of the school, as well as the school routines and rituals needed to create order and learning effectiveness.

Routines and rituals: The heart and soul of school climate

There is a difference between rituals and routines. Routines are essential for young children. They are the manner by which young children tell time and learn to regulate their internal clocks. In pre-kindergarten children discover that after story time comes center time. They learn to predict what will happen next, feeling empowered to tackle the task. Our brains are pattern-seeking devices. The clearer the patterns are for young children, the more brain enriching is the environment. Routines add predictability and consistency to the program. They are the skeleton that supports the school family, just as our skeleton supports us. Use the following brain compatible practices as a checklist to discern where to begin strengthening your program.

1. For young children pre-kindergarten through first grade, the daily routine is represented by pictures and displayed to be "read" with ease. For older children the daily schedule is posted in writing.

2. Write down all the routines for the day so you can be clear about what you expect your children to do and know. Ask yourself the following questions as a guide:
   a. What do I expect children to do upon arriving to my program? (arrival routines)
   b. What role do children play in management task routines? (attendance, lunch

count, permission slips, cleaning up routines, etc.)

c. What do I expect from children during transition times? (transition routines)

d. What do I expect children to do when lining up? (lining up routines)

e. What do I expect children to do during snack and lunch time or in the cafeteria? (eating routines)

f. What are my hygiene expectations of the children? (toilets, hand washing, nose blowing, teeth brushing, etc.)

g. What do I expect children to do for program dismissal? (dismissal routines)

©1999 Loving Guidance, Inc.

The daily routine displayed in pictures is essential for young children.

3. Systematically teach the routines to your children. Writing down or thinking through all the routines helps make you aware of the amount of sequencing the child is asked to learn and retain. The second step is to decide which routines will be taught first and what strategies will be used to teach them. Many teachers try to make rules to teach routines (Be prepared for class, line up with hands to yourself, etc.). This will not be as helpful as systematically teaching the routines to children.

Rituals: Creating a caring culture

Rituals are not routines. Routines have predictability as their goal. Rituals have connection as their goal. Rituals are sacred spaces designated for togetherness and unity. Holiday rituals typify this. Many gather on Thanksgiving to bond the family in gratitude. Birthday rituals, such as someone preparing your favorite meal, are forms of honoring each other. Rituals are the glue that hold the mosaic of love together. Street gangs create rituals as they bond. These rituals replace the emptiness left by a life void of meaningful connections. We must create healthy rituals with our children, or they will form them the best way they can. The choice is ours.

Rituals are sometimes hard for teachers who are trained so deeply in using every moment to teach cognitive skills. It may be hard to release the "teaching" and begin allowing moments where the number one goal is connection, not learning per se. The good news is that these rituals require very little time and often ask children to apply their academic learning.

Rituals are the most important part of creating a school family. Without them the school family will collapse. Rituals soothe the lower centers of the brain. These centers deal with survival issues. They respond quickly to perceived threat with a flight or fight orientation. Therefore, rituals produce a calming affect on children. This effect is more noticeable on hyper-anxious children. Children who perceive the challenges of school life as threatening will need rituals if they are going to succeed academically.

Ritualization results in a calming effect. This means children count on a specific thing happening at a specific time in a specific way. My mom used to say, "Nite, nite, don't let the bed bugs bite." She always said it standing by my bedroom door just before she clicked the lights. As you and your children create rituals for your classroom, make sure they are ritualized. They must occur in the same location, at the same time and for the same reason of connection. They must occur day after day. Trust is established in this way. Trust is essential for healing the hurting children who have yet to learn the world is a safe place and adults can be trusted to guide them. Without trust, children will not relax their defenses enough to be guided. Without guidance there is no discipline. The following ten rituals will help create a culture of caring:

1. Greeting ritual: Select a location you will stand every morning to greet the children. Greet children both nonverbally and verbally. Nonverbally you can greet with your eyes or with a touch. Verbally you can say, "Hello, good morning, I'm glad you are here today," or "I was waiting just to say hello to you." Part of the greeting ritual may be to have children notice the morning message written by a classmate.

2. School family song: Each classroom can create a school family song or chant. The song or chant can represent the values of the classroom. It is sung daily at specified times. The following represents one school family song. It is sung to the tune *You Are My Sunshine* and is followed by a chant created by Ms. Levitt's 4th grade class in Gainesville, Florida.

You Are My School Family
You are my family,
My school family.
I feel happy,
When we are here.
I hope you know friends,
How much I like you!
(make eye contact and point to a friend)
When we're apart,
I'll keep you here!
(cross hands over your heart)

Ms. Levitt's class anthem (chanted)

"We are intelligent thinkers who persevere through difficult obstacles. We show compassion to people around us. We practice self-discipline in our work and actions. Together we can help each other make the world a better place."

3. I see song (3-6 year olds): The *I See Song* is a ritual of noticing. It allows each child to be seen by the teacher and receive individual attention in a group setting. Young children struggle to get enough attention to sustain them when in group settings. This ritual is one of the ways teachers can began to meet the needs of young children in group care. In the song, the teacher describes what she or he sees the children doing. It is important not to mention jewelry, glasses or clothing. The song is about valuing and seeing the child, not the "stuff." The *I See Song* is sung to the tune of *Frere Jacques*.

"Hello (state child's name)." *Children echo the sentence sung.*

"I see (state child's name)." *Children echo the sentence sung.*

"Her hands are going like this!" (demonstrate hand positions)
Children echo and copy the movements.

"Her legs are going like this!" (demonstrate the leg positions)
Children echo and copy the movements.

4. Connecting and appreciation rituals: At specified times during the day, take time for connecting and/or appreciation rituals. Connecting rituals are those activities that ask children to consciously touch one another and/or make eye contact. Appreciation rituals are verbal and written expressions of caring and helpfulness. Two appropriate times for a connecting ritual are during the brain smart routine in the morning and during the closing rituals at the end of the day. *I Love You Rituals* is a book I wrote which has 79 connecting activities that can be used with young children (3-8 years of age). They also can be sent home for homework and used in your reading buddy program.

5. Absent child rituals: The school family can brainstorm things they could do for a child who is absent. The message to send is, "We noticed you were gone, we missed you and we are glad that you are back." Some classes make cards or poems. Others write songs. The following is an example of a song that could be used. It is sung to the tune of *Frere Jacques*.

"We missed _____." (insert child's name)

"We missed _____." (insert child's name)

"Yes we did! Yes we did!"

"Glad that _____ is back" (insert child's name)

"Glad that _____ is back' (insert child's name)

"Now we are all together."

"Now we are all together."

63

6. Welcome new child rituals: I have frequently said teachers are always pregnant, they just don't know when the next child is coming. With the increased mobility of our society, children leave and enter new schools frequently. These life transitions need to be marked with accepting rituals. The rituals can be developed by your class. One second grade classroom made t-shirts at the beginning of the year. Children decorated the t-shirts with their hand prints. Extra t-shirts were made with all the children's hand prints in case a new child enrolled and joined the class. When the new child came, the t-shirt was presented during a welcoming ceremony the children had designed.

7. Moving child rituals: Just as children come, they also leave. Rituals are needed to mark the transition as children move to new schools. One first grade class decided that they would make a goodbye video for the child leaving. Similar to the process done at weddings, children in the class had the opportunity to say something on camera and take video footage of the school and classroom.

8. Life change and holiday rituals: Life changes include birthdays, deaths, graduations, the births of new siblings and losing teeth. Most classrooms mark these transitions in some way. Design a series of fun and/or reassuring rituals for these occasions. If you include holiday rituals make sure you cover diverse cultures and how they celebrate holidays.

9. Closing and goodbye rituals: As the school day draws to an end, another critical transition occurs. Children end their time as students and teachers end their time as teachers. Many teachers end the day with a report from the Kindness Recorder (a classroom job suggested on page 70) and a song. Each child is then personally sent off with a goodbye. One kindergarten teacher says to each child, "Tomorrow I will see your smile, crocodile," and then gives a hug. She has a different saying for each week of school.

10. Testing rituals: With more and more emphasis placed on testing, testing rituals are needed. In one school, the principal took each fourth grade teacher a single rose one week before the test. In front of the class, the principal presented the rose and said, "Mrs. Luther, you have worked hard all year teaching these students. They are ready for the upcoming test. You can relax knowing you have prepared them well." In the same school, kindergarten children wrote "you can do it" notes to the older students and held a parade two days before the test. A second grade teacher involved parents by asking each family to write a note to their child. After the test, each child was presented with a "you did it" certificate and the note from home.

All cultures create rituals. The classroom is a unique culture with different ritual styles. There are many different ritual styles, some of which are no more reassuring than the "have a nice day" offered by the bored and tired clerk at the gas station. To be successful, your class rituals must be authentic expressions of togetherness and joy. The following are different ritual styles seen in the classroom. What kind of rituals are promoted in your school? What type of rituals do you have in your classroom?

1. **Minimized rituals:** These rituals are not emphasized in classrooms. Academic achievement is the goal. Little attention is placed on the whole child, specifically social and emotional intelligence. Holidays and birthdays might be celebrated if time permits, work is complete and children have earned the break by demonstrating good behavior.

2. **Interrupted rituals:** Interrupted rituals usually indicate some sort of crisis has taken precedence. This crisis could be the changing of teachers, long-term illness of a teacher, push by the county or state for some immediate program changes, natural disasters, bomb threats and other human tragedy.

3. **Rigid rituals:** Rigid rituals are created by the teacher and are done the same way year after year regardless of the make-up of the classroom. Trying something new is out of the question. Everyone's role is highly prescribed. The emphasis is on doing the ritual correctly instead of connecting. Those who do the ritual "wrong" are excluded from the activity. Playfulness and humor is not allowed.

4. **Imbalanced rituals:** Imbalanced rituals occur in classrooms that conduct only a small range of rituals. Instead of having good morning rituals, absent child rituals and the like, only holidays and birthdays are emphasized. Sometimes the curriculum is driven by holidays with October being Halloween and November focusing on Thanksgiving, etc. These rituals usually represent one ethnic heritage.

5. **Obligatory rituals:** Obligatory rituals exist because they "should," because they are the thing "to do." They lack true connecting. The good morning song is sung as a way to start the day, not as a way to connect with each other. Teachers do not stop to talk about the meaning and importance of caring and helpfulness. Rituals become more like routines that mark the passage of time instead of meaningful events. A tired flight attendant routinely saying goodbye to 300 people exiting a 747 is an obligatory ritual.

6. **Authentic rituals:** Authentic rituals are true, positive rituals. They are jointly created by the teacher and students. They evolve out of the "family" framework presented by the teacher. Authentic rituals are flexible, capturing and reflecting the current needs of the members of the community. They offer a sense of continuity and connectedness throughout time. Authentic rituals bring cohesiveness to the school family. They emerge and dissolve with spontaneity and delight. They are sacred space that is set aside to put the classroom values into action. They help establish relationships, mark life changes, heal wounds from hurtful experiences, voice the beliefs of the "school family" and celebrate life itself.

Building the school family

Conscious Discipline advocates creating a positive school climate through the creation of the school family. "School family" is a term that represents a way of thinking about the school environment, not just the activities within it. In today's world, it is urgent that we reach beyond the domain of the self. Children and adults need to feel a sense of belonging. The Power of Unity teaches us that what we offer to others, we experience within ourselves. Essentially this means giving and receiving are one. Teaching children to care for others allows them to care for themselves.

The teacher's job in the school family is to keep the classroom safe. The student's job is to help maintain classroom safety. In order to do this, children must learn ways to be helpful. The school family is the vehicle we use to teach children their job description. Through the school family we teach helpfulness by having each student live in and contribute to a climate of caring.

Certain physical classroom structures/centers are suggested to support *Conscious Discipline*. Each of the structures is paired with a power and a skill to support the learning introduced in each chapter. Ideally, as you begin this chapter you will have a safe place and circle time/morning meeting from chapter one already in practice in your classroom. The specific structures to support the creation of the school family are:

- ☑ Friends and family board
- ☑ Job board
- ☑ Ways to be helpful

The complete list of all the centers suggested in the *Conscious Discipline* program are listed below. Each classroom center ultimately contributes to the creation of the school family, however, different centers are introduced in different chapters.

1. Safe place (chapter 1)
2. Circle time/ morning meetings (chapter 1)
3. Friends and family board or book (chapter 2)
4. Job board (chapter 2)
5. Ways to be helpful board or book (chapter 2)
6. Time machine/instant replay (chapter 3)
7. Picture rule cards (chapter 4)
8. Celebration center (chapter 5)
9. We care center (chapter 6)

Physical structures that contribute to the creation of the school family

The three physical structures suggested to aid in creating a positive school family are **1)** the friends and family board or book, **2)** the job board and **3)** the ways to be helpful board or book.

☑ **Friends and family board or book:** The purpose of the friends and family board or book is to display pictures of children and their families. Either a bulletin board or a book may be used for this purpose, depending on your needs and preferences. Displaying pictures helps students get to know one another and feel secure at school. For young children, family pictures can be taken on home visits. When the children arrive at school, the pictures are already up on the wall (or in the book) and become a point of security and conversation. Older children can bring in pictures of their families or have pictures taken at school. In schools where poverty prevails or there are other obstacles to obtaining home pictures, disposable cameras can be sent home with children. It is vital that you include your own family on the board or in the book. Additional pictures of classroom friends (principal, speech language pathologist, police officer, etc.) are displayed as the school family grows. The friends and family board or book is not static, it evolves through the year as children come and go. It provides a visual, concrete way for young children to register friends versus strangers in the school setting.

A friends and family bulletin board is a positive visual classroom tool, but teachers may elect to create an equally effective friends and family book instead. Once the pictures are assembled in a book, students may check it out, bring it home and "read" it to their families. This allows the children to introduce their school family to their home family.

☑ **Job board**: Each child in the classroom should hold a job. These jobs contribute to the functioning of the classroom and the health of the school family (see page 68 for a sample listing of jobs). The purpose of the job board is to manage the administration of the jobs. One way to administer jobs is to place library card pocket holders on poster board. On each pocket put a picture of the job to be performed or write the job's name (depending on the grade level). Have the children glue a photocopied picture of themselves on the top of a popsicle stick. Each stick will be placed in one of the pocket holders. The sticks are rotated each week as children change jobs. At the beginning of the year you must teach each job. This takes time and lesson planning. Integrate the teaching of these jobs into your language arts program. After the initial lessons, each child teaches the child whose job it will be the next week.

☑ **Ways to be helpful**: The purpose of this bulletin board or class book is for the children to illustrate concretely what behaviors are expected in the school family. The teacher announces her job description the first day of school. "My job is to keep you safe." She then announces the job description for the students. "Your job is to help keep the classroom safe." From this point on, the teacher works with the students to teach them their job description. The children decide what it looks like, feels like and sounds like to be helpful. The many forms of helpfulness can be drawn and displayed or written about in a class book. It is essential for teachers to help the children be specific in this process. Many children may suggest ways to be helpful such as being nice, sharing and taking turns. The teacher must then guide the children into specific scenes so they know the language and actions to use to be nice, share and take turns.

Principle # 2: Contributing to the welfare of others builds self-worth.

It is important that children believe they are meaningful contributors to the school family. Meaningful contributions build self-worth and value within the individual. An internal feeling of self-worth extends outward as kindness, sharing and cooperation. During a drought in Florida, we had severe fires. Firefighters from all over the country came to put them out. As the fires came closer to my home, the smoke became intense. I decided to volunteer at a nearby shelter to help those who were forced to evacuate their homes. While at the shelter, I felt I was truly helping others. The feeling of being blessed poured over me. I knew I was worthy, valuable and loved. Many of you have had similar experiences. You know the feeling. Children *need* the opportunity to be significant contributors to others. Children can undertake the following activities to facilitate this sense of contribution:

1. Meaningful classroom jobs for all children

2. Service projects for the school or community

3. Noticing children's contributions to others

Skill # 1: Meaningful jobs for all

Years ago, farm life depended on children doing their share of the labor. Without their contributions, the family wouldn't survive. As society has changed from agriculture to manufacturing to the information age, children can be perceived more as a burden than an asset. News headlines calculate how much money each child will cost to raise. The numbers are staggering. It seems our priceless children now have a price tag.

Many parents, rushed for time, find it easier to do home tasks themselves or to hire help rather than systematically teach and rely on their children. Chores are often seen as a way to earn money instead of being the child's contribution to the household. Schools and homes must support children's contributions. Every child in the classroom needs to have a job. If you have 28 children you will have 28 jobs. To discern what jobs are needed do the following:

1. Make a list of all the class management task you do. From this list decide which jobs can be turned over to children.

2. Involve the children. Ask for their assistance in coming up with the jobs and creating the job board.

3. Think in terms of the social and emotional support children need and enjoy. The following social and emotionally supporting jobs may spark your thinking:

☑ **Morning message writer:** This person's job is to write (or draw a picture of) a welcoming and encouraging idea for children to see as they enter the classroom in the morning. The message may be, "Welcome to school. I hope you have fun today," or "I am glad you are in my class." Encourage children to speak from their hearts. Older students might look up inspirational quotes to share.

☑ **Greeter:** This job involves greeting children as they enter the classroom. It also includes extending a helping hand. The greeter(s) might say, "Good morning! Do you need help with your backpack?" The greeter(s) might also decide to give handshakes, pinky hugs or thumb touches to students as they enter class. Have the class brainstorm ways they would like to be greeted in the morning. Write down all these wonderful ways and put them in a jar or box. The person(s) who are the greeter(s) can reach in and select the greeting method for that week or day.

☑ **Kindness recorder:** This person's job is to notice all the kind acts children perform during the day. At the end of the day, the kindness recorder can share with the class all the wonderful times of caring demonstrated during the day. The anecdotes can be bound at the end of the year and called, "Ms. Bailey's Fourth Grade Random Acts of Kindness." For young children the teacher will notice the acts of kindness and record them on paper. At the end of the day a child's job is to be the "Blue Bird of Happiness." When the teacher shares the kind act, the child with a Blue Bird Puppet flies over to the children involved and "kisses" them on the arm.

☑ **Encourager:** This person's job is to notice children who are feeling discouraged with school work, home life or friends and to offer encouragement. The encouragement can be a poem, a note saying "Hang in there," a card, a pat on the back or a class heart that says, "We care about you and want you to succeed." Older children can write and design encouragements as part of their language arts program. Younger children can draw pictures and hand out prefabricated hearts. The teacher might say, "Marissa seems very sad. Her grandfather was visiting and he went home today. Whoever is the encourager for this week, start thinking about how you could let her know we care."

☑ **Visitor greeter:** This person's job is to greet the guests that come into the classroom. The child must be taught what to do and say through demonstration and role play. One classroom had a guest book for visitors to sign. When I arrived at the door, I was greeted and presented with the book. I felt like I was entering a bed and breakfast. Upon leaving I wrote a wonderful note back to the class. You might have your visitor greeter do the following:

1. Walk over to the meet the visitor.

2. Say, "Welcome to Mrs. Grier's class. My name is _____."

3. As the other person introduces him or herself you may want to teach to the child to extend his or her arm for a handshake and say, "Nice to meet you."

4. The child would finish the interaction by asking, "How may I help you?"

☑ **Absent child committee:** This job can belong to a person or a committee. Their job is to do something for an absent child that communicates the message, "We noticed you were gone. We are glad you are back." This could be done by making a welcome back card, song or poem. If the absent child has a phone, a message could be left wishing him well.

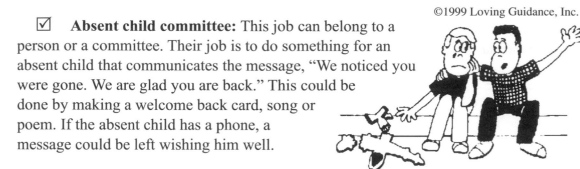

☑ **New child buddy:** This person's job is to be the buddy of a new child who enters the school and classroom. The job of the buddy can be developed by the class. Ask the children, "How would it feel to enter a new classroom with no friends and not knowing anything about the school?" From this discussion develop a list of duties the buddy would be involved with. The buddy's job is a big one and occurs randomly throughout the year. This job could be role played with a friend and video taped for later reference. The following are example duties:

1. Sit next to the new child and introduce him to others

2. Give the new child a tour introducing the office staff, media specialist, etc.

3. Walk in line with the new child and play with him at recess

4. Sit together at lunch, showing the new child the necessary rules and procedures

5. Help the child learn the daily routine, secure necessary supplies and understand how we treat each other in the school family

☑ **S.T.A.R. person:** This person's job is to lead the class in breathing activities. This could be done as part of the brain smart start of the day routine. At the specified time, the S.T.A.R. person holds up a star-tipped wand, puts on star sunglasses or uses some other star symbol to signal the class to **S**mile, **T**ake a deep breath **A**nd **R**elax. Throughout the day the S.T.A.R. person may also help to calm students who appear tense or frustrated. The S.T.A.R. person might walk over to the upset child, use the star symbol and say, "Breathe with me. You can do it (or some other encouraging statement)."

☑ **The sprinkler:** The sprinkler has the job of sprinkling children with kindness. Younger children will delight in a wand with streamers hanging from it to symbolize and support this job. The children must be taught what may and may not be sprinkled on one another. Practice helpful phrases such as, "Way to go," "You did it," and "Good for you." Children may also sprinkle appreciation in the form of joy, happines, humor, peace, brain power, safety and love. The wand may be used to help the child *sprinkle* these positive emotions over fellow classmates.

☑ **Wish well leader:** This student's job is to lead the wish well activities that are created by the class or the teacher. Wishing well is something the class might do when a fellow classmate is sick, upset or going through a difficult time. The wish well leader can help the class sing the lyrics below to the tune of *The Farmer in the Dell.*

"We wish you well!
We wish you well!
All through the day to day-
We wish you well!"

Skill # 2: Service jobs for the school or community

Each child at age four or older can offer service to the school or community. Young children up through grade three would offer their services to the school. Older children in fourth and fifth grade can offer their services to the community. Examples of services include the following:

1. All children can work to keep the playground and school clean.

2. Children of any age can decorate the cafeteria including making centerpieces to bring more humanity to the eating rush.

3. Younger classrooms can be cheerleaders for older children who take part in state and national tests. They can write or draw supportive letters, cheer during a parade and/ or make banners reading, "You can do it. We love you."

4. Older children can do community projects. Efforts like adopting "grandparents" at a nursing home or helping the homeless may be explored. These efforts may be tied to curriculum areas, adding meaning to academics.

Skill # 3: Noticing children's contributions to others

Proactively notice all helpful, kind acts children perform. Notice these acts privately to the child and publicly to the class. During the first six weeks of school notice at least ten kind acts per day. The following are suggested steps to get started:

Step 1: Start the statement with the word "you" or the child's name followed by the word "you."

Step 2: Describe in detail what the child did.

Step 3: Relate how the child's behavior helped someone else or the entire class. You can do this by continuing the sentence with, "so _____."

Step 4: End with a tag by saying, "That was helpful! That was kind," or "That was caring."

Some "noticing" examples follow:

- ❤ *"You* put all the puzzle pieces back into the box *so* who ever plays with the puzzle next will be able to be successful. *That was helpful."*

- ❤ *"Jim, you* held the door open *so* all the children could walk through without bumping each other. *That was helpful."*

- ❤ *"You* noticed that Becca needed some paper *so* you offer her some of yours. *That was thoughtful."*

- ❤ *"You* helped Maddie practice her spelling words, *so* she would be more successful on the spelling test. *That was helpful."*

The basic formula:

You _____ so _____ . That was _____ .

Activity to notice acts of kindness

Notice the following acts of kindness. Verbalize your answers out loud.

Situation 1: Kyle and Kimberly were working on a turtle project. Kimberly was getting frustrated with reading. Kyle helped her with some of the more difficult words.

Situation 2: Arlie was upset and could not find her carpet square to sit on for story time. Marcia waved to her and said, "You can sit with me."

Situation 3: After working on some math problems, Alexander cleans up his table space and organizes his materials.

Situation 4: Mrs. Ramsey, the principal, walked into Mr. Hall's third grade class. Some students saw her and said, "Be quiet, get busy, it's the principal."

Helping children know their unique gifts

To feel adequate, children must feel useful and know their contributions count. Help children feel useful by identifying their talents and suggesting ways they might use them to contribute to the classroom. In addition to noticing kind acts do the following:

1. Notice children's assets and strengths. Ask children to share them with the others.
"Malcolm, you sound out words when you don't recognize them when reading. This is a skill that is very helpful in reading. Would you share how you do this with Tyree?"

"Ashley, you take time to plan how you are going keep your work together. That is called an organizational skill. Would you show Melissa how you organized your notebook and see if she has any questions or needs help with hers?"

2. Have the child represent or symbolize their strengths and assets. Helping children write or draw about their strengths and assets is helpful. Avoid activities that say, " I am special because ___." Special implies *better than, less than* categorization. Instead of focusing on being special, use sentence stems to encourage children to think about their strengths and helping others. Use phrases like, "One thing that I do in school that seems easy for me is ___," or, "I enjoy doing ___ most of all in school." Then have the students list two ways they can help others with their strengths.

3. Structure the environment so that children's gifts are made public. At circle time, class meetings or during whole group instruction, bring someone's sharing of their gifts to the attention of the group.

"Today during reading, Malcolm, who sounds out words he does not recognize when he is reading, helped Ashley with a word. That was very kind of him."

"On the playground, Ashley, who is has the ability to double jump rope, showed two of her friends how they could be successful. That was very helpful."

4. Have a bulletin board that is titled, "I can help." Have pictures of the children helping one another, pointing out each one's contributions to the success of the school family.

Activity to notice children's strengths

Notice the following children's strengths. Discuss how you would share these publicly with the school family.

Caroline: Oh, how she loves to spell. She meticulously copies all the words off the word wall into her personal spelling dictionary. She is able to spell or look up most any word she needs. Carl struggles with spelling.
To Caroline you say: "_____
_____."

If Caroline chooses to help Carl, you could highlight this by saying to the school family: "_____
_____."

Chance: Chance would rather draw than do almost anything. His drawings are exciting with much detail and color. Joseph struggles with writing and with illustrating his work.
To Chance you say: "_____
_____."

If Chance chooses to help Joseph, you could highlight this by saying to the school family: "_____

_____."

Principle # 3: How you "see" others defines who you are.

Activity to define "Who am I?"

Write the answer to the question, "Who am I?" in the space below.

_____

_____

_____

_____

Each of us have tried to answer the question, "Who am I?" The answers usually have not been helpful. We have tried to answer this question as if we were a separate self, some kind of self-sufficient island. In doing so, many of us answer this question by making a list of attributes about ourselves or the duties we perform. Answers to the activity might include such attributes as woman, husband, mother, teacher, happy, competent and loving. Each list we create presents us with an unanswerable paradox. If you believe yourself to be loving, are there not times when you are unloving? If you believe yourself to be competent, are there not times when you make mistakes? What happens to your self-worth then? Usually, we feel inadequate. If you listed a role in your answer such as teacher, you probably are carrying within you some definition of a "good" teacher and a "bad" teacher. What happens to your sense of worth when you perceive yourself as not being the "good" teacher, husband or mother? The dilemma is, "how do I know who I am without setting myself up to feel inadequate?"

It appears we cannot answer the question, "Who am I?" as a seperate self because that is not the truth of the situaion. Our answer is found in our interactions with others. It is about unity. The way we perceive and interact with each other answers, "Who am I?" in one of two ways: "I am worthy," or "I am unworthy."

> How you answer the fundamental question
> "Who am I?"
> colors how you interact with everything.

Modern physics yields two profound truths that impact the way we define ourselves and each other. The first of these is the idea that there is no objective truth out there. We give value and meaning to situations based on our past experiences and beliefs. Teachers have an awesome responsibility to be conscious of the meaning they attribute to life events. The manner in which a teacher "sees" others, events and situations trains his or her students to "see" these things in the same way.

The second fact we learned from modern physics is that the energy from which we are created is not seperate from the energy of others. In the material world, when you give something (a toaster) to someone else, you no longer possess it. The other person has the toaster and you do not. In the realm of thought and energy, however, the same does not apply. You can't give your negative (or positive) thoughts to someone and expect to be rid of them. Thoughts, unlike toasters, never leave their source. Your thoughts of others effect both you and them. In essence, the manner in which you perceive others ultimately defines who you are. The judgements, criticisms, complaints, engouragement, joy and love that we think we are giving to others, are really gifts to ourselves.

Teacher A who "sees" a child off task walks over and comments, "What should you be doing? You better get busy. You will never finish if you continue to waste time." This teacher did not err in what she said. Her mistake came in her perception. In "seeing" the child off task, the teacher saw the child acting "poorly." The teacher discourages herself first by seeing what was not good enough, then discourages the child. Both teacher and child are left feeling disconnected and inadequate. In addition, the teacher has trained the other children in the class to view this child in the same way.

Teacher B "sees" a child who needs help focusing. She walks over and offers assistance by saying, "What would help you, right now, to focus on your math problems." Seeing the child's behavior as a call for help, this teacher feels encouraged to act on the child's behalf and extends this encouragement to the child. In addition she trains other children in the class to see "misbehavior" not as a sign of "badness," but as a call for assistance. As children start seeing misbehavior as a call for help, they have the opportunity to respond in a helpful manner, contributing to the classroom community in positive ways. These actions build self-worth as children become meaningful contributors to the welfare of others.

Self esteem is not earned through accomplishments, it is created each moment in how we "see" other people. If we see others as lacking, we will feel inadequate ourselves. In this state of inadequacy, we experience ourselves as isolated and separate. Loneliness and pain separate us from our real selves. Life seems empty and fears are projected. Teachers project their fears daily in comments such as, "If you don't do your work, you will fail. Is that what you want?" Seeing the best in others creates worthiness within ourselves. From this state of worthiness, we experience ourselves as connected to others. A sense of belonging permeates our being, safety is present and love is extended to others. A teacher who has maintained her own self-worth is capable of extending love. She might say to the same child, "Looking at all those problems can be overwhelming. What help do you need to get focused?" A caring school family cannot be created unless teachers change their perceptions of misbehavior and conflict.

Skill #4: The "call for help" perceptual frame

Teachers play a significant role in how children perceive each other and view misbehavior. We have a choice. We can teach children to see others who act inappropriately as bad and deserving rejection, or we can teach children that these behaviors are a call for help.

At any given moment, children feel safe and are extending love to others through helpful behaviors, or they feel threatened and are calling for help by acting in hurtful ways to themselves or others. The teacher's response to misbehavior dictates the perceptual framing of a call for help. The following are examples of teachers who either respond to a child's call for help, or respond by unconsciously labeling the child as bad.

Situation 1: Jeb is sitting at a table with four other children. They are independently working on journal writing. Jeb is not focused on his writing. Instead, he is talking and fidgeting.

"Call for help"—A two-step teaching process:

Step 1: Empower the students to respond to Jeb
The teacher, noticing the disruption, walks over to the table. She speaks first to the children who seem distraught with Jeb's behavior by saying, "Is Jeb's talking and fidgeting bothering you?" If the response is affirmative, the teacher then teaches the students how to assertively communicate with Jeb. She might say, "Tell Jeb: *I can't focus on my work when you are talking. Please be quiet!*"

Step 2: Using a "call for help" perceptual frame
The teacher then turns to Jeb. She might say, "Jeb it seems you are having a problem focusing on your journal. What could you do to help yourself stay focused?" The teacher could also elicit assistance from the children by saying, "Jeb seems to be having a problem staying focused on his journal. What could we do to help him?"

Labeling the child bad—A one-step process:

Step 1: Deliver the prescribed consequence to Jeb
The teacher notices the disruption and walks over to the table. She speaks firmly and directly to Jeb. She might say, "Jeb, what should you be doing? Focus on your journal writing. You are bothering the other students at your table who are trying to work. Go put your name on the board."

76

Situation 2: Eileen enters the classroom with a grumpy look on her face. Her body language is tense. She bumps into several friends, knocking them out of the way. The friends scream for the teacher.

"Call for help"—A two-step teaching process:

Step 1: Empower the students to respond to Eileen

The teacher responds to the situation by going to the children who were bumped and saying, "Eileen walked by you and bumped your arm. It seems like it really hurt."

The girls shake their heads "yes," so the teacher continues. "Did you like it?"

"No," responds Cara.

"Then tell Eileen: *Watch where you are going. It hurt when you bumped me.*"

Step 2: Using a "call for help" perceptual frame

The teacher then turns to Eileen and says, "Eileen you seem grumpy and tense this morning. Something frustrating seems to be bothering you. What could you do that would help you feel better?" The teacher could also elicit assistance from the children in the classroom by saying, "Eileen seems to have had some frustrations getting to school this morning. What could we do to help her feel better?"

Labeling the child bad—A one-step process:

Step 1: Deliver the prescribed consequence to Eileen

The teacher hears the cries of the children and goes directly to Eileen. She looks at her disapprovingly and says, "Eileen it is not nice to push your friends. You must pay attention to where you are going. How would you feel if they bumped into you like that? Go take a slip from the box. If you get two more slips you will not have recess today."

Children "call for help" in many ways.

©1999 Loving Guidance, Inc.

Activity for "call for help" practice time

In the following situations role play a "call for help" perceptual frame. Use a partner if possible.

1. Michael is walking very slowly in line. He is holding up others who are getting very irritated with him.

2. Several children are working on a collaborative project. Mariah is constantly grabbing items from others.

Principle # 4: We are all unique, not special.

Our true nature is unity. We are all unique expressions of a common energy. There are no two people that are alike, just as no two snowflakes are identical. Our interconnectedness does not erase our individuality, it accentuates it. Each person contributes to the whole. The body is a good metaphor to use for the simultaneousness of unity and uniqueness. All cells in the body are interrelated. Yet each cell does specific, unique functions to support the whole. Without each and every one, the whole organism suffers. We are cells in the body of humanity. Our job is to discover our unique gifts and offer them back to the whole.

Systems created out of separateness create a sense of inadequacy as people strive to be better than or avoid being less than others. This competitive striving creates the winners and losers, the "haves" and the "have nots." From this sense of striving, individuals seek to be special. It becomes important to wear the right clothes, say the right things, own the right house and stand out to be noticed. Our western culture is based on being special instead of truly connecting with others. Specialness is based on comparisons instead of contributions. By dividing people into "better than" and "less than" categories, equality is impossible. Schools who seek to embrace diversity, yet have systems relying on specialness, will not obtain their goals

Most schools have competitive, individualistic orientations. Children who are special are rewarded. Specialness was thought to contribute to self-esteem. Children were asked to be special helpers or write in their journals, "I am special because ____."

> **Unworthiness creates a need to be special. Specialness prevents people from feeling connected to one another.**

Programs that seek to help children feel special teach children to focus on *getting*. Children are taught certain ways to gain attention or recognition. Adults operating under the same mind-set are also attempting to *get*. We seek to get material goods, get children to behave, get our needs met or get approval as a way of filling up the emptiness inside ourselves. Programs that are based on the Power of Unity teach children to focus on *giving*. Giving of yourself is valued as children learn to offer their unique talents for the benefit and enjoyment of others.

How can we build classrooms so children choose to connect with each other with trust and respect instead of through excluding others and creating common enemies (you are not my friend, we don't like the girls)? The answer comes from drawing on the Power of Unity. To access the Power of Unity, we must relinquish the need to be special. This runs against the grain of American culture, which places a premium on being special. To become conscious of your desire to be special, ask yourself, "Do I want to be special (right) or do I want to connect?" This is an important question, *especially during conflict.*

If you must feel special to feel worthy, you will push the children to be special. One way this is done is with the words we choose to praise and encourage the children. When we judge children instead of noticing their efforts and accomplishments, we train them to seek being special. It's as if we carry around a yellow highlighter at all times. With this imaginary marker we highlight for children those aspects of life we deem important for them to notice. One teacher might say, "Good job, Beth. You got a 100 on your spelling test. Three more of these and you will earn a spelling pencil with your name on it." Another teacher might say, "You did it Beth. You worked hard on your spelling, and look what you did. You can now help others with spelling difficulties." Both responses celebrate the child's success, but they do it in different ways. The first response fosters specialness, the second one supports connecting. The choice is ours.

Principle # 5: Some forms of praise can be discouraging. Effective praise relies on describing, not judging.

You will get more of the behaviors on which you focus. Your focusing also determines what you strengthen within yourself and others. It's like holding a flashlight in a dark room. Where you point your flashlight illuminates what you value. By shining the beam on certain things, you teach children what to value. If you focus on children being "good," you teach them to please others and seek specialness in order to feel worthy. If you focus on children being "bad," you teach them to rebel and seek to be special through negative attention. If you notice their strengths, you teach them about their abilities. If you encourage their contributions, you teach them the importance of sharing their gifts with others.

How many times have you heard a young child say, "Look at me!" A million times? If they are standing on one foot you might hear, "Look! I am standing on one foot." Children want and need to be seen. Your attention by itself is greatly encouraging and your role as teacher is quite straightforward. You can respond simply with, "Yes, I see you," and the child will be tickled. If you want to foster their brain development, you can expand on their words and say, "Wow! You are balancing on one foot, your arms are like this (demonstrate arm position for the child)." All you really need to do is describe the efforts or accomplishments you see from the child. In effect, you become the child's mirror.

Children ask to be seen, not judged. Teachers tend, though, to judge instead of see. The child might say, "Watch me on the monkey bars." Instead of replying, "Look at you climbing so high," you might say, "Good job, honey." Instead of describing the child's action, you have judged it. If you replace seeing with judging too often, the excited 4-year-old child who shouts, "Watch this!" grows into an anxious 8-year-old who asks, "Is this okay?"

How we praise children can be encouraging or discouraging. Yet new skills cannot be developed unless we change ourselves first.

Assessment # 2: Do you tend to encourage or discourage yourself?
Remember, how you treat yourself is how you will treat children. The following quiz can help you pinpoint your major tendency:

1. During the course of one day, I tend to focus more on (a) my assets and strengths or (b) my liabilities and weaknesses. _____

2. Typically, I (a) accept myself as I am or (b) focus on what is wrong and needs changing (too fat, too thin, too something). _____

3. I generally talk to myself in a way that (a) builds self-confidence or (b) makes me feel confused or inadequate. _____

4. During the day, I tend to think about (a) what am I currently doing or (b) what should I be doing. _____

5. I notice (a) my efforts and improvements or (b) that I am not where I think I should be. _____

6. As life unfolds I tend to (a) notice the turn of events without the need to judge or (b) judge events as good or bad. _____

If you scored high on (a)'s you are probably good at encouraging yourself. If you scored high on (b)'s, you may tend to discourage yourself. If you routinely discourage yourself, you will unconsciously discourage your children. Change begins with you, then extends to your children. Today, decide to be kinder and more encouraging toward yourself. To begin the process of change, say the following aloud:

☑ I will recognize and honor my own contributions to a better world.

☑ I am willing to allow myself to make mistakes and I will forgive myself.

☑ I will encourage myself to be successful.

☑ I will accept praise other people offer me because I know I am a valuable human being.

☑ I will suspend my judgments long enough to allow my love to shine through.

> **If you change how you treat yourself,**
> **you will naturally change**
> **how you treat your children.**

Ways praise can be discouraging

One important way to encourage children is through praise. It seems logical that praising children would foster enhanced self esteem. However, two decades of research have shown that this is not always true. Research indicates the following kinds of praise can inhibit a child's self esteem.

☑ **If you use too much general, all-encompassing praise, you can unduly burden the child. General praise can make a child feel pressured to live up to unrealistic standards.** Perhaps you grew up hearing, "She is so sweet and *always* helpful." Hearing this again and again left you with two options. You could try to live up to the perfect image that adults had bestowed upon you or you could "act out," hoping that your parents would see the real you. Be careful with such comments as, "Shantelli is a wonderful student. She *always* turns her work in on time and pays attention."

☑ **If you use praise that relies on value judgments too often, you teach children that "good" equals "pleasing others" and "bad" equals "displeasing others."** Many of us praise children by imparting value judgments such as, "What a great job." Praise based on judgment has side effects. **1)** Children can become judgment junkies. They will ask, "Is this good? Did I do this right?" with anxiety. **2)** It trains children to focus on what others think of them as opposed to listening to their own inner wisdom.

☑ **If you use praise that focuses on how you think or feel about the child's behavior, you teach your child to seek approval.** If you praise your children to *make them* behave well, your praise will backfire because it is a form of getting, not giving. You might say things like, "I like the way Jeb is sitting quietly," or "I like how Tiffany is working on her math," in hopes of future good behavior or influencing others to straighten up. But that tells the child, "I like you when you please me." She may conclude, "I am worthy when I am pleasing to others and not good enough when others are displeased."

☑ **If you praise children only for successful, completed tasks, you teach them that effort does not matter—only accomplishments matter.** Many adults give children commands, only offering praise when those commands are carried out. When the toys are all put away, you may say, "Good job." Imagine how boring a football game would be if the fans sat in silence until their team made a touchdown. Football fans don't act that way—they scream throughout the game to encourage the players. If we treated our children like we treat our favorite athletes, my guess is that we would create a true home-court advantage. Children need to learn that the process counts as much as the product. You must focus on your child's efforts and the small steps they take, not only on the touchdown.

> **If you praise only finished jobs that are done well, you teach your child to devalue effort.**

I'm sure many of you recognized the examples above and the long-term outcomes of misguided praise. You may know people who desperately seek the approval of others or seem obsessed with winning. Perhaps you have friends who strive to be perfect and deny mistakes they make. Maybe you fear being who you truly are for fear of losing the love of your dearest ones. We can praise differently and produce different long-term outcomes. There are two major ingredients necessary to effectively encourage children. **1)** Notice your children instead of being a judge. **2)** Link your child's actions to enjoyment and satisfaction instead of tangible rewards.

Trying to pump people up from the outside doesn't build self esteem on the inside.

"Great swing, Joe!"

©1999 Loving Guidance, Inc.

Learning to notice

When you judge children, you tell them who you think they should be. Judgment shows *conditional* love—love that makes demands. Encouragement is about accepting children for who they are. Acceptance notices and describes behavior or actions that exist. Acceptance underlies *unconditional* love—love which makes no demands. Here are some examples:

Praise (judging)	Noticing (describing)
⃠ "Good job, Erica."	❤ "Erica, you put your toys in the bin and carefully matched the toy with the label on the shelf."
⃠ "That was excellent."	❤ "You did it. You finished all your homework!"
⃠ "That was a great slide!"	❤ "You did it! You came down the slide feet first and landed right in my arms."

Here are some guidelines to help you notice children instead of judging them:

☑ **Start your sentence with the child's name or the pronoun "you." Alternately, start with "You did it!" or "Look at you!"** This is an important step in breaking the judgment habit. Judging statements generally start with "good" or "great." Practice statements like, "Corey, you climbed in and fastened your seat belt," "Max, look at you skip!" and "You did it, you dressed your doll!"

☑ **Next describe exactly what you see.** Pretend you are a camera. Before you speak, ask yourself, "Can a camera record what I am about to say?" If not, then you are still judging. You might be about to say, "Thank you, Kevin, for being so kind." A camera can not record that. Immediately rephrase the statement. Say, "You found Mia's blanket and gave it to her." A camera could record this kind of statement.

☑ **End your description with a tag**. Tags can help you wean yourself from making judgments and move towards acceptance. At first, you may feel your words are not complete without saying, "Good job." If so, you may use those phrases as tags. For instance, "Chris, you completed all your math problems. Good for you." Beware, though, of judgmental tags. Instead, use tags that describe attributes for your child or values you admire. Eventually try dropping the tags entirely. Below is a list of different types of tags and their suggested usage.

    ❤ **Tags that judge—use sparingly.**
        Good for you!
        Good job, honey.
        Doesn't that feel great?

    ❤ **Tags that describe attributes—use regularly.**
        That took determination.
        That was gutsy.
        You sure are organized.

    ❤ **Tags that describe values—use lavishly.**
        That was helpful.
        That was thoughtful.
        That was kind, caring, loving etc.

> **Awareness is a necessary first step to change.**

Never say, "Good job?"

You may ask, "Can't I ever tell children that they did a wonderful job?" Of course you can, but don't overuse that kind of general, judging praise. Such comments are like antibiotics—when overused they can cause serious long-term problems.

Phase out or stop replacing encouragement with rewards

The popularity of behavior modification through reward and punishment has caused many teachers to hand out stickers and other tangible items in place of freely giving affection and verbal affirmations. We replaced human connections like noticing, acknowledging and appreciating children with material rewards like stickers, gummie bears and treasure boxes. Such material rewards either become meaningless over time or teach children that their value as humans depends on how many things they can acquire. Using rewards with children has shifted our focus from establishing and honoring relationships to valuing material goods. Phase out your reward programs and replace external motivation with the internal joy of being part of a school family.

> **Praise is about forcing our judgments of who we think they should be onto our children. Encouragement is about accepting children for who they are.**

Principle # 6: Children need encouragement especially when they have made "poor" choices.

We all make inappropriate choices. The last thing we need is a lecture. Focus on encouraging children to solve their own problems. Some examples follow:

- ♥ "I have confidence you will figure out another way of handling this."
- ♥ "You'll figure out a way to be helpful. I know you, inside you do not like to be hurtful."
- ♥ "That's a rough spot you are in, but I know you can work it out. Let me know if you need help."

♥ "We all make mistakes. What could you do now that would be helpful?"

♥ "You can do it."

> ## Encouragement is basically a dose of hope. People need hope to feel safe.

Becoming brain smart

Children who feel picked on, left out and threatened in school generally do not function optimally. They are likely to exhibit behavior problems. They are also the least likely to change those behaviors. This occurs because the frontal lobes of the brain that deal with perceptual mapping and complex behavior are unable to be engaged in stressed children. Blood flow and electrical activity in the brain is diverted from the frontal lobes to the brain stem, which controls survival functions. With survival as the main goal, the child becomes less capable of receiving information and problem solving. They also become more defensive and helpless when faced with the demands of school.

The brain functions optimally when stress is low and security, challenges and stimulation are high. Any system of learning that relies on controlling others through rules, punishments and rewards will be harmful to all children in the long run, and especially damaging to children considered "low achievers."

Activities that are challenging and exciting to one learner may be threatening to another. Children can and must be used as valuable resources to one another. Children can offer comfort, support, ideas, feedback and encouragement. Brain research states that the most important factors required for optimal brain functioning are safety, security, feedback and encouragement (Jensen, 1997). We must teach children to seek help from each other, offer help to each other and create an atmosphere of trust, caring and mutual respect. The most creative, complete thinking occurs when learners are not threatened and feel safe with their peers.

The skill of encouragement is rooted in the Power of Unity which, in turn, encompasses all the other powers for self control. Here is how encouragment works:

☑ You must accept both yourself and your situation as they are, not as you think they should be (Power of Acceptance).

☑ You must focus on what you want instead of what you don't want (Power of Attention).

☑ You must own your own upset (Power of Perception).

☑ You must attribute positive intention to yourself and to others (Power of Love).

☑ You must acknowledge your own free will and the free will of others (Power of Free Will).

☑ You must view conflict as an opportunity to teach or learn (Power of Intention).

Self control and encouragement represent two sides of the same coin. Encouragement allows you to deeply connect with others, fully appreciating their unique qualities. It lets you drop your self-centeredness so you can reach out, rejoice in others and focus on giving rather than getting. Encouragement affords a deep sense of belonging.

The benefits of encouraging children take several forms. A school gains psychologically and academically when its members have a strong sense of belonging. An encouraging environment builds a child's self-esteem. An encouraging atmosphere also offers neurological benefits. It actually sculpts your child's brain for a lifetime of healthy adjustments. Discouraging environments shape brains that are prone to depression, violence, addictions and impulsivity. To foster an atmosphere of encouragement, you *must* practice the Seven Powers for Self Control. As you master the powers, your capacity to offer encouragement will grow.

> **Self control and encouragement are two sides of the same coin.**

No time like the present!

Start right now. Use the skill of noticing to encourage yourself and your children. It will take practice and persistence to break the judgment habit. The following tips will help you to be more successful:

☑ Notice your tendency to judge. At least three times a day, catch yourself before you issue a judgment. Instead, make a comment that shows you have noticed a child.

☑ Consciously notice and encourage each child three times daily. Use this formula to get started:

1. Start your sentence with one of the following: Your child's name, "You," "Look at you," "You did it," or "I noticed. . ."

2. Describe exactly what you see.

3. Add a tag if desired. Use one of the following: "That was helpful," "Good job," or "Good for you."

☑ After a command, praise the child if he chooses to listen to you. Praise him, even if you had to repeat yourself five times. He still decided to cooperate. It just took longer than you thought it *should*. Cooperation, no matter how long it takes, deserves a celebration.

☑ Create a job board. Have a job for each child in your classroom.

☑ Create rituals to build your school family.

☑ Set up the "friends and family board" and the "ways to be helpful board" as your classroom centers.

> **Acceptance notices what exists and describes it.**
> **Acceptance is the cornerstone of unconditional love.**

 ## Look for these teaching moments

Notice the following types of behaviors and encourage them:

Helpfulness	Thoughtfulness
Kindness	Sharing
Taking turns	Cooperation
Caring	Concern

Notice each time a child chooses to comply with one of your commands and praise him or her. Use acts of kindness as the core of your character-building curriculum. Take a moment right now to notice the changes you have made within yourself and your classroom. Calmly say to yourself, "You did it," and specifically describe those changes.

Chapter 3

Assertiveness

**Saying, "No!" and being heard:
Setting limits respectfully**

What you focus on,
you get more of

Assertiveness
Saying "No" and Being Heard: Setting Limits Respectfully

Power: The Power of Attention
  What you focus on, you get more of

Value: Respect

Purpose: Set limits and expectations

Brain Smart: Telling children what to do aligns their physiology with their willpower

Emotional Development: Healthy boundaries are essential to healthy relationships

Assertiveness Principles:
1. What you focus on, you get more of.
2. When you are upset, you are always focused on what you don't want.
3. Passivity invites aggression, aggression begets aggression and assertiveness dissipates aggression.
4. Children must learn that they teach others how to treat them. They must learn to assertively deal with the intrusive behaviors of others.

Principle #1: What you focus on, you get more of.

The motto to promote this month is, "What you focus on, you get more of." It is represented by the icon of the miner's hat. The light on the hat is to remind us that we control the focus of our attention. Right now take a slow deep breath. As you breathe in, say these words: "What I focus on." As you exhale say the following: "I get more of." Do this three times, letting the phrase and its meaning bathe your brain. Take a moment to reflect on your own life. Where do you focus your attention? Do you focus on what is not done, how much you have to do and how little time you have to do it in? Are you critical about your body shape, looks and weight? Do you focus on the strengths of your spouse or his or her shortcomings? In heavy traffic, do you upset yourself with being "stuck" or do you patiently use your time to notice clouds, listen to tapes or talk with your children?

I am going to describe two scenarios in which a teacher sets a limit in a classroom. Teacher A sees two children off task and launches into a diatribe: "What are you two doing? What is our rule about visiting during work time? This is no way to act. Do you want your name on the board?"

Teacher B sees two children visiting instead of working and focuses on what the children need to do in order to be successful. She walks over to the children, calls them by name and says, "Focus your attention on the math problems. I want each of you to complete problems two through four. I will watch so I know you understand what to do to be successful with your work." As the children shift their focus from each other to their work, the teacher encourages them by saying, "There you go. It's hard to keep your focus on your work. You must help each other stay focused. You may visit together at recess in twenty minutes."

Teacher A chose to focus on what was wrong or "not good enough." Teacher B focused on the action needed to solve the problem. What do you want to focus on, the error or the answer? Both are present in each moment. The choice is yours!

Before you can teach children what you expect of them in a situation, you must clearly define for yourself what you want to happen. Often we carry on about the things we want children *not* to do, to *stop* doing or what we will *not allow*. Think about these commands and questions: "Stop talking! Don't hit! Don't run in the halls! What is our rule about ___? Do you want to go to time out? Why are you talking?" We focus on what we don't want instead of what we *do* want. Learning to focus your attention on the outcome you desire will bring you enormous power. *Focusing on what you want is probably the most important technique you can learn for finding success and joy in life.* Focusing on what you want lays the foundation for all the skills in this program. It is a cornerstone because it creates the opportunity for change to occur. On the other hand, by beginning an interaction focusing on what you don't want, you shut the door on permanent behavior change.

Becoming brain smart

Only when you are willing and capable of permanently changing your own behavior can you begin to help children change theirs. To change yourself or help anyone else change, you must first focus on what you want. Many people have tried to change their own behaviors without success. New Year's resolutions are great examples. "I will stop smoking, eat less junk and spend less time at work" are common resolutions. Usually, people keep these commitments for only a few weeks before backsliding. Why? The main reason for failing is we are trying to change behaviors, both in ourselves and in our children, by focusing on what we don't want. If I told you, "Don't think about a purple alligator," what would pop into your mind?

Watch a toddler. If you say, "Don't touch the lamp," what does the child do? She will look at you, look at the lamp, point to it, touch it and then look back at you— usually with a big smile. Her brain heard, "Touch the lamp," so she looks at you

92

proudly as if to say, "Hey! I did it! I touched the lamp!" Imagine her confusion when you growl, "What did I tell you?" and push away her little hand. No wonder we all need therapy!

Instead of focusing on what you don't want, redirect the child. When she spots the lamp, you could say, "You see the pretty lamp. Put your hand in mine and I will show you how to touch delicate objects that might break." Perhaps you do not want to teach the child how to touch the lamp. Then you could say, "You see the pretty lamp. Let's look at this truck. I will roll it to you. Whee!" Then push the truck over to the child. Have fun with the alternative you choose. Children, like all of us, respond to enthusiasm.

As an adult, you probably make the connection between a negative command ("don't hit") and a positive alternative ("talk through your problems"). For young children, this is impossible. Children younger than five or six simply do not understand conjugated verbs such as "don't." When you say, "Don't talk with your mouth full," you actually increase the chances that your child will "disobey" and that you will get to watch them grind broccoli in living color.

Focusing on what you don't want also pits your body chemistry against your willpower and cuts down your chances for success. Let's say that you want to eat fewer sweets. You may tell yourself, "That's it, no more sweets for me. I'm not eating them, at least not after seven o'clock at night." In saying these words, you are focusing on sweets. Your brain hears the word sweet and the brain region which regulates your body chemistry (the hypothalamus) actually adjusts your body for an influx of sugar. Your blood sugar drops and your insulin levels change at the mention of the word "sweet."

> **You must tell your brain what to do.**

So, this is how you begin your diet. Your mind is focused squarely on "no more sweets," while your body's physiology is urging you to run to the next vending machine. As the week drags on, you feel increasingly lethargic. Eventually, to get your adrenaline pumping, you may become self-righteous and start lecturing friends on the harmful effects of sugar. By the end of the week, you are likely to feel exhausted and tell yourself, "I've been good all week. I deserve a little treat." At this point, a hot fudge brownie delight hits the spot. Full of remorse, you swear off sweets again and the next day your blood sugar once again plummets, launching you on yet another week of denial followed by excess. To successfully cut back on sweets, you must tell your brain passionately, "I love fruits and vegetables. I want more fruits and vegetables in my life." After vigilantly doing this for 21 days, your body will be naturally drawn to the produce section in the grocery store.

Activity to find where the attention is being focused

Read the following scenarios and determine where each teacher's focus is directed.

Scene 1: "Michelle, why did you hit Jake? Would you like someone to hit you? Hitting hurts. Go to time out and think about your behavior. Then come back and be nice."

Teacher's overall focus: _____.

Scene 2: "Mark, what is our rule about fighting? You march yourself down to the principal's office. Fighting is not allowed in this school. Fighting is a serious offense."

Teacher's overall focus:_____.

Scene 3: "Cameron you wanted a marker. You didn't know the words to use to get it. You may not grab. When you want a marker say: *May I borrow your marker, please?* Say that now."

Teacher's overall focus: _____.

Scene 4: Think about the last discipline encounter you had with a child. Bring up a specific scene with dialogue. Write the dialogue in the space below:

_____
_____.

Your overall focus: _____.

In Scene 1, the teacher's focus was on hitting. In Scene 2, the focus was on fighting and in Scene 3 the focus was on communicating the idea, "May I borrow your marker, please?" Where was your focus? Remember, what you focus on, you get more of.

This month, pay attention to the many occasions when you tell yourself what *not* to do and what you *don't* want. Then consciously begin to redirect your attention by focusing on what *to* do and what you *do* want. Do this in every arena of your life—the food you will eat, the video you will rent, the behavior you want from your spouse. Remember the universal principle, "What you focus on, you get more of." If you focus on stopping your children from pushing while standing in line, you create more opportunities for conflict. If you focus on your children standing in line with their hands by their sides, you create an opportunity for change.

> **Commitment # 1:** I am willing to spend one month of my life discovering where I focus my attention. I am going to be conscious of my outer and inner speech. I want more joy in my life!
>
> Signature _____ Date _____

Principle #2: When you are upset, you are always focused on what you don't want.

Think about the last time you felt upset and bring the scene fully to mind. As you recreate that moment you will see that you were focused on what you did not want. You badly wanted someone to stop doing something. To focus on what you *do* want, you must be a calm model of self-control. Stop reading and take a deep breath. Take one more. Relax your shoulders. Allow your mind to repeat to itself, "When I am upset, I am always focused on what I don't want." Allow your mind to reflect on your most recent upsets to prove to yourself that this statement is true. Notice that even during minor upsets, you were still focused on what you didn't want to happen.

When I discuss the Power of Attention with teachers, they listen, laugh and nod their heads as if they can really relate. However, when I finish explaining this power, a teacher will invariably ask, "How will this help me make my first grade students stop fighting?" I again guide them toward an awareness of where they have put their attention by saying, "Think about what you do want the children *to do*." The usual response is, "Stop hitting." Most of us have a deeply ingrained mental habit of focusing on outcomes we do not want. In these cases, I continue to walk them through the process. I'll ask, "What skill do you want your students to use instead of hitting? Do you want them to say: *Give me back my paper* or: *Stop! I don't like it when you call me names!*"

You must focus on the specific action you want your child to take instead of focusing on actions you want them to stop. Imagine going to a carpet store and telling the clerk, "I want to replace my carpet." The clerk would ask how much carpet you need. You respond, "I don't want to get home and not have enough." This sounds absurd, but this is how we handle our children day after day. Be clear when you tell your children what you want. Specificity and assertiveness are essential when you address children.

Skill #1: Pivoting, "About face!"

We will all get upset. The goal is not to eliminate life's frustrations, but to regain self-control before you deal with your children when you become upset. *You must discipline yourself first and your children second.* This month practice pivoting. Pivoting is an about-face during which you shift your focus from what you don't want, to what you do want. When you feel frenzied, stop, take a deep breath and talk to yourself. Say, "I feel upset. If I am upset, I am focused on what I don't want. Do I want more of this in my life?" If the answer is no, shift your mind to what you *do want* and calmly state it to yourself or others specifically and assertively. If the answer is a loud "I don't care," go ahead and act like a nut, but remember to forgive yourself later. Pivoting is a military term. I used it deliberately. You must be firm and vigilant to retrain your mind. This is internal boot camp — be firm with yourself.

Activity to pivot

Stand up and practice physically making an about-face. Walk three steps, rotate on the balls of your feet and turn to go in the opposite direction. Take three more steps, tell yourself to pivot (about-face) and make the turn again. Experiences that enter our body through motor activities are more likely to be remembered. The more you physically pivot the more likely you will mentally and emotionally pivot. Now sit down and role play pivoting in each of the following situations.

Situation 1: A child is repeatedly talking when you are trying to teach. In your frustration you say, "Meredith, stop talking this minute."

Situation 2: In the middle of telling a child what you want him to do, he makes a face and says, "You're stupid and I don't have to listen to you." You snap back, "Don't you ever talk to me like that again."

Situation 3: Two children are pushing and shoving in the back of the room. Eventually this form of bonding gets out of hand and one child hits the other. You arrive on the scene and yell, "Stop this nonsense. You know better than this!"

During the role play allow yourself to do the following:

1. Get upset and tell the child what not to do.
2. Recognize your upset and say to yourself, "Okay, I feel upset. If I am upset I am focused on what I *don't* want. Do I want more of this in my life?"
3. Pivot by telling the child specifically what you want him or her *to do*.
4. Reflect on the process with your partner. Assess if you focused on what you wanted the child to do. Use the *Dead Person Assessment* below as a guide.

Dead Person Assessment: If a dead person can do it, you have *not* stated what *to do*. If a dead person can do it, you are not giving usable information. For example, "Can a *dead person* stop talking?" The answer is yes. This means that you are still focusing on what you *don't* want. "Can a *dead person* sit quietly, crossing his legs with his hands in his lap and listen?" The answer is no. This means you are focusing on what you *do* want.

Focusing on what you don't want creates more of what you don't want in your life. The Power of Attention will enable you to create opportunities for yourself and your children to change.

96

> **Commitment #2**: This month I will focus on *pivoting*. When I am upset, I will take a deep breath and switch my focus from what I *don't* want to what I *do* want the children to do. I will tell children what I want them to do and why. My "why" will be related to safety and/or building community.
>
> Signature _____ Date _____

Skill # 2: Assertiveness—adults must set limits respectfully

Assertiveness is a communication skill. To effectively learn assertiveness, we must learn to reverse negative programming and become acutely aware of our passive and aggressive communication tendencies.

Picture your second grade classroom littered with the remains of a class project. If you approach the students with the goal of control, you might focus on what was done wrong and ask, "Why are all these materials on the floor?" Instead, use the Power of Attention and positively say, "Half of your materials have been put away. Pick up the other half and you are ready for lunch!" Fear focuses you on what you don't want, while love focuses you on what you do want.

When you focus on what you want, assertiveness comes naturally. Without that focus, you may be passive or aggressive in your limit setting. If you are passive in setting limits (hoping to *make* children happy to avoid upset), you teach your children to allow others to intrude upon them. You actually create a victim mentality (learned helplessness). If you are aggressive in setting limits (hoping to *make* children mind to avoid conflict), you teach children to hurt those that intrude upon them. You act as a bully and model bullying tactics. How you choose to set limits with your children defines their psychological boundaries.

Activity to reverse negative programming

Many times we tell children what not to do, but fail to give them information about what *to* do. Change the following "don't" statements into "do" statements. Give children usable information! Your goal is to create descriptive mental images to help them be successful. The brains of young children are governed by mental pictures, not words.

1. Stop fidgeting with your papers.
2. Don't throw objects, they could hurt people.
3. Don't push your friends, that's not nice.
4. Stop talking when I am talking.

Sample answers are provided on page 129.

Saying "no" and being heard

A colleague of mine, we'll call her Nancy, once lent other professors my books without asking my permission. She simply left me a note that began with the classic words, "I hope you don't mind, but . . ." and went on to explain what she had done. I was livid. I felt intruded upon. Nancy had clearly crossed a line.

You may relate to my subsequent behavior. Instead of telling Nancy how I felt about her presumptuousness, I complained bitterly about her to three other people. This was like reacting to static on my radio by changing the oil in my car.

Now the assertiveness plot thickens. I asked myself, "Why didn't I speak to Nancy?" I answered with statements like, "What good would that do now?" "I don't want to hurt her feelings," and "I don't know what to say." The first response indicates that I felt my voice lacked power. The second response was simply lying to myself, since telling people about her rudeness would surely hurt her. The third response indicates I lacked a major communication skill. All too often, teachers will talk *about* their colleagues when problems arise rather than *talking to* them.

Teachers seldom tolerate children who behave like I did. Children constantly come to us with, "He poked me," "She took my marker," and other intrusions. We constantly demand they deal with the source of the problem or ignore it. Children cross boundaries with each other frequently. Teachers, in turn, often expect them to know how to deal with these conflicts. We expect children to possess skills we have yet to develop. You simply cannot teach skills you do not possess.

Children also engage in conflicts with adults quite often. Your reactions to these conflicts act as models for the development of interpersonal skills for your class. If the children disobey and you scream in response, you teach them to be rude to people that don't do their bidding. If you permissively allow children to ignore your limits, you teach them to infringe on others and let others infringe on them. Your style of setting limits teaches children how to set and hold boundaries in their future relationships.

Teachers In The Lounge

©1999 Loving Guidance, Inc.

Assertiveness begins with ourselves and extends to our children.

You teach others how to treat you!

In all your relationships, you actually teach others how to treat you. People who seem doubtful or unsure invite other people to boss them around and "help" them, even when they don't want or need help. Your use of assertiveness lets other people know your limits. Assertiveness lets you set boundaries on what behaviors you consider appropriate, safe and permissible. Assertiveness enables you to say *no* to children and teach them how to say *no* to others when appropriate. Assertiveness also enables you to say *yes* to interactions that support you and to teach children when *yes* is in order. In sum, assertiveness is the medium through which you can teach children the value of respect.

Flipping from passive to aggressive - A school culture epidemic

Our goal with children is to teach them that speaking is more powerful than attacking verbally, hitting or kicking. However, you cannot teach children the power of words until you have learned it yourself. All teachers, especially women and people of color, must become comfortable with their assertive voices. Generally speaking, people who have historically been disempowered in a culture did not need to develop an assertive voice because society did not allow them to use it. Their voices were simply ignored. Disempowered people tend to believe they must be passive or aggressive to be heard. Assertiveness, however, is the key to communication for *all* people.

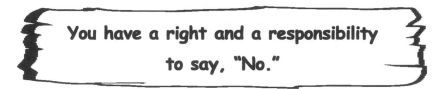

You have a right and a responsibility to say, "No."

Many teachers have developed the habit of approaching children from a passive position. They say things like, "Line up at the door, okay?" "When you are quiet, I will begin," or "I'm waiting!" These comments put children in charge of the classroom. Two responses are typical. Children who seek approval will immediately become attentive in hopes to gain your favor. Children who seek control will often ignore or answer nonverbally. These children might continue talking (indicating, "No, I'm not ready for you to begin.") Teachers faced with what they perceive as disobedience often flip to an aggressive position. A teacher might shout, " Listen to me. Do you want to have your name on the board? Then get quiet!" Having taken an aggressive position, some teachers will feel guilty. Guilt then prompts a switch back to the passive mode.

Blocks to assertiveness

To be assertive, you must express your feelings, thoughts and wishes without diminishing those of other people. This *sounds* simple, but to clearly state your thoughts and desires, you must feel entitled to have them, recognize them and own them. In short, you must value yourself. You must shift your focus from what you assume others are thinking and feeling, to being conscious of your own mind's contents. You can acquire assertiveness. It is not a personality trait that some people have and others lack. Like passivity and aggression, assertiveness is learned behavior. To learn it, you must do the following:

☑ **Achieve self-awareness.** Do you tend to interact with your children in a passive way, an aggressive way, with a passive-aggressive flip-flop or are you already assertive?

☑ **Monitor your own thought patterns.** How do you talk to yourself? Do you address yourself passively, aggressively or assertively? Once you learn to talk to *yourself* more assertively, you will naturally use this skill with your children.

☑ **Teach and utilize assertiveness in all your relationships.** By becoming more assertive with yourself and other adults, you will model this skill for your children.

When children in your classroom complain to you, "Emily pushed me," or "Nathan is looking at me," you will be ready to teach them what words to say in order to assertively state their limits.

Self-awareness: Being polite and respectful

Early in life, we internalize guidelines for social conduct—rules about what is good, polite behavior and what is rude, bad behavior. We learn early to conceal and share certain kinds of feelings early in life. We absorb these rules from parents and other role models.

It is difficult, but important to remember that these rules are not cast in stone. We can change them if we consciously decide to do so. Do the following exercise to help you become aware of certain beliefs that can block your efforts to be assertive:

Assessment to become self-aware
Read the beliefs listed in columns A and B. Check off each rule that you learned as a child and continue to follow as an adult. The check marks in column A show how often you rely on passive aggressive behaviors. The extent to which you identify with the behaviors listed in column B will show your degree of assertiveness.

Column A: Passive/aggressive beliefs	_Column B: Assertive beliefs_
You should have an appropriate response for every situation.	You have a right to make mistakes.
Mistakes are shameful, especially if someone's feelings get hurt.	Mistakes, not perfection, are a part of being human.
It is selfish to put your own needs first.	You have a right to put yourself first sometimes. It models responsibility.
You should not waste others' time with your problems. They have problems, too. You should be grateful for what you have.	You have a right to ask for help and emotional support. This gives others the opportunity to request help and support.
When someone is in trouble, you should always help them.	You have a right _not_ to take responsibility for someone else's problem. They are strong.
If you cannot convince others that your feelings and opinions are reasonable, then your feelings must be wrong.	You can feel and think the way you want. You can accept your feelings and opinions as legitimate, regardless of other people.
You should be intuitively sensitive to the needs and wishes of others.	You should not be expected to mind-read or figure out the needs and wishes of others.

101

Always try to accommodate others so they will like you.	You have a right to say, "No."
You should always be logical and consistent.	You have a right to change your mind.
Knowing you have done something well is its own reward. People do not like showoffs.	You have a right to receive recognition for your work and achievements.
You should always have a good reason for what you say, feel and do.	You do not have to justify and defend yourself to others.
If you are criticized, you have been rejected as "not good enough."	You have a right to hear feedback and filter out that which is of no value to you.

*Reprinted with permission from *Messages: The Communication Book*, by McKay, Davis, and Fanning. New Harbinger Publications.

Now mentally pick two beliefs from column A that you are going to drop. From column B, pick two new beliefs that you are going to adopt.

 ## Activity to make the commitment

I'm going to adopt the following beliefs: (Write them to boost your commitment.)

1.

2.

Are you passive, aggressive or assertive?

The first step towards assertiveness is learning to distinguish between assertive, aggressive and passive behavior. Decide to become aware of how you currently communicate with yourself and others. This awareness is a critical first step for change. If you beat yourself up with your awareness, you stop all possibility of change. The following formulas may help you:

Awareness + Acknowledgment + Forgiveness = Change

Awareness + Acknowledgment + Punishment = Repetition

Principle #3: Passivity invites aggression, aggression begets aggression and assertiveness dissipates aggression.

Read Principle #3 slowly three times. Think of personal experiences in your life where you have seen this principle in operation.

Passivity

The goal of assertiveness is clarity. When we communicate passively, the goal is not clarity, but to please others. A passive person's speech and actions constantly say, "Approve of me, love me." A passive teacher manipulates her children to behave. In the process, she gives her power to them. A person's power is their ability to have an effect in the world. Passive people relinquish this power by leaving decisions to other people. "Where should we eat?" is a passive message a wife may send to her husband. A mother who says, "Let me hang up, honey, then Mommy will talk to you," is asking the child's permission to talk. By putting another person in charge, the passive person skirts blame if something goes wrong.

Passive people long to be "perfect" so everyone will like them. They seldom express direct desires for fear that their desires may not be the "right" ones. Instead, they drop hints like, "Wouldn't it be nice if we had faculty gatherings?" Sometimes they say what they don't want. "I don't want to be work all day with people I don't know." They may ask questions instead of making statements. "Don't you think it is important for the faculty to bond?"

If you surrender your power to your children, you hope the children will use that power to make the "right" choice (to act nice). If they don't act nice, you are likely to feel frustrated and this frustration often begets aggression.

A passive teacher in action

Mrs. Lee announces to the children it is clean-up time. She gives them a two-minute warning, eliciting a few whines, so she immediately extends her warning to five minutes to accommodate the whiners. Finally, after waiting as long as possible, she begins to sing her cleanup song. While the song ripples through the classroom, she begins to help those who are having trouble. "Etta, it's time to clean up now, okay?" Etta busily puts the blocks on the shelf. "Cody, try to put all the same toys in the same bin, okay?" At this point, Alison asks the teacher for assistance and Mrs. Lee replies, "Let me finish here, and I'll be over in a minute." As circle time approaches, Mrs. Lee walks around the room one last time to help the stragglers. "Latisha, are you ready for circle time?" Latisha stares at Mrs. Lee and continues to paint. Mrs. Lee, now a bit frustrated, asks, "What time is it, Latisha? Where should you be? What should you be doing?" Latisha still ignores Mrs. Lee, continuing to finish her last rainbow color. Mrs. Lee is now feeling very frustrated.

Some of the children who had gone to the circle area on signal were starting to horse around. In frustration, Mrs. Lee shouts, "Latisha, stop right now! Don't make me have to send you to time out!" Latisha continues painting. Mrs. Lee continues her empty threats, "I'm warning you. This is not very nice behavior. Why are you doing this?"

Mrs. Lee demonstrated almost all the behaviors of a passive teacher. At the beginning, she changed her time limit to accommodate the whining of a few children. She did this unconsciously to meet her needs for the children to be happy and to like her as a teacher. She then repeatedly put the children in charge of her through comments such as, "Etta, it's time to clean up, okay?" This asked Etta's permission to clean up. Etta could have said, "No, I want to play longer!" Mrs. Lee was giving the children choices when they really had none, which probably stems from a belief that giving commands is rude and impolite. Mrs. Lee asked Cody to accomplish the intermediate, nonspecific goal, "Try to clean up." Mrs. Lee gave her power away without any repercussions until she ran into Latisha.

The problem with giving your power away is you never know if you are giving it to Mother Theresa or Stalin. When Mrs. Lee gave Latisha a choice about being ready for circle, the child opted to continue painting. In Mrs. Lee's frustration, she demonstrated other typically passive behaviors. She made statements that failed to communicate what she wanted Latisha to do, not giving her any usable information. Statements such as, "What time is it?" and "Where should you be?" do not direct a student to take action. These non-action questions confused Latisha and aggravated Mrs. Lee into threatening time out. In this threat, Mrs. Lee sent the message that Latisha was in charge of the teacher's decision. Mrs. Lee was blaming Latisha for her own passive choices when she said, "Don't *make me* have to send you to time out." The teacher's powerlessness was the true cause of Latisha's punishment. Further demonstrating her passivity, Mrs. Lee did not follow through with the consequences she had threatened.

Through her verbal and nonverbal actions, Mrs. Lee was teaching the children how to treat her. As she gave her power away, she put the children in charge, unconsciously modeling irresponsibility. She fulfilled her need for approval at the expense of the children's need for clearly stated expectations. By putting her children in control of her, Mrs. Lee unconsciously modeled irresponsibility. Having given her power away, she found it difficult to regain. She also tried to fulfill her need to avoid upset at the expense of the children's need for useful information. The following are characteristics of the passive person:

1. **A passive person asks the child to accomplish an intermediate, but nonspecific task.**
   Examples: Asks the child to make an effort. Try to be nice. Try your best to clean up. Try to clean up all the paint.

2. **A passive person asks the child questions about his or her behavior that don't give usable information.**
   Examples: Where should you be? Why are you doing that?

3. **A passive person does not follow through on consequences and will adjust events to accommodate the child's emotions.**
   Examples: The next time you speak to me like that you're going to time out! I'm warning you, just one more time.

4. **A passive person gives power away to the child, putting the child in charge of the adult.**
   Examples: When you are ready, I will begin. Let me finish here and I will help you.

5. **A passive person holds the child responsible for the adult's anger and out-of-control behavior.**
   Examples: You are *making* me send you to time out. Don't *make me* have to take your papers away!

6. **A passive person gives children choices when there are none.**
   Examples: It's time to clean up, okay? Are you ready for rest time?

7. **A passive person may ignore a situation completely, in hopes that unacceptable behavior will magically disappear.**

Passivity gives away power. Once you have put others in charge of you, it is difficult to get your power back. This occurs in all relationships. At home you may find yourself giving power to your spouse by saying in a passive, people-pleasing tone, "Honey, I'm feeling kind of dirty, so I'm thinking of taking a quick bath before coming to bed, okay?" In essence, your fear of rejection or disapproval makes you tiptoe around, justify your need for a bath, ask permission to take one and promise to make it quick. If you use such people-pleasing language, don't be surprised if your spouse starts questioning you later. "Where are you going? What are you doing? Why didn't you talk to me before you did that?" You may find yourself angry, thinking, "Why do I have to tell him what I'm doing or ask his permission? He does what he wants, when he wants," when you have actually encouraged this behavior from him. We teach each other how we want to be treated based on our beliefs about what constitutes good behavior. If you change your beliefs about you and your behavior, the techniques and skills of assertiveness will begin to develop naturally in your interactions.

Aggression

Aggressive communication aims not to clarify, but to win by overpowering. "Winning" means getting the other person to do what you want. An aggressive teacher often states his wishes with "you-me" statements. Instead of telling children clearly what to do when children are talking, an aggressive teacher might say, "*You* always interrupt *me*." *You-me* statements focus on the other person, not the problem. When a teacher makes remarks about children instead of stating his own feelings or thoughts, the teacher is attacking. If a teacher says, "*You* hurt *me*," a child feels attacked. If a teacher says, "I feel hurt," no attack is implied. Because *you-me* statements focus on the person and not on the problem, the recipient generally feels she must respond defensively. With adults, we call the resulting exchange an argument. With children, we call it talking back.

Aggressive people often speak for others and act as mind readers. They will describe the other person's viewpoint (often wrongly), but seldom express their own. An aggressive teacher may say, "You think you can get away with acting like that in my class. You think because it's okay at home it is okay at school. You better think again."

> ### "You-me" accusations
> ### leave a child feeling attacked.

Aggressive people also use the words "always" and "never" as forms of attack. "You never remember your lunch money." "You always put off big projects." With such extreme statements, you suggest the child is all good or all bad. By generalizing, you teach children to generalize about themselves and others. The children may grow up saying things like, "I never do things well." "All computer wizards are nerds."

An aggressive teacher in action

Anne Wall is having a rough day. She sees three children spraying each other with water at the water fountain and shouts, "What are you doing by that water fountain? How many times have I told you to stay in your seats? I don't care if you are dying of thirst, get back to your seats. You never listen." Laura tries to explain to the teacher saying, " Mrs. Wall, Karri has a cut on . . ." Mrs. Wall interrupts, "You are just using Karri as an excuse to get out of doing your work and make a mess in this classroom." "But, Mrs. Wall," whines Tara. "Don't you talk back to me, young lady. Now get to work before I put your name on the board. You think you can do whatever you want, but you're wrong. I am in charge of this classroom and you are keeping other children from learning. You children are so selfish," Mrs. Wall says. As the children grudgingly begin to return to their seats, Mrs. Wall begins to threaten them. "You don't have to act like that. You ought to be grateful I don't send you to the principal or call your parents."

Anne demonstrated most of the characteristics of aggressive people:

1. **She made "you" statements that focused on the other people, not the problem.** "You children are so selfish."

2. **She spoke for others, often wrongly describing their viewpoints. She seldom expressed her own thoughts and feelings.** "You are just using Karri as an excuse to get out your work and make a mess in this classroom."

3. **She used the words "always" and "never."** "You never listen."

4. **She viewed others as attacking her.** "Don't you back talk me, young lady."

5. **She used empty, punitive threats.** "Now get back to work before I put your name on the board.

Although Anne did not act in the following ways, aggressive people often do:

6. **Imposing consequences that are overly severe.** "Detention for two weeks."

7. **Physically responding to a child out of anger.** Shaking or squeezing the child's arm, jerking, threatening to hit or actually hitting the child.

> **Any statement about the other person, rather than statements about one's own feelings or thoughts, tends to have an attacking quality.**

Assertiveness

The goal of assertiveness is clear communication. When you communicate assertively, you make straightforward statements about feelings, thoughts and wishes. It is assertive to say, "I want pizza." It is not assertive to quiz others ("What would you like?"), think for them ("You probably want Chinese food like always."), or try to control them ("Everyone loves pizza. Why not you?") You cannot be assertive if you often think about what others think of you. Nor can you be assertive if you fret about what someone will do or say in response to what you do or say. You cannot set a limit and take care of another person's feelings at the same time. To be assertive, you must concentrate on yourself instead of focusing on what someone else might think.

> **Assertiveness comes from the Power of Attention.**
> **Focus on what you want to happen.**

To be an assertive teacher, you must:

☑ **Tell children what to do.** State your wants, needs and expectations clearly and simply. "Give me the scissors. These are too sharp. They could cut you. I will get you a plastic pair."

☑ **Send the nonverbal message "just do it" in the tone of your voice.** Match your nonverbal and your verbal communications. If your nonverbal cues are too passive, your child may easily choose not to comply. If your nonverbal cues are too aggressive, your child will resist in self-defense. When your nonverbal and verbal communication match, you let your child know you mean what you say. Before your child decides whether to comply with a command, she will read your facial expression, tone of voice and gestures. You increase the chances she will obey if you appear confident and in control, sound sure of yourself and use gestures to provide information.

☑ **Be clear and direct.** Give children choices only when choices really exist. "Are you ready for a story?" implies that your child has the choice of being ready or not. If you say, "It is storytime. Sit quietly and listen," you leave your child no choice. You have stated plainly what will happen.

☑ **Give children usable information.** Give commands that contain usable, helpful information and avoid asking rhetorical questions. "Sit down and check to see if your friends have enough space," is assertive. "Who can show how to sit nicely?" is not.

☑ **Own and express your feelings *directly*.** If you say, "I feel angry when you interrupt me," you are being assertive. "Look what you made me do" and "can't you be quiet while I am talking" are indirect (passive/aggressive) ways to express anger.

☑ **Speak in concrete terms.** Abstractions like good, bad, nice, etc., can be confusing for young children. Teach children what it is to be good and nice specifically, without relying on the labels. "Ask your friend if you can play by saying: *May I please play*," is assertive. "Be nice to your friends," is not assertive.

☑ **Be conscious of the intent behind the communication.** The intent behind assertive communication is clarity. Clarity will help the child be as successful as possible in your classroom. Show respect for your child and enforce rules without teasing, embarrassing or bullying. Being respectful means focusing on improving behavior rather than on getting children to feel bad about their actions. The intent behind the words is more powerful than the actual choice of wording.

An assertive teacher in action

Frances Canipe has been teaching for two decades. Over the years, she learned the value of assertiveness in structuring her classroom. Megan is what could be called a "spacey" child. She seems to have trouble staying on task. Megan's passive aggressive mother is convinced that she has a hearing problem. However, Megan's ears have been checked twice and all is well. During open house at the beginning of the year, Mrs. Canipe observes Megan and her mother. Mom repeatedly attempts to get Megan's attention by saying, "Megan, look at me, I am talking. Megan, are you listening to me? Megan, do you hear me? I am not going to speak to you again. Megan!" Mom then gets extremely frustrated and grabs Megan's arm and starts lecturing her on topics such as respect and listening. Sometimes Megan's mom would threaten her with the loss of a trip to McDonalds or some favorite toy. Mrs. Canipe approaches Megan differently. She walks over to Megan and gets down on eye level about six inches from Megan's face. She waits for Megan to notice her and make eye contact before beginning to speak. With a firm voice she says, "Megan, walk over and take your mother's hand. It is time to go home. I look forward to seeing you tomorrow at school." Mrs. Canipe waits for Megan to make any motion toward her mother that would indicate a response to her command. When Megan begins to move, Mrs. Canipe quickly says, "You did it, you looked for your Mom so your could find her hand."

> **Assertiveness clearly tells children what to do so they may successfully meet your expectations.**

Activity to find your assertive voice

With a partner, use a passive, an aggressive and an assertive voice to give the assertive command, "Sit down and look at me." Give the command three times, using the voice as indicated. Record how each voice felt, sounded and looked on the chart.

	Feels Like	Sounds Like	Looks Like
Passive			
Aggressive			
Assertive			

Assessment to identify your style

In the spaces below, assess your current communication style. Note the percentage of time you speak to your children in each communication style. Remember, to be assertive you must clearly tell children what you want.   Date _____

Passive Communications	Aggressive Communications	Assertive Communications
_____%	_____%	_____%

Young children turn fearful situations into a game

As a teacher, you need an assertive voice. An assertive voice is calming to children. An aggressive voice sounds angry and all anger is rooted in fear. Imagine someone cutting you off on the freeway. You might curse with fury, but beneath your rage would be fear of an accident. Anger is a secondary emotion. All anger is really fear in disguise. When angry with children, we may fear we won't know how to respond if the misbehavior continues or fear bigger problems may arise.

When you get angry, children sense your fear and it frightens them. A frightened child will turn a scary situation into a game. Do you remember 2-year-old Jessica who fell into the well in Texas? Rescuers dug for two days to reach her. When found, she was singing. She had turned her dreadful predicament into a game to master it. You see children do this everyday. Most children watch cartoons featuring about 25 violent acts per hour. Cartoon violence can frighten young children. Often, they respond by begging for toys based on the TV shows. Once they own these figures, they can master the fearful situations they witnessed by manipulating the characters in play.

An aggressive voice sounds angry and children sense the teacher is out of control. The anger scares the children. On the other hand, if you speak passively, you put the child in charge. As a child, being in charge is also quite scary. Children know they are not equipped to be in charge of adults. When young children hear either an aggressive or passive voice, they feel frightened and make it into a game to regain a sense of control. Toddlers do this with great panache.

Karen wanted her 2-year-old daughter Christina to get in the car seat so they could keep a doctor's appointment. Karen said, "Christina, get in your car seat. Over here honey, here is the car seat. Come get in. Come over here." Christina paused for a moment to watch her mother and Karen got nervous about her dawdling. Karen's nervousness quickly flared into anger and she shouted, "Don't start with me. Get over here now and get in your seat." Karen was angry because she was afraid they would be late. Christina could practically smell her mother's fear. In response, Christina ran away, looking back at Karen over her shoulder and giggling as if they were playing tag. Karen chased her daughter, shouting threats. Karen finally caught Christina, gave her a swat on the rear and forced her into the car seat.

Similar problems arise when parents or teachers use an aggressive or passive voice to send older children to time out. The child may refuse to go, go with an attitude or play when they get there (singing or picking paint off the chair). Again, they are turning the fearful situation into a game in order to master it.

Karen had interpreted Christina's running as disrespect, but it was really a reaction to the fear her mother's voice contained. In cases like these, children turn tense situations into games adults do not want to play. To avoid such problems, use an assertive voice and keep fear out of your conflicts with children.

Overview of the three voices			
	Assertive	**Passive**	**Aggressive**
Intent:	Clarity	Avoids conflict through pleasing	Avoids conflict through dominating
Tone:	Just do it.	Asking permission?	Or else!
Power:	Within	Given away	Taken from others
Feelings:	Owned with *direct* expression	Projected with *indirect* expression	Projected with *indirect* expression
Information:	Usable, what *to* do	Non-usable, confusing	Non-usable, attacking
Belief:	I am enough	I am not worthy	You are not worthy

Assertive skills needed to work with children

The following assertive skills are needed to successfully guide children:

Skill 1 Assertive commands (individual and group)

Skill 2 Tell and show

Skill 3 I-messages (direct expression of feelings)

Assertive commands

We often confuse requests and commands. A command relays to children what you expect or want them to do. It does not offer a choice about the situation. Think of the daily routines you expect children to perform. Some examples at home are getting up, getting dressed, bath time and bedtime. School-time examples include cleaning up, walking with the group in line and being quiet when the teacher is talking. A request is when you ask a child to do something for you. "Would you please run this down to the office?" "Would you please hand this pencil to Melissa for me?"

Many of us grew up with ambiguous commands, commands worded as if they were requests. For example, "Keith, would you take out the trash?" actually means,

"Get up now and take that trash out to the curb." Granted, this ambiguity in the language took a while to comprehend. Keith, depending on his personality, may have figured it out after a few lectures, yellings or even spankings. This presents two problems. First, as a child, *you* must figure it out. This can take anywhere from two to five years. In that time, a lot of frustration, unnecessary anger and hurt feelings can develop. Second, adults growing up with this type of language eventually stop hearing they have choices. Life becomes one obligation after another. Thus, if an acquaintance asks you to dinner, you hear this as a command. If you do not obey, you could feel the guilt associated with childhood lectures. What we often do in such a dilemma is lie. Your mind goes into high gear, thinking of a viable excuse for saying no. Finally, you respond: "I'd really love to go for dinner, but I haven't been feeling good. I'd better stay home and just hope I can make it to work tomorrow." This passive, people-pleasing attempt to say no is not only confusing to the caller, but the guilt you so tried to avoid now creeps in for lying. Some people feel so guilty they actually make themselves sick and miss a day of work after all. Learning to give assertive commands eliminates such ambiguity and helps children and adults become successful.

Assertive commands can be given to individual children or to a group of children. The first step in any assertive command is to get the attention of the child or children. If talking with an individual child, you can do this through proximity. If you are talking with a group, you can do this with a pre-established signal such as blinking the lights or through a unifying experience like a song or a finger play.

Skill #3a: Assertive commands to individuals

1. Move to the child, get down on eye level and make direct eye contact. To establish eye contact with a young child you must adjust the distance between your face and the child's until he notices you. For easily distracted or disengaged children, this distance may be as close as six to eight inches. Children from some cultures are educated not to make eye contact with adults. This is under very specific situations, usually when they are being reprimanded. Giving a command is not a reprimand.

2. State the child's name.

3. Verbally tell the child what you want him or her to do.

4. Touch the child gently on the arm or place your hand on her back or shoulder (if possible and appropriate).

5. Use visual cues through gesturing to support what you want the child to do. Point to all the papers and books on the tables, then use your arms and hands to show where they are to be placed as you say, "Remove all papers and books and put them in your desk."

112

In short, assertive commands use all the senses:

1. Kinesthetically, move into proximity with the child
2. Visually, utilize eye contact and gestures
3. Auditorily, state the child's name and your expectations
4. Tactilely, through touch
5. Energetically, with a loving positive intent for clarity and success

 ## Activity to give assertive commands

With a partner, role-play giving assertive commands in the following situations:

☑ Helping a child who is dawdling at his table line up

☑ Assisting a child walking around the room to return to her seat

Assessment #3: Individual Assertive Commands

1. Did you wait for the child to make eye contact before saying a word? If yes, say to yourself, "I did it." If no, do it again.

2. Did you use your arms like a traffic cop gesturing to visually support your vocal command? If yes, say, "I did it. I used my hands to be helpful." If not, do it again.

3. Were you conscious of your intent, as well as your words? If yes, say to yourself, "I'm becoming more conscious and it feels ____." If not, do it again and pay attention.

Skill #3b: Assertive commands to groups

Use a signal or unifying experience to get the group's attention. Teach an auditory and visual signal. Children who spend time in group settings need a signal to help them stop what they are doing and shift their attention to another activity. Many teachers and child caregivers use blinking the lights, a musical instrument such as a drum or triangle, or a specific transition song. I encourage each teacher to provide children with two signals, one auditory and the other visual. Children can be given the auditory signal first, then the visual one, as shown in the following classroom example.

At the beginning of the year, Mrs. Pinder decides to use a drum as her first or auditory signal, and children raising their hands as the second or visual signal. She selected the drum because she has Native American heritage and wants the children to understand that at one time drums were used for communication. She frames her discussion of the drum in a Native American folklore story and her personal experience. The children come to understand that the drum was a means for people of different

113

languages to communicate with one another. She states clearly that when the children hear the drum beat, they are to stop what they are doing, take a deep breath to help them focus, look for the teacher and listen for the instructions that will follow. She provides the children practice time to stop, breathe, look and listen. "Pretend you are drawing at your table and you hear the drum. What will you do?" or "Pretend you are talking with your friends and you hear the drum. What will you do?" She then has the children engage in activities that require actual talking and movement. Next, she organizes the class into small groups to play several get-acquainted games which allow the children to truly practice "Stop, breathe, look and listen." Each time the children successfully stop what they are doing and shift their focus, she celebrates this accomplishment. Some children are so focused on what they are doing that they don't hear the drum. When this happens, Mrs. Pinder explains the importance of everyone helping each other by raising their hands up over their heads. When friends see the raised hands, they will know it is time to stop, breathe, look and listen.

When the signals fail

Sometimes signals just do not work. The children are so scattered about the room that chaos seems eminent. When things seem to be getting out of hand, a unifying experience is usually more effective. The following steps are recommended:

1. Conduct a unifying chant or movement activity. "Everybody do this, do this, do this. Everybody do this, do this now," is a follow-the-leader chant that can be fun as long as the "do this's" are challenging or silly. Once you have their attention, have the class be a S.T.A.R. (**S**mile, **T**ake a deep breath **A**nd **R**elax).

2. Praise the children who stop. "Phillip, Reynaldo, Wayne, Ashley, each of you stopped, took a deep breath, looked and are ready to listen. You heard the signal and are ready for what will happen next" or "Most people heard the drum and began to stop, breathe, look and listen. Then you noticed that some of your friends did not hear the drum signal and you put up your hand to help them. That was very helpful."

3. Verbally tell the children what you want them to do. As soon as you have the children's attention, begin telling them what you want them to do. Having children wait, especially young ones, just creates problems.

Assessment to reflect on your current "signal" practices
1. Have you taught your children the class signal? Does it have an auditory, a visual and a kinesthetic (breathing) component? How many specific lesson plans did you utilize to teach the signal? Did you teach and practice it for 21 days to form a habit?

2. Have you framed the experience so that children who hear the signal can help those who missed it to also be successful?

3. Do you encourage children who follow the signal by describing what they have accomplished ("You stopped what you were doing, took a deep breath and looked for me")? Do you judge children, fostering dependency ("Good listening")? Do you manipulate children by using your affection for them ("I like the way _____ is listening")?

4. How are you going to modify your practices? Renew your committment by writing: I'm going to _____

_____.

Skill #4: Tell and show

If children do not follow your assertive command they are indicating they need additional support to be successful. One strategy is *tell and show*. It involves *telling* children what you want them to do, then following up by *showing* them how to do it.

Step 1: Give an assertive command. If the child complies, praise him or her through encouragement. If the child ignores you, continue to Step 2.

Step 2: Say, "There you are." If a child continues to ignore you, the tendency is to shout from a distance to get his attention. You might say, "Jason, did you hear me? Jason, I am talking to you. Jason look at me." Sometimes we approach the child and physically turn his head toward us to make eye contact. These actions frustrate us and send children the message that "getting" their attention is the adult's job rather than their own responsibility.

Instead of taking the actions above, walk over to the child and get as close as necessary until the child looks up at you and makes eye contact. For some children, a successful distance is three feet, for others it may be six inches. Once the child makes eye contact, you can say, "There you are." (For older students you can say, "Hey, there you are! I thought we had lost you.") These words build a connection between you and the child. This connection is the cooperative link necessary for a child to choose to listen to you. Next, follow the "there you are statement" with the original command. If the child chooses to be cooperative and listens to you, remember to praise him or her. You might say, "That's it! You are doing it! You got your book open and are ready to go. Good for you."

Step 3: Say, "I'm going to show you what I want you to do." Say, "I am going to show you how to. . ." Guide the child gently and instructively to finish the task. For example, tell the child, "Jason, pick up all the puzzle pieces and put them in this box labeled *horse*." If Jason begins to pick them up, you would encourage him for his choice. If he ignores the command and continues to play with the puzzle, move toward him, make eye contact and say, "I am going to show you how to pick up the puzzle pieces and put them in the box." Then take Jason's hand and guide them to the pieces, helping him to physically begin the task. You might also model the behavior by saying, "Watch me. I am going to pick up two at a time and put them in the box. Now you can pick up two." If Jason chooses to cooperate, encourage his choice and effort. "Jason, look at you! You picked up two at a time and put them in the box. You are going to make sure you have all the pieces so you can make this puzzle again."

Tell and show is a wonderful skill for children who are so busy growing and playing that they tend to ignore the rest of life, including us. It is instructive and it gives usable information. The message is, "Here is what is expected of you. I will assist you in performing it successfully." If a child doesn't choose to comply with our commands, we must change the structure to help the child be successful. Ask yourself, "What can I do to help this child successfully meet both my expectations and his own need at the same time?" Children need to feel competent, responsible, capable and helpful. Because adults can abuse this skill, however, our intention must be clear. If you intend the child to be successful and capable, your actions will be guided accordingly. If your intention is to force the child to comply, you will communicate this also. If a child chronically ignores commands or refuses to comply, ask yourself if your expectations are appropriate and your intentions loving.

©1999 Loving Guidance, Inc.

Tell and show is a very powerful teaching skill for young children. I often wonder why this skill was rarely used even though it is so effective. I came up with the following hypothesis to explain the oversight: In the beginning, as wisdom was being delivered to the multitude of teachers, a wise but faint voice rang out, saying, "Remember always to tell and show." The teachers listening intently heard the message and with great insight shouted back, "Show and tell! We can do that." So instead of using the assertive skill, *tell and show*, teachers began the educational practice of show and tell.

Skill #5: I-messages help when frustration sets in

Children will disobey you. It is part of their developmental journey to find limits and test them. It is your journey to be conscious of how you hold and set the limits. You, like all teachers, will feel frustrated with the children's behaviors and find them exquisitely annoying. You can express this frustration passively, aggressively or assertively. The passive and aggressive approaches are indirect, sideways methods of venting your feelings. Assertiveness provides you a direct way of communicating even while you feel intense emotions.

Assessment for direct or indirect expression

Read the following statements. Discern for yourself if you indirectly or directly express your feelings (especially frustration).

1. **Indirect through labeling:** "You are rude to interrupt."
   Direct: "I don't like it when you interrupt. I can't remember what I was saying. Please be quiet."

2. **Indirect through commands:** "Sit down, be quiet, stop running."
   Direct: "When you run through the house while I am trying to work, I feel distracted. I can't think."

3. **Indirect through questions:** "What did you do? What's wrong with you?"
   Direct: "Something seems to be bothering you. I feel concerned. Would you like to talk about it?"

4. **Indirect through sarcasm:** "So you finally decided to join us for dinner, how thoughtful."
   Direct: "Our dinner time is important to me. I like it when we're all here together. Please come when I call you."

5. **Indirect through accusations:** "You don't care about anybody but yourself. You should be ashamed."

Direct: "When you keep ignoring me and what I am telling you to do, I feel furious. I'm going to go calm down and then I will talk with you."

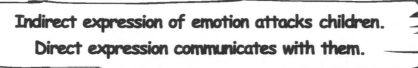

Indirect expression of emotion attacks children.
Direct expression communicates with them.

Activity for favorite indirect styles
I tend to indirectly express my frustration in the following ways:

1. _____   3. _____
2. _____   4. _____

Commitment #2: This month I am willing to be conscious of my feelings and how I express them. I am going to work on directly expressing my frustration by saying "When you _____ I feel _____," followed by telling children what to do. Or by saying "I don't like it when you _____," followed by telling children what to do.
Signature _____ Date _____

How to give an I-message

I-messages are skills that originate from owning one's feelings and claiming one's power. If you believe children *make* you angry, you will be unsuccessful. Remember, the person whom you believe to be in charge of your feelings you have placed in charge of you. It is time to take back your power. Own your feelings, then express them directly through I-messages. I-messages could be called responsibility messages because an adult who sends an I-message takes responsibility for **1)** her own inner condition and **2)** for being open enough to share this self-assessment with others.

When adults have feelings of upset triggered by children, they have an expectation that the children are not meeting. The dilemma is how to express this frustration without blaming the child. The I-message is the least guilt-producing method of directly expressing to the child how her actions are affecting you and possibly her peers. The I-message is a way of informing children about your problem. It does not communicate "You did something wrong" or "Here is how I want you to change." It communicates the way the child's behavior has impacted you. It tells the child, "You have the power to influence other people by your choices." I-messages are nonjudgmental statements that allow children to cognitively reflect on their actions and find their own ways to choose to change.

An I-message describes the behavior that is annoying or disruptive, the feelings the adult is experiencing, and the tangible impact of that behavior on the adult. Here are some examples:

❤ "When your toys are left on the floor, I feel scared because I might trip and hurt myself or break a toy. Pick up the toys and put them on the shelf."

❤ "When you talk when I am talking, I feel frustrated because I can't remember what I was saying. Sit quietly while I talk."

❤ Make sure the word following "feel" is a one-word description of an emotion (irritated, annoyed, worried, upset). Do not say, "I feel like you don't care." That is a thought, not a feeling. It brings you right back to expressing your feelings indirectly.

When a child infringes on you, use an I-message

"I-messages" tell children that you believe they have infringed upon you. Children are not born knowing the difference between respect and disrespect. They must be taught. I often see children attacking teachers physically and verbally. I have seen teachers dodging blows and retaliating by saying words to hurt the child, removing the child to time out, sending the child to the office or delivering some negative classroom consequence. I seldom see them use the disruption to teach assertiveness.

Mrs. Bailey works with at-risk, 4-year-old children. She instructs the children it is clean up time. One child's response is to make a growling sound, ball up her fist and punch the teacher in the arm. The teacher responds, "Why did you hit me? Do I hit you? We don't hit in this classroom." The child screams, "No" and begins to cry. As she cries, Mrs. Bailey asks, "Why are you acting like this?"

This teacher forfeited a teaching opportunity. She asked irrelevant questions and failed to offer any usable information. The child was hurtful and the teacher needed to assertively set a limit by saying something like, "Ouch! It hurts when you hit me. I don't like it. Say: *Mrs. Bailey, I have something to say*, if you want my attention." If the child hit her again, Mrs. Bailey could restrain her hands and tell her, "You may not hurt me or anyone else. I will hold you until I think you are safe and I am safe." If this is too much to remember, simply say a firm, "I don't like it when you hit me."

Another child and his mother were discussing soccer practice. She said, "You play better when you don't get so mad." The child snapped back, "Shut up Mom!" She then said, "You are so rude. Do you want to be grounded?" Her words do not teach, they scold.

Imagine trying to learn division, making a mistake and hearing someone say, "That's wrong, stupid. Be ashamed. Make another division mistake and you're getting a referral." This type of response cannot help you master division. You do not see your mistakes or how to correct them, and your feelings about math are likely to be negative. Behavior works the same way. When you are treated with disrespect, you need to respond assertively. If you respond aggressively, you are treating your child with *disrespect* while trying to teach *respect*. The soccer mom could say in an assertive voice, "I do not like it when you speak to me like that. If you disagree with me, you can say: *Mom I disagree.* If you say that now, I will listen. If not, I am leaving the room. I will not be treated with disrespect."

Activity to practice I-messages

There are several ways to deliver an I-message. Pick the form that is most comfortable for you. The most important point to remember is to speak from your *heart*.

Style 1: "I don't like it when you _____."
(describe the child's action)

Style 2: "I feel _____ when you _____
(Use a feeling word)   (describe the child's action)
because _____."
(relate to safety)

Remember, when giving an I-message, you are upset and seeking to set a boundary for the child. Make sure your face (stern) matches your tone (firm and assertive). After giving an I-message, complete the process by telling the children what you want them to do through problem solving or by delivering a consequence.

"You" statements often do the opposite of an I-message.
- ⊘ "You" statements send a message of blame. "It is your fault I am acting this way."
- ⊘ "You" statements send a message that the child is in charge of the adult. It gives the adult's power away.
- ⊘ The purpose of a "you" statement is to make the other person feel guilty.

Speaking from your heart, respond to the following situations with an I-message.
1. You repeatedly ask the children to settle down. They continue to talk.
2. A child calls you a "stupid idiot."
3. A child hits you.

Principle #4: Children must learn that they teach others how to treat them. They must learn to assertively deal with intrusive behaviors.

Teaching assertiveness to children—He hit me.

"He pushed me. I had it first. She called me stupid. He started it." Sound familiar? Children constantly struggle to establish boundaries with other children. If you are passive and aggressive with your children when setting limits, they will be passive and aggressive with each other. You must assertively set limits for your children and teach them to do the same with others.

Skill #6: Tattling as a teaching tool.

Tattling is a wonderful opportunity to teach children assertiveness instead of helplessness, dependency, aggressiveness or withdrawal strategies. Children who tattle bring their problem to the adult for assistance and are simply saying, "I don't have a clue how to handle this—could you help me?" Typical teacher responses include: "We don't tattle on our friends. Are you bleeding or dying? What is our rule about tattling? Use your words and work it out." None of these are helpful. Even the last one, "Use your words," does not teach the child which words to use. Punishing children who ask for assistance is a missed opportunity to teach.

Children who do not come to the adult for assistance are taking care of the situation the best way they can by hitting, manipulating, teasing, harassing and only occasionally using helpful words. Whatever skills they are using, regardless of appropriateness, they are taking action. With luck, there will be a child willing to tattle. This provides the adult the opportunity to teach both victim and aggressor new skills for interacting.

Helping children assertively deal with intrusion

Martin says to you, "Logan pushed me." When a child brings you a problem involving a perceived intrusion by another, the first question to ask is, "Did you like it?" This may seem odd, but it is critical for three reasons. First, it helps you to assess how much assertive energy the tattler possesses. Second, "no" has a great deal of assertive energy and your question makes that energy instantly available to the child. Third, you help the child focus on herself and her own feelings instead of on the other person.

When your child responds with some form of *no*, take note of it. Was it a head shake, a firm *no*, an aggressive *no*, or a weak, passive *no*? An assertive *no* reveals a high-confidence level while passive and aggressive *no's* reveal low confidence. If the *no* reveals high confidence, say to your child, "Go tell Logan: *Stop, I don't like it when you push me.*"

If your child demonstrates low confidence with his *no*, you must teach both the words to say and tone of voice to use. A child with a passive temperament must learn to use their "big voice." If you send a child off to talk to a classmate in a passive voice, that child will get hit when you turn your back. It is almost guaranteed.

The following example outlines this process for tattling:

121

High confidence
> Child: Tiffany hit me!
> Adult: Did you like it?
> Child: No.
> Adult: Go tell Tiffany, "I don't like it when you hit me."

Low confidence
> Child: Andrea took my sweater.
> Adult: Did you like it?
> Child: No (in a whiny, little voice).
> Adult: Go tell Andrea, "I don't like it when you take my sweater." Say that now for practice.
> Child: I don't like it when you take my sweater. (still in a small, whiny voice)
> Adult: Yes, that's it. Now say it again, matching your voice to mine. "I don't like it when you take my sweater." (modeling a firm, confident voice)
> Child: I don't like it when you take my sweater.
> Adult: That was much louder. I heard you that time. I will walk with you while you tell Andrea.
> Child to Andrea: I don't like it when you take my sweater. (whiny voice, but somewhat stronger)
> Adult to Andrea: I am here to let you know it is important to listen to your friends.

In this example, the adult spent some time modeling an assertive voice for the child, however, modeling alone is not the answer. The child has beliefs about herself that prevent her from feeling confident. These beliefs must ultimately be addressed. For now, the adult models the skill needed and accompanies the child for support.

The language you provide for children will go through a progression depending on the developmental level of the child. For young children (2 years), children with developmental delays or those with language or speech disorders, you might say, "Go tell Jeremy: *Stop! No!*" As children progress in both their cognitive and language abilities, the words we provide must also change. The following responses represent the developmental progression of assertive language skills we can provide for children. Approximate development ages are provided as a guideline only.

> **Level 1:** Stop! No! (Toddlers)
> **Level 2:** I don't like it. (3 to 4 years)
> **Level 3:** I don't like it when you take my pencil. (4 to 6 years)
> **Level 4:** I don't like it. Get your own pencil. (6 to 9 years)
> **Level 5:** I feel frustrated when you take my pencil. I can't finish my work. (9 to 12 years)
> **Level 6:** I feel frustrated when you take my pencil. I can't finish my work. Get your own pencil. (12 and up)

Children must be taught the exact words to use.

Children use whatever skills they possess.

Nonverbal or developmentally delayed children

While shopping at the mall, I heard some crying and looked up to see a mother pushing a double stroller with a 4-year-old in back and an infant in front. I watched the 4-year-old use the infant's head like a drum as the baby cried. To soothe the crying infant, the mother (who was unaware of the hitting) was pushing the stroller back and forth. The woman looked exhausted. I commented on her lovely children and asked if I could take a closer look. I bent down, looked at the 4-year-old, waited for him to make eye contact with me and said, "See your brother's face. He's crying. He is saying: *I don't like you to hit me. Stop.*" The boy had an awkward look on his face as he processed the information. I could almost hear him thinking, "So *that's* why he's crying."

You must teach older children to read the faces of younger, nonverbal children. "Look at her face, she's smiling. Her face is saying: *I like it when you sing and touch my hands.*" When one child hugs another too hard, teach her to listen to the nonverbal child by saying, "See his face. It's red. His lips are quivering. His face is saying: *You are squeezing too tight, hold me gently.*" Guide the child's hands to reinforce your words. As a teacher, you must talk for nonverbal children until they can talk for themselves.

Passive/aggressive tattling: Attempts to get revenge

1. **What it looks like in your life**. Have you ever wanted something so much you could taste it? Perhaps you really wanted a significant other to share a special something with you and he or she refused? Think of such a time in your life, then think of all the techniques you used to persuade the other person to change his or her mind. Usually, we try various forms of seduction and manipulation, but as our prospects dim, we bring out heavy-duty artillery like, "I do so and so for you, I can't see why you won't do this for me." Or perhaps, "You are just trying to be hateful. I don't know why I married (hang out with, put up with) you anyway." When these attacks also fail, we usually formulate some plan of revenge. "I'll go and have a good time, then you'll see just how much fun you missed and you'll be sorry." The purpose of the revenge plan is to make the noncooperative person feel as bad as we do. This same process operates with children, except their manipulation skills are less developed.

2. **What it looks like in children.** Often, when a child is unsuccessful in influencing another's behavior, she attempts to get that child punished in some way. The child may directly communicate her frustrations with the other child or to an adult. She may also indirectly imply that a problem exists through passive aggressive tattling.

Passive aggressive tattling involves a child telling on others who are breaking a rule
> **Child:** Stephanie is not cleaning up!
> **Adult:** Are you telling me to be helpful or hurtful?

Child: Hurtful.

Adult: What could you do that would be helpful?

Child: I don't know.

Adult: You could say, "Stephanie, would you like some help cleaning up?"

Child: Well, she pushed me!

Adult: Did you like it?

Child: No.

Adult: She pushed you and you didn't know what to say to let her know how frustrated you were. So you came to me hoping to get her in trouble. When she pushes you say, "Stop! I don't like to be pushed. It hurts." Say that now. I will walk with you while you talk directly to Stephanie.

If the child answers the first question with "helpful," you could then say, "How is telling me about Stephanie being helpful?" Then you listen for the answer and continue with the process. The goal is to reframe the child from attempting to get another child in trouble, to being either a helpful friend or learning to express his or her frustration directly.

Tattling out of fear: The classroom is not safe, do something

When children see other children being hurtful or getting hurt, the natural response is to tell an adult seeking assistance to restore the situation to safety. The adult response to this is vital. When a child tells you, "Mark hit Latisha and she is crying," your response is to reassure the child you will take care of restoring safety to the room.

©1999 Loving Guidance, Inc.

Responding to tattling teaches children respect for authority.

You could say, "You were concerned about your friends, I will take care of the situation so that our classroom is safe." Then you proceed to the *victim* first to begin the healing process. Describe what you see, "Latisha, you are holding your arm and crying." Then inquire, "Something happened?" Wait for Latisha to explain the situation. Listen closely, reflecting back to her what you heard so she can clarify if needed. "Mark wanted your notebook, you said *no* and he hit you on the arm?" Once you have clearly perceived her side of the story, go to Mark, teaching him, "Mark, you wanted a notebook? You may not hit. Hitting hurts. When you want a notebook and a person says *no*, come ask me for assistance. What could you do that would be helpful for Latisha right now?"

 ## Activity to use tattling as a teaching moment

Children exhibit three basic types of tattling; each one gives a different message.

Type 1. **Child has been victimized.**
Message: "I feel powerless."
Response: "Did you like it?"
"Go tell _____ . I _____."

Type 2. **Child sees someone getting hurt.**
Message: "I don't feel safe."
Response: "My job in this classroom is to keep it safe."
"I will take care of _____."

Type 3. **Child wants to get someone in trouble.**
Message: "I feel angry at ___ for not being my friend and not doing what I wanted them to do. I don't know how to express my anger directly."
Response: "Are you telling me this to be helpful or hurtful?"

Below are four tattling situations. First, discern the message the child is relaying. Does the child perceive her rights have been intruded upon? Does the child perceive the classroom is unsafe? Does the child seem to have an ulterior motive behind her comments? Respond to the underlying message using the methods taught. Role-play these situations:

1. Child comes to you and says, "Martin is not lining up."

2. Child comes to you complaining, "Marissa wrote on my paper."

3. Child comes to you whining, "Meredith pushed me."

4. Child comes to you and says, "Mark pushed Kevin off the swing."

Physical structures that support the Skill of Assertiveness

Each of the skills of *Conscious Discipline* are supported by learning centers in the classroom. The "safe place" center supports the skill of composure and becomes the hub of your anger management curriculum. The same is true for the "centers that build the school family." There are two centers that are helpful in teaching children their assertiveness voices. One is the "time machine/solution station" mentioned briefly in chapter 2. The other is the "instant replay" center.

Time machine/solution station

The purpose of the time machine (as stated in chapter 2) is to provide a designated space for children to go back in time and change hurtful interactions into helpful exchanges. The following is an example:

While working independently on a math assignment a fourth grade teacher over heard Lasandra say to Marcus, "Shut up." The teacher approaches Marcus (going to the victim first) and says, "Marcus, Lasandra just told you to shut up. Are you willing to work with her and help her learn another way of talking to her friends?" Marcus answers, "Yes." The teacher then turns her attention to Lasandra and says, "Lasandra, are you willing to learn another way of communicating with your friends?" She agrees. Both students and the teacher walk over to the time machine (a string of lights hanging on the wall). The teacher facilitates the process by saying, "Lasandra, you wanted Marcus to be quiet so you could focus on your math problems and you told him to shut up. Can you think of another way you could have told him to be quiet?" Lasandra thinks for a minute and says to Marcus, "Marcus, would you please be quiet. I can't think when you are talking." Marcus responds by saying, "Yes, I can. I'm sorry." Both students return to their seats and continue their math project. The rest of the class watched and learned valuable communication skills they may need in the future.

Instant replay

The purpose of the instant replay is the same as the time machine. It provides an opportunity for the teacher to take moments of conflict and use them to teach. The center consists of a yellow flag similar to those used by referees in soccer or football. To introduce the instant replay concept, the teacher could ask students if they have seen an instant replay on the television, if they know the function of a referee and if they can demonstrate ways a referee might signal a foul has occurred in the game. As children share their knowledge of the instant replay process in sports, the teacher can explain how it will work in class. The process can be summed up in the acronym **F.A.I.R.** *F* represents there has been a **F**oul committed. One person has said or done something hurtful to another. *A* stands for asking, "**A**re you willing to do an instant replay to change the interaction from hurtful to helpful?" *I* is for **I**gniting the brain. This will involve the children taking a deep breath to calm down and taking a moment to think about how the situation could be handled differently. The final step is represented by the letter *R* which stands for **R**eplay the scene. The parties involved now replay the situation using helpful communication skills. The teacher may need to assist the children with the words to be used. Instant replay is summed up below.

F = **F**oul committed
A = **A**re you willing to be helpful instead of hurtful
I = **I**gnite your brain by breathing and thinking
R = **R**eplay the scene using helpful communications

No time like the present!
This month vigilantly practice the following:

☑ **Consciously pay attention to your focus.** Are you focusing on what you *do* want to happen, or what you *don't* want?

☑ **Pivot when you are upset.** Say to yourself, "Okay, I'm upset. If I'm upset I am focusing on what I don't want. Do I want more of this in my life?" If the answer is *no*, breathe deeply (be a **S.T.A.R.**: **S**mile, **T**ake a deep breath, **A**nd **R**elax). Then tell your children specifically and firmly what to do and why. Relate the "why" to safety.

☑ **Breathe deeply and affirm the following principles three times a day.** "What I focus on, I get more of. When I'm upset, I always focus on what I don't want."

☑ **Go to the victim first in conflict situations.** Empower victims to deal with bullying situations.

☑ **Use tattling as a teaching opportunity.**

☑ **Set up a time machine or instant replay center.**

☑ **Transform passive and aggressive language into assertiveness.**

Look for these teaching moments

The curriculum for teaching assertiveness and respect will come from *your* children in *your* classroom. Look for moments when children intrude in others' spaces . They may do this physically or psychologically. Use tattling as a teaching opportunity.

Intrusive behaviors

Physical:

Pushing	Shoving
Grabbing	Hitting
Pinching	Kicking, etc.

 **Intrusive behaviors**

> *Psychological:*

Name calling	Looking provocatively at each other
Excluding others	Racism and sexism
Teasing	Intolerance of physical differences
Tattling	

Sample answers to "Activity to reverse negative programming" page 97.

1. Stop fidgeting with your papers.

    Kevin, work on problem number 3. (Point to #3). If you need help ask Marcus or raise your hand.

2. Don't throw objects, they could hurt people.

    Mary, you may throw balls outside. Take the blocks and stack them up into a tall tower like Marcus is doing.

3. Don't push your friends, that's not nice.

    Kurt, you wanted Chad to move. You may not push, pushing hurts. When you want Chad to move say, "Chad, move please."

4. Stop talking when I am talking.

    Melinda, sit quietly so you can hear the story.

Chapter 4
Choices
Building self esteem and willpower

POWER OF FREE WILL

The only person you can make change is yourself

Choices
Building Self Esteem and Willpower

Power: Power of Free Will
The only person you can *make* change is yourself

Value: Empowerment

Purpose: Empowers children while setting limits

Brain Development: Choice changes brain chemistry so that learning is optimized

Emotional Development: Builds self esteem and willpower; reduces impulsivity

Choices Principles:
1. The only person you can *make* change is yourself.
2. Giving your power away sets you up to blame.
3. Ask yourself, "How do I help the child more likely choose to ____ ," rather than, "How can I get the child to ____ ."
4. Making choices builds willpower and self esteem.

Principle #1: The only person you can make change is yourself!

The motto for your program this month is, "The only person you can *make* change is yourself." Think how often we believe it is our job to *make* others act a certain way. Take a deep breath and say to yourself while inhaling, "The only person I can *make* change." Then on the exhale slowly say to yourself, "is me." The icon for this month is a road sign signifying two paths that are possible. Life is filled with choices. One of the most fundamental choices is whether to actively change ourselves, our attitudes and our actions, or whether to spend energy trying to make others change.

I recently stayed in a lovely hotel in Chicago, in a room on the 36th floor. One morning, I rode the elevator with a woman who was irate because the elevator kept stopping. She was choosing to be a nut because the elevator had stopped for people. It wasn't behaving the way she thought it should. I thought to myself, "This is what elevators do." Why did she want to be a nut? Why do any of us want to be a nut? Why do we give our power away to elevators, children, spouses and institutions? What is so attractive about choosing to be a victim?

Reclaim your choices and you reclaim your power. If you say, "Don't make me have to take away those counting bears," you have given your power away to the child. You have put the child in charge by telling him that he is *making* you respond in a particular way. You can reclaim your power by acknowledging you are free to choose how you respond to situations and free to choose how you initiate interactions with others. You could say, "If you choose to throw the bears, I will take them away. You can count with them or play the matching game. What will you choose to do?"   In saying this, you maintain your self-control and send the message to the child that you are in charge of your choices and he is in charge of his. You have modeled responsibility and empowerment. Power comes from choice, not force.

> ## Power comes from choice, not force.

Free will has been and continues to be one of the hardest powers for me to embrace. I find it difficult to acknowledge free will in myself and others. I keep making two mistakes.   First, I continue to believe that outside forces can make me choose certain things in my life. My speech reveals this. I hear myself saying, "I have to exercise," or "I should call Michael." Such decisions are choices, not externally forced situations. I could just as easily have said, "I am going to exercise," or "I will call Michael." Second, I believe I can make others choose to act in ways I desire.

These mistakes are two sides of the same coin. If I believe others can make me act a certain way, it is reasonable to assume I can make others act in a certain way. Both these beliefs are false. Still, these beliefs are widely held, causing great trouble in relationships and profoundly shaping how we handle discipline situations.

 The belief that adults can *make* children mind and *get* them to change is as common as air. Most people consider it the parent's responsibility to *make* children behave. Since teachers operate in place of parents, they too feel the pressure to *make* children mind and *get* control of them.   This pressure creates enormous guilt in both teachers and parents since making others change is ultimately impossible. Certainly we can threaten someone into submission, however, you have probably run into a child who does not respond to threats, removal, loss of privileges or other forms of control. We have been operating under the illusion that we can *make* children mind us. No matter how much pressure we put on them to behave, it is their choice to submit their will to us.

The message that one person can control another and make others think, feel and behave in certain ways is taught daily. Teachers have parent conferences so that parents will *make* their children behave better in the classroom. Art teachers have conferences with a child's regular classroom teacher so she or he will *make* the child listen more appropriately during art lessons. Teachers send children to the office so the principal will *make* them shape up. Teachers in the classroom can be heard using comments like, "Look what you made me do, look how you made her feel, don't make her late for class." We must discipline ourselves first by changing our beliefs. By changing our beliefs, we also change our thoughts. This changes our feelings, which changes our behaviors. If a person truly believed that one could not make others change, new practices would emerge. Parent-teacher conferences would be designed to create a cooperative plan between parent and teacher to help the child become more successful at school. The same would occur between the regular classroom teacher and the special area teachers. Principals would come to cover classes so teachers would be free to work one-on-one with difficult children. Teachers would say, "see her face, she looks sad," instead of, "look how you made her feel." These might seem like slight modifications, but they are reflections of quantum shifts in beliefs.

We must rethink our beliefs. Can we *make* children behave in a certain manner? Can we make anyone, regardless of age, do something that they are set against doing? Is it possible to make an 8-month-old baby who is refusing peas actually swallow them? Is it possible to make a child who refuses to do his homework finish the assignments? It seems impossible to me to *make* others go against their own wishes. If we try to *make* others do things, we prime ourselves to rely on force. Our strong-arm tactics teach children it's legitimate to use force to influence others. Through force, we attempt to remove other people's choices. By removing their choices we remove their self-esteem and their willpower. We can no longer continue on this path, kidding ourselves by having self-esteem lessons on Friday.

Practice the Power of Free Will by consciously becoming aware of how often you think others are making you do things. Is the child *making* you put his name on the board or call his parents? Are the children talking during story time *making* you upset? Notice how often you use the words "have to" and "should." Practice changing "should" into "could" and changing "have to" into "I'm going to." Move from operating in a victim position into operating in an empowered state. Victim language absolves you of responsibility and thus removes your power. If you hear yourself saying, "The children are driving me nuts," change it to, "I am choosing to go nuts over the noise in this classroom." If you hear yourself saying, "I have to get that paper work in by Friday," change it to "I'm going to get the paper work in on Friday." By making the change from "should" to "could," you will transfer responsibility of your life from others to yourself. This puts you in charge. It also allows you the opportunity to teach the same skills to your students. Learned helplessness, victim perceptions and apathy are epidemic in our culture. It is time for a change.

Principle #2: Giving your power away sets you up to blame.

Giving your power away to children means you have put them in charge of your behavior. Many children take the power given to them by the teacher and try not to abuse their reign. When you say, "Don't make me have to speak to you again," these children straighten up and immediately try to regain love and approval. They seek to please others. They learn that their power comes from pleasing others, not choosing for oneself. Other children respond differently. When a teacher says to them, "You're making me angry, behave," they seem to take this information and experiment. It's as if they are thinking, "If this makes her angry, what would it take to make her cry?" They seek to control others. They learn that their power comes from controlling others, not from their own choices. When you give your power away to children, you never know what type of personality will respond. You don't know if you'll face a little Stalin or a Mother Theresa. Either way, once you give your power to others, you must seek to get it back, or live as a victim to life's experiences.

> **Giving your power away to children sets them up to be "pleasers" or "controllers."
> It also sets you up to blame.**

Below are some common phrases used by teachers who unknowingly give their power away to children. When we give our power away to children, we believe we are entitled to receive obedience due to our status as teachers. We model entitlement instead of empowerment. Each one of these phrases sends the false message that the child controls the teacher or classroom.

1. When you are quiet, I will begin.

   _____

2. Let me finish reading the story and I will help you.

   _____

3. Don't make me have to speak to you again.

   _____

4. You are driving me nuts.

   _____

5. Look how you made your friend feel.

   _____

6. You are ruining the story for everyone.

   _____

7.   I should do these grades tonight. I have to have them in by Monday.

   _____

8. Line up for lunch, okay?

_____

Activity to move from entitlement to empowerment

Rewrite each of the statements or questions above. Change them to empowering statements. Write your changes in the lines provided. Sample answers are provided on pages 155-156.

Activity to reclaim your power

List three common phrases you use to give your power away to children. After each phrase, rewrite the phrase from a position of entitlement (they owe me their obedience) to empowerment (I am committed to being responsible for my thoughts, feelings and actions).

1. Old phrase _____
New phrase _____
2. Old phrase _____
New phrase _____
3. Old phrase _____
New phrase _____

Most of us grew up hearing these statements (or ones like them at home). After years of such messages, we now feel a lingering sense of inadequacy. If we controlled our parents, why couldn't we *make* them happy? Why couldn't we *make* them get along with each other? Why couldn't we *be* better and *make* everything better? Of course, the reason is that we never really were in charge. We were simply given that false message by our well-meaning parents.

The blame game

If we believe we can make others change and we fail to perform our duty, another belief takes over our thoughts. We believe we are inadequate. We fight these feelings of inadequacy by starting a blame game, whereby teachers blame parents, parents blame school systems and both, when exhausted, blame children. In actuality, the blame game ends with us. We feel inadequate to handle the situations life presents.

We make decisions in every moment of every day, yet we often blame others for our own choices. "He made me do it," your child might cry. "Don't make me have to tell you again," you might warn. "Now look what you made me do, we missed the turn," your spouse might say. These examples show the kinds of words we say when we blame our own reaction or behavior onto an outside situation or another person. We move through most days on automatic pilot, forgetting that *we* are the ones in charge of our own decisions.

> Change "don't make me have to" into "I'm going to" and you will reclaim your power as a teacher.

In fact, we often choose to forget we are making choices. Life seems to "happen" to us because we lack the awareness that we *choose* to perceive things a certain way and we *choose* the thoughts we think. You come home from work moaning, "Boy, did I have a bad day." The big question is, who decides how your day will go? Does the day choose your thoughts about it? You complain, "Traffic today is horrible." Is it horrible, or are there simply many cars on the road? Traffic is not inherently horrible, but you can choose to perceive it as such.

Giving your power away results in upset. Upset usually is followed by blame. Blame removes the possibility of finding solutions because you are focused on what you don't want. What you focus on, you get more of and the cycle continues. At any moment you can seek to administer blame or look for solutions. You must choose.

Principle # 3: Ask yourself, "How do I help the child be more likely to choose to _____," rather than "How can I get the child to _____."

To shift from *making* children behave to relying on *choice,* you must change the question you ask yourself. Generally teachers ask, "How can I get the children to stay on task?" Asking, "How can I *get*," is the same as asking, "How can I *make*." These questions ask your brain to come up with every feared, forced, coercive or manipulative strategy you have ever been taught. If you ask a new question you will get new answers. By asking yourself, "How can I help the children be more likely to choose to stay on task," you will ask your brain to come up with a different set of answers. These new answers will be more creative, will be based on changing the structure of the classroom, and will be asking you to reflect upon yourself and the needs of children. This new question directs you to come up with developmentally appropriate discipline strategies. Start today by paying attention to the questions you ask yourself when you run into a child or a problem that is perplexing. Once you hear yourself say the word *"get"* or *"make,"* let that be a signal for you to change yourself first and children second.

Becoming brain smart

Research indicates that the brain acts differently when choice is offered (Glasser, 1985; Harter, 1982; Jensen, 1997; Mager & McCann, 1963; Seligman, 1987). Choice changes the brain's chemistry. When we feel we are lacking in choices, the brain produces norepinephrine. Norepinephrine is part of the brain's alarm system. In this state, motivation and morale are low and learning efficiency is poor. Choices, on the other hand, trigger the release of the brain's optimal thinking chemicals. These chemicals, known as endorphins, increase motivation, reduce stress, create positive attitudes and foster an optimistic "I can" attitude. In short, the child experiences a general sense of well-being and confidence (Ornstein, 1991).

One key to giving choices is that the child must be able to recognize he has a choice. Perceiving a choice is critical. Understanding this key is integral to your success when using the skill of choices. You must be conscious of your intent and the child's perception simultaneously. This requires practice and a willingness to make mistakes.

Commitment #1: I am willing to take responsibility for my choices. I understand that if I choose to believe that others are making me behave in certain ways I give my power away, stress my body, and put myself in the frame of mind to blame and punish someone.

Signature_____ Date _____

Reframing blame

"He made me do it! It wasn't my fault! He pushed first!" These are common phrases uttered by many children. Children have internalized the notion that offering blame instead of solutions is the best possible approach to life's upsets. Children tend to blame others in direct proportion to the amount and severity of the punishment they receive. Children who are rarely in trouble and have compassionate teachers/parents are most likely to respond, "I hit him, but he pushed me." They are not afraid to own their choices and take some responsibility for them. Children who are chronically in trouble and live on a diet of regular punishments at home/school are more reluctant to stand up and declare their role in misbehavior. It is more likely that they will lie out of fear.

For children to begin making wise choices and own the choices they are making, the fear of punishment must be minimal. The focus must be on solutions and problem solving. The "who is the boss of you" skill below will help children who tend to blame others for their actions reclaim their power.

Child statement	Teacher response
1. "Ernie made me do it!"	"So Ernie is the boss of you?"
"No!"	"What could you do differently if you were the boss of you?"
2. "Ernie made me do it"	"So Ernie is the boss of you?"
"Yes!"	"How sad! That must be hard for you with Ernie bossing you all the time."

 ## Activity to reframe blame behavior

Role-play the following blame situations. Reframe the blame in your response:

1. Child says, "Bryan made me pull the fire alarm."

2. Child says, "It wasn't my fault, he pushed me first."

Two positive choices

Young children, still developing a sense of their own autonomy, often need to assert themselves when they hear an adult command. Instead of giving an assertive command, you can offer children two acceptable choices. These choices allow children to comply with your wishes while having the "last word." By offering children two positive choices, you help them do the following:

- ☑ Attend to the task you deem important
- ☑ Comply with your wishes
- ☑ Learn decision-making skills
- ☑ Feel empowered, thereby reducing power struggles
- ☑ Redirect their behavior and learn impulse control
- ☑ Establish and maintain self control

Ms. Barry is working with Mara to help her control her impulses and follow through in cleaning up after center time. She goes to where Mara is playing, kneels down close by and waits for her to make eye contact. Then Ms. Barry gives an assertive command such as, "Put your toys in the bin. You can tell where each toy belongs by looking at the pictures on the containers." Ms. Barry consciously points to the bins and the pictures as she speaks. She knows nonverbal gestures will help Mara attend to her words. Ms. Barry also waits for Mara to begin putting the toys away so she can praise her for choosing to comply with the command. Once Mara seems focused and on task, Ms. Barry leaves to assist other children.

Several minutes later, Ms. Barry checks on Mara. The child has emptied the toy bin and is sitting in it, taking off her clothes. With a deep breath, Ms. Barry reaffirms to herself what she wants Mara to do and offers her two positive choices. "Mara, you have a choice. You may climb out of the bin and put on your shirt, or you may climb out and put on your shoes. What do you choose?" Mara begins climbing out and says, "Shoes." With that decision, Mara empowered herself to take action. She channeled her will and curbed her impulses to continue playing. She committed herself to putting on her shoes.

In this story, Ms. Barry offered Mara two positive choices. Most of us were not raised in this fashion, so thinking in this manner may seem awkward at first. We are accustomed to giving a positive choice and a negative choice. Growing up we heard our parents say, "You can eat what is offered or starve." "You can go to sleep now or never have another sleepover." I call these false choices. They have coercion as their intent. When you offer a false choice, you set children up to believe when they think, feel or choose differently than you, they are bad, wrong or disrespectful instead of simply making a choice. You can guess the devastating effects this could have later in life in marriages when each person tries desperately to have all household members think, feel and act like him or her.

Skill #1: The five steps in delivering two positive choices

The following steps will help you deliver two positive choices:

Step 1: Breathe deeply. Think about what you want the child to do. Make a conscious decision.

A positive and negative option is not really a choice but a manipulation.

Step 2: Tell the child, "You have a choice!" in an upbeat tone. Your positive attitude will lighten up the situation, especially if the child seems resistant. It will also help the child in perceiving the options as choices. For older children you might say, "Seems to me you have a couple of options."

Step 3: State the two choices you have created to achieve your goal. Say, "You may _____ or you may _____." For older children you might say, "Feel free to _____ or _____. What would be better for you?"

Step 4: Complete the process by asking the child for a commitment. You might say, "What is your choice?" If the child hesitates, you may want to repeat the options.

Step 5: Notice your child's choice. Do this by saying, "You chose_____ !" in a very encouraging voice with loving intent. Be sure to make this final comment. It will bring crucial awareness to your child about his choice. Remember, most people make their choices unconsciously and end up feeling controlled by life. Children who are aware of their choices will not only feel less controlled, but will also have greater self control.

In order to deliver two positive choices to children, you must:

☑ Give children true choices. Offer either two positive options or two options that are both acceptable to you.

☑ Think in positive terms about what you want children to do.

142

Two positive choices optimize the chance for cooperation.

Activity to make two positive choices

Below are scenarios in which you might elect to use the discipline skill of two positive choices. Think first of what you want the child *to do*. Then offer two choices that will allow him to achieve that goal. Express these options to him in an upbeat manner.

Scene: Playing with food

Nathan (age 3) is busily pounding his fist on his pizza during lunchtime. Breathe deeply. Think about what you want to happen. Now decide which choices you will offer Nathan. You might say, "Nathan you have a choice. You may _____ or _____. What will you choose? You chose to _____!"

Scene: Listening

Meredith (age 8) is playing with an eraser cover instead of listening to the teacher. Think about what you want Meredith to do. Select two options that would achieve that goal and present them to Meredith. You might say: "_____
_____."

Scene: Finishing work

Cameron (age 10) is sketching B-2 bombers on his notepad instead of completing his math problems. Take a breath. Think about what you want Cameron to do. You might say: "_____."

Sample answers can be found on page 156.

143

The "what if's"

By now I'm sure that "what if's" are running wildly through your head. "What if the child doesn't choose either option?" is probably your biggest anxiety. Remember fear always manifests itself as resistance. Resistance is the enemy of learning. If you have been obsessing about what could go wrong, take a deep breath, go back, reread the sections and do the exercises.

Principle #4: Making choices builds willpower and self esteem.

A person's ability to make choices and commit to those choices is a measure of self-esteem. To really make a choice, you must make a decision and accept the consequences of that decision. Therefore, it is vital to help children who have trouble making choices and/or accepting the consequences of their choices. You can only help your children if you choose to help yourself first. Does this conversation sound familiar?

"Where would you like to have lunch?" asks Melinda.

"Wherever, doesn't matter," responds Barb.

"Doesn't matter to me either. Really, whatever you like is fine," says Melinda.

"You're driving, you decide," answers Barb.

In our society, women are socialized to please others. It is impossible, though, to make your own choices and simultaneously please others. As a teacher, you cannot set limits and take care of the children's feelings at the same time.

> **It is impossible to make your own choices and simultaneously please others.**

Children who have trouble making choices

Children who have trouble making choices fall into the following four categories:

1. Those who refuse to make a choice
2. Those who resist the structure given (given a choice of A or B, they pick C)
3. Those who change their minds (given a choice of A or B, they pick A, then switch to B, back to A, etc.)
4. Those who developmentally do not understand what a choice is

Helping children who refuse to choose

Lisa was given a choice—put her backpack on the shelf in her cubby or hang it on the hook. Lisa stood staring at her teacher, then suddenly burst into tears. For Lisa, the decision was overwhelming. Perhaps you can relate to Lisa. Have you ever felt so stressed that you thought you simply couldn't handle one more thing? Tremendous anxiety is brewing within children who find decision-making very difficult. This difficulty is their way of saying, "My world is overwhelming." A child's overwhelmed feelings could come from developmental issues. Imagine the length of your arm changing daily or your vocabulary doubling in a month. Rapid change like this can be taxing. The anxiety may have its roots in major life stresses like moving or a death. It may also stem from everyday aggravations such as disappointing your parents or yourself, changing teachers, fighting with friends or having been teased by classmates.

Depending on their temperament, some children get overwhelmed easily. Others seem to roll with life like a surfer on a wave. Don't fight the child's temperament. Instead, learn how to best respond to it. To assist children who have trouble with choices, do the following:

1. **Point out to the child the many choices they are always making.** For instance, when they decide to color with crayons, say, "I see you chose to draw today." Whenever possible, show the child the choices he or she is always making. The child may look at you as if to say, "Duh." That's great—it means that they are aware of their own actions. Slow, discouraged or at-risk learners generally have inappropriate self-convincer strategies (Jensen, 1997). Simply put, they often don't know what they know. It is our job to make their choices conscious by announcing and describing them.

2. **Offer the child small choices that involve closeness with you.** For example, say, "Marvin, you have a choice. You may hold my left hand or right hand to walk in the building. Which do you pick? You chose my right hand! I like holding hands with

you." Making choices demands autonomy. At certain times, autonomy is scary for some children. To ease the child towards independence, use closeness with you as a starting point.

3. Model acceptance of mistakes. Children who refuse to choose may fear disappointing others or being wrong. Model the fact that everyone slips up. Use the skill called "think aloud."

"Gary, you chose to stack the blocks on top of each other."

©1999 Loving Guidance, Inc.

Skill #2: Think aloud

When you think aloud, you say your inner thoughts out loud. This allows the children to see how you handle making a mistake. An example follows:

A teacher says, "Where is my stapler? You children know better than to take things off my desk. Who took it? Speak up! It's important to respect other people's property. There will be no recess today." Carmen said, "But teacher, Mrs. McElwain borrowed your stapler yesterday." The teacher then realized she had made a serious mistake. She had not only blamed her children, she had attacked them. She also realized this was a perfect time to use the "think aloud" technique. Speaking aloud, she began, "Well, I made a big mistake. I was mad about the missing stapler. I thought you children were being disrespectful and not asking me first. Actually, I was the one who was disrespectful to you. I blamed you and tried to make you feel as rotten as I felt."

146

She continued, "I will take a deep breath and forgive myself for my mistakes. I owe you an apology. Children, I am sorry for my behavior. Next time I feel upset I am going to breathe deeply and collect some information instead of blaming."

Thinking out loud, this teacher modeled the constructive handling of mistakes. She modeled learning from a mistake and making a commitment to change her behavior. Many children learn that no matter what you do, an apology will eliminate the problem. Children must learn that while it is important to express regrets about misdeeds, you must also (and more importantly) change misguided behavior.

Helping children who resist the given structure

Some children will use structured choices you offer as an opportunity for a power struggle. Such children, when offered two options, consistently create a third option in order to maintain control of the situation. Asked to pick A or B, they select C. You might say, "Megan you have a choice. You may walk next to me in the hall or hold my hand. What is your choice?" At this point, the child chooses option C and simply runs off.

Before we discuss how to handle resistance, we need to understand the reason control matters so greatly to these children. We must explore the events in a child's life that prompt him or her to oppose any or most of the structure created by an adult. Developmental opposition and learned opposition are two reasons children who *habitually* resist structure behave this way. Both types of opposition are explored and helpful solutions are given on the following pages.

Developmental opposition

All young children go through a process that researchers call *individuation separation*. This process transforms a helpless, dependent infant into a person with a unique identity. During this journey towards selfhood, the child starts to define himself as that which is "not Mom" or "not Dad." Any assertive stance from an adult prompts the child to react with the opposite behavior. Children in the oppositional years often show their resistance by ignoring the structured choices an adult presents. These children are testing, not trying to "make" you angry or see what they can get away with. They are simply testing to figure out who they are (where they end and you begin) and to discover their uniqueness.

To help a child who resists structured choices for developmental reasons, do the following:

☑   Realize that if you allow yourself to be dragged into a power struggle, you have become part of the problem not the solution. To avoid this trap, take a deep breath, become conscious of your thoughts and focus on what you want the child to do. If you slip into focusing on what you don't want (stop crying, stop talking, don't hit) you will be *in* the power struggle.

☑   Once you are in control of yourself, recognize that your child will or will not choose to operate within your framework. Coercion is the problem, not the answer. Consciously choose to rely on the Power of Free Will. You both have a choice of how to behave. You can control your actions, but not the child's.

☑   Use the parroting technique. This involves repeating the options you have presented to the child in a calm, assertive voice.

Skill #3: The parroting technique

An example of the parroting technique follows:

Parent: "Joseph, it is time to put away these toys. You have a choice. You can begin by picking up small blocks or large ones. What is your choice?"

Joseph: "No!" He begins throwing the blocks.

Parent: "Joseph, it is time to clean up. You have a choice. Small blocks or large ones. What is your choice?"

Joseph: "You can't make me. I hate you."

Parent: "Small blocks or large ones. What is your choice?"

As you continue to calmly repeat the choices, one of three things is likely to occur. **1)** Joseph may start to put away blocks. He may do this begrudgingly. **2)** He might escalate in his verbal assault on you and resort to physical aggression like hitting. **3)** He might also attempt to escape the situation through a temper tantrum or by running away.

If Joseph escalates in his opposition you can disengage from the fight by saying, "You are right Joseph, I can't make you clean up. I hope you choose to be a part of this school family." Turn and walk away. When Joseph recovers have him clean up his mess and celebrate his accomplishments with him. For further information on how to deal with and prevent power struggles, listen to the audio tape entitled *Preventing Power Struggles* by Dr. Becky Bailey.

If your child chooses to cooperate with you, celebrate his choice. Recognize how much willpower and energy the child harnessed to transform his negative response into a positive one and to engage in the cleanup process. This is close to a miracle, celebrate it!

Have you ever been so upset that your negative thoughts about another person or situation blew up in your own mind to reach the point of outrage? Have you ever felt unfairly treated? Have you ever felt determined to prove that your point of view was correct? Think about how much strength it takes to stop a landslide of blaming, anger and self-righteousness in order to become cooperative again. The child who chooses to comply has just completed a difficult process, one adults struggle with mightily. From the depth of your heart, praise your child and celebrate his victory of love over fear. Your words will be perfect if your intention is to show true thanks for his gift of choosing cooperation over opposition. Any leftover huffs and puffs your child may mutter are just the bleeding off of the adrenaline that was rushing through his body during the conflict.

Learned opposition

The second type of child who resists choices has learned resistance as a way to get needs met. Children learn resistance in three basic ways. It is learned due to parenting that fails to meet the child's needs, permissive parenting and family troubles.

Permissive parents either cave in to the child when he becomes upset or try to dance around an issue to avoid upsetting him. These kinds of actions teach a youngster to fight limits and misbehave to get his way. They also teach children that adults don't mean what they say. The sad part of this is that when a permissive parent looks at their child and says, "I love you," the child can't believe that either.

The second way a child learns to resist structured choices begins in infancy and pertains to the way a baby's needs were met or not met. When a baby has a need (hunger, warmth, comfort) he enters an aroused state. When an adult fulfills the baby's need, a relaxed state is produced. If the parent responds to the baby, but cannot soothe him (due to colic, premature birth or other physical problems), the baby will remain in a overly-aroused state. From the infant's perspective, his needs were not met. That baby may come to believe that he must attempt to run the world in order to have his needs met. As he grows, the child may become controlling and resist imposed structure. These children expend a lot of energy trying to steer the world their way because they believe this is their only chance for survival. Such children do not resist structure to test the boundaries of their power. Instead they try to control others in order to feel safe. They have a low tolerance for frustration.

One last way a child learns to oppose structured choices is through the experience of serious family trouble (divorce, death, a depressed, drug-abusing or alcoholic parent). Such troubles create enormous stress, leaving the child feeling overwhelmed and unable to make choices. This child attempts to control a life that seems out of control.

You can help a child who has learned to oppose structure

To help children who have learned to oppose structure, diligently practice all the techniques of *Conscious Discipline*. Although an oppositional child will challenge your patience, you *must* maintain self-control to help him. Children who are willful and controlling are not likely respond to the old fear-based approach to discipline. Regardless of the discipline style you use, power struggles may be common. Power struggles always require two willing participants. Without two players, the struggle cannot exist. A one-person struggle is like a one-handed clap or playing tug-of-war with only one player. It is impossible.

With two willing participants, power struggles escalate.

Power struggles always require two willing participants.

©1999 Loving Guidance, Inc.

You will need to use the steps listed below to enable both you and the child to heal after a power struggle has occurred.

☑ **Forgive yourself.** Forgiveness takes place in three steps, the three R's of forgiveness. First, *recognize* and accept your feelings. Tell yourself, "I feel angry and anxious and that's okay." Second, *reframe* the experience. Forget about finding a good guy and a villain. Admit that given your states of mind, you did your best and so did the child. Third, *request* help. Calmly ask your child to work with you in forging new patterns of behavior.

☑ **Engage the child in solving problems.**

☑ **Help the child feel powerful.** Do this by giving him or her the chance to participate often in activities he enjoys and at which he can succeed.

☑ **Spend time with the child to develop a trusting relationship.**

Some oppositional children may have neurological imbalances. They may have attention deficits or sensory integration issues. Chronic issues like these require evaluation and some children may need medication. Misbehavior is a call for help. Sometimes the call is for mental health services, social services or medical services.

Helping children who change their mind

Morgan's teacher offered her the choice of milk or juice for a snack. She selected milk. When the teacher served the milk, Morgan pushed it away and said, "No. Juice." The teacher then passed her some juice and Morgan said, "I want milk." Understandably, the teacher was ready to dump both drinks on her head.

Children like Morgan may have self-esteem issues. They may, at an indecisive moment, be feeling down on themselves or their world for many reasons. She could be tired or stressed by a family problem. She might be having a rough morning. Through indecisiveness, Morgan is trying to control her environment. Children who pick "C" after being given a choice between "A" and "B," are launching a direct confrontation. You could call them aggressive. Children like Morgan, on the other hand, could be called passive aggressive. They use passive rather than direct means to control others.

Helping these children begins with a diagnosis. The first question Morgan's teacher could ask herself is whether this is a developmental issue or a learned behavior. Is indecisiveness a new behavior for this child? Is it occasional or chronic?

When an inability to choose appears from nowhere and occurs infrequently, the child may be overwhelmed by stress. Children who are stressed often regress developmentally (they revert to behaviors you would expect from a much younger child). When children regress, they need assertive commands rather than choices. The teacher could say, "Morgan, you are having trouble choosing for yourself this morning. Here is the milk, drink it if you like." Commands teach children what to do. Choices teach children how to make decisions and keep commitments. Teaching decision-making to a 6-month-old infant would be silly. The same is true for highly stressed children.

If the problem is chronic, there is a good chance it is a learned behavior. The child gets more attention by changing her mind than she does for being cooperative. This is a side-effect of living in a "hurry up" world.

Helping children with developmental delays

Children with special needs may require structured assistance in understanding the concept of choices. They may need physical adaptations in the environment in order to make their choices. To assist in this process the adult can do the following:

☑   Point out to the children they are always making choices.

☑   Observe children playing to see what toys they prefer. Present the child with a favorite toy and a different type of toy. Generally, the child will select his or her favorite toy by eye gaze, pointing, touching or verbalizing. As the child makes the selection, reinforce the idea the child has made a choice. You might say, "You made a choice to play with the block. You chose the block. Here it is for you to play with." This same exercise can be done with pictures of toys.

Cindy loves horses. She would spend the entire day with the plastic horses if the teacher would let her. Mr. Worrel uses this information to assist Cindy in understanding the concept of choice. He puts a firetruck and a horse in front of Cindy and says, "Cindy, you have a choice. You can play with the firetruck or the horse. What is your choice?" Cindy reaches for the horse with a loud squeal. "I see you chose the horse. Here it is. You made a choice. How exciting," says Mr. Worrell with encouraging, loving intent.

You chose the horse!

Children who are physically challenged may need adaptive devices in their environment to facilitate their ability to make choices. Many toys can be adapted to include switches that allow the child to manipulate the toy with the strength and coordination he does possess. Children who need assistance in talking can be provided communication boards to enable them to communicate choice through pictures. The child points at the pictures or uses eye gaze to indicate what he would like to have happen, the help he may need or simply to engage in conversation. See the reference section at the end of this book for more information on adapting toys for children with special needs.

Exercising the power of free will brings lasting changes

Becoming aware of our choices as adults and passing this awareness on to our children is a wonderful gift. You can become conscious of your choices as you *interact* with your child or you can opt to remain unconscious of your choices and simply *react* to your child. Once you accept that you are constantly making choices, you take charge of yourself. You realize your power lies within you, not in your ability to manipulate others. You can become a conscious choice-maker or you can become controlling. The choice is yours alone.

Go conscious, not crazy!

Physical structure that support the skill of choices

The physical structure that will support the skill of choice is the picture rule cards. The picture rule cards were introduced in Chapter 2 as part of the structures that build the school family (page 61). The purpose of the picture rule cards is to provide children with visual images of helpful choices they can make when they find themselves involved in hurtful actions.

Picture rule cards

Most schools require teachers to post the rules. Often these rules are written for children of all ages whether they can read them or not. A more effective way to display the rules in the classroom is to provide visual rules. By putting the rules in picture form, children can use the information more effectively. Young children encode information in pictures. They do not use inner speech to govern their behavior. Like a gymnast, young children need visual images of successful behavior. Each rule in the card set provides children with two helpful choices and one hurtful choice. If children find themselves making a hurtful choice, they are visually provided options to redirect their behavior. The cards are also helpful reviews before an activity to show the expected behavior. Before leaving the room, the teacher could show the children their options with the cards. The children have the choice of walking with their hands by their sides like soldiers or walking more relaxed with arms swinging casually.

No time like the present!

This month vigilantly practice the Power of Free Will by taking these steps:

☑ Listen consciously to your inner and outer speech. Notice how often you say the words *get, have to, should, ought to, must* and *don't make me.* Consciously choose to reframe these words into more powerful statements. Convert your *make me* language into choice language. Instead of saying, "Don't make me stop this car," say, "I am going to stop the car until you have your seat belt on." Instead of saying, "You are driving me nuts," say, "I feel crazy. Too much is happening at once." Then assertively tell the children what to do. "Sit down at your tables and take four deep, slow breaths with me."

☑ Catch yourself saying, "How can I make the child _____?" and "How can I get the child to _____?" Change the question to, "How can I help the child be more likely to choose to _____?"

☑ Change "should" to "could," then make a choice. When you hear yourself saying, "I *should* run to the dry cleaner," catch yourself. Own your choices and say instead, "I *could* run to the dry cleaner." Then decide whether you will or will not. There is no *should* or *ought to*, only choices. Start choosing.

**You may line up
in your own space.**

**You may line up
with your hands by your sides.**

**You may not push and shove
when you line up.**

154

☑ Practice allowing others to have their own thoughts and feelings. Resist the urge to try to *make* others happy or convince them you have all the answers. Ask yourself, "Would I rather be *right* or *happy*?"

☑ For one day, give up the attitude, "I don't know and I don't care." It allows you to avoid making choices. Act as if you *do* know. If a friend asks where you'd like to eat lunch, state your preferences clearly. "I'd like Chinese food."

☑ Post picture rule cards in the classroom. Use them to help children learn rules and make choices.

☑ Use the skill of two positive choices.

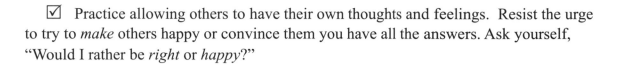 ## Look for these teaching moments

Giving children choices is one way to be assertive while empowering children at the same time. Any time you give an assertive command you could just as well have given two prescribed choices. Sometimes children resist assertive commands and operate better with choices. Sometimes children resist choices and operate better with assertive commands. This you must discover as you work with your unique children.

 ## These children often benefit from two positive choices

Children who do not follow the directions the first time

Children who have difficulty focusing and staying on task

Children who are somewhat defiant and like to boss other children around

Children who have trouble making choices

Children who seem to be feeling powerless

Children who appear to have low self esteem

 ## These children often benefit from assertive commands

Children who chronically change their minds

Children who are overly stressed or easily overwhelmed

Sample answers to "Activity to move from entitlement to empowerment," pages 136-137:
Remember there are no right answers. To change these statements you must at times make up pretend situations to address. Your pretend situations are just as valid as mine.

1. When you are quiet, I will begin.

    <u>It is time for announcements. Sit quietly.</u>

2.   Let me finish reading the story and I will help you.

       <u>I will help you when I am finished reading the story.</u>

3.   Don't make me have to speak to you again.

       <u>What can I do to help you remember to keep all four legs of your
       chair on the floor?</u>

4.   You are driving me nuts.

       <u>I feel out of control. I am going to breathe deep and slowly. I want
       you to breathe with me.</u>

5.   Look how you made your friend feel.

       <u>See her face, she seems sad. Her face is saying, "I didn't like it when you hit
       me."</u>

6.   You are ruining the story for everyone.

       <u>Sit quietly so everyone can hear the story.</u>

7.   I should do these grades tonight. I have to have them in by Monday.

       <u>I could do these grades tonight. I must decide.</u>

8.   Line up for lunch, okay?

       <u>Line up for lunch. Look around and see if anyone needs help.</u>

Sample answers to "Activity to make positive choices," page 143:

"Nathan, you have a choice. You may eat your pizza or take your tray to the trash can.
What will you choose? You chose to eat some more. I can see your teeth working hard just like
this (imitate chewing motions)."

"Merideth, you have a choice. You may put your eraser away and listen from your desk
or sit here (point to new location) to listen to the directions. Which will you choose? You
decided to listen from your desk."

"Cameron, it seems you have a couple of options. You can work on your math by
yourself or you can ask for help. Which would be better for you? You decided to get some help.
In our school family we help each other be successful."

Chapter 5

Positive Intent

Creating teaching moments

Power of Love

See the best in others

Positive Intent
Creating Teaching Moments

Power: Power of Love
         See the best in others

Value: Diversity

Purpose: Create teaching moments especially with oppositional or aggressive children

Brain Development: Thoughts physically alter the cells in the body

Emotional Development: Improves self-image and builds trust

Positive Intent Principles:
1. See the best in one another.
2. What you offer to others, you strengthen within yourself.
3. Children arc cithcr cxtending love or calling for love (help).
4. Attributing positive intent creates teaching moments by transforming resistance into cooperation.
5. Attributing negative intent to children teaches "gang readiness" skills.
6. Children cannot *behave* differently until they are *seen* differently.

Principle # 1: See the best in others.

This month the motto for your program is "see the best in others." This motto represents the Power of Love. Love looks for the best in people and situations. It sees the beauty in differences. The icon for the Power of Love is a pair of eyeglasses with hearts in the center to remind us it is possible to look at the world differently. The glasses remind us to look at the world through loving eyes. When we search for beauty, it is always found. When we search for meanness, it is always found. The choice is ours.

Take a deep breath. As you inhale, say to yourself, "I am willing to see." As you exhale, say to yourself, "The best in others." It is easy to see the best in others when they act appropriately. It is much harder to hold this perception when they make "poor" choices. The paradox is that children who make "poor" choices feel poorly about themselves. They are the ones who have not consistently had others see the best in them. Positive intent has the power to turn children around, changing aggressive children into cooperative members of your classroom and helping bullies learn other ways of feeling in control and safe. This skill will also send you home feeling better about yourself.

Principle #2: What you offer to others, you strengthen within yourself.

The overriding principle from which *Conscious Discipline* is founded is, "What you offer to others you strengthen within yourself." One of the myths we have grown to embrace is that we can attack others (verbally or physically) without harm to ourselves. Recently, a friend of mine said, "I will never forgive my niece." She has decided to hold on to her anger with the misguided illusion that the anger inside her will somehow change her niece. Anger, like other emotions, is energy in motion (e-motion). Each energy is designed as a signal. Anger is the signal of change. Unfortunately, we have taken the position that anger directed outward at others changes the other person. In reality, anger is a signal from within that says we need to change our own attitude or actions. Each emotion creates a biochemistry within our bodies. Anger and fear emit a hormone called cortisol. Cortisol has the capacity to kill brain cells when in excess. It actually damages the hippocampus in the brain, reducing one's capacity to store memories. Alzheimer's patients have severe damage to the hippocampus. Cortisol may also be responsible for other degenerative diseases.

There is an African proverb that states, "What you see with your eyes you value with your heart." If this is true, many of us value hurting, hatred and exploitation.

To grasp the power of this principle, I want you to do an exercise with me. Stop reading for a moment and think of someone you love. Silently and with a full heart, wish that person well. If no one comes to mind just take a moment to be grateful for some aspect of your life—your home, health, job, whatever. Now notice how you feel inside. When we wish others well, we tend to "well up" on the inside with warm feelings of comfort. If we offer gratitude, we tend to feel grateful and blessed.

> **If you offer others love and gratitude,
> you will feel warm and blessed.**

The same kind of mirroring occurs when we look at the world and focus on what is wrong or lacking. It's a paradox, but it is true. Your sense of self esteem does not come from how other people see you, but from how you see other people. If you choose to see what's missing, lacking and not good enough, you not only inhibit change from occurring, you destroy your own sense of value. Feeling powerless, you are primed to blame someone for your discomfort. Those who are blamed deserve punishment. Punishment is derived from the intent to hurt. As you hurt others, you value hurting and hurt yourself.

Judging the intentions of others

Pretend a friend had committed to call on Friday to discuss a very important issue with you. Friday rolls around and there is no phone call. You call her house and there is no answer. At this point you start trying to figure *why* your friend did not respond. You spend an enormous amount of time trying to figure out why she is taking certain actions. Most of us are unaware of how much time we spend trying to figure out the motives of others. We are constantly trying to figure out what people are "really up to." We take in every subtle cue available from words, facial expressions, gestures and body posture to make our conclusions. Using this information, we make up our theories as to why people are acting a certain way. These theories are tested by asking calculated questions and checking responses. This is only the beginning! Then we put all this information into our brains and go over the data bit by bit, playing back the conversation like court transcripts in our heads. We check this new information with data from previous conversations and evidence we've heard from other sources. All this, just to make a guess at the other person's true intentions. Once we have a relatively complete theory, we draw in friends to discuss the possibility that we are correct in our assumptions. These conversations could last hours or days, involving more and more people. Finally, after all this investigative work, we decide we have *the* answer. And whether we are right or not, we treat the person as if we know their motivation. This treatment, based on our biased conclusions, will dictate how we treat the other person and how they respond to us.

Why is figuring out the intentions of others so crucial that we would spend this enormous amount of time and energy on the task? We think we *must* figure out the intentions of others because if we don't, we will not know what their actions mean and we will not know how to respond. If we do not know how to respond, how will we protect ourselves from attack or some sneaky trick that may leave us humiliated? On the other hand, how will we know when good is being offered so we can be thankful and encourage more of the same? Somehow, we have come to believe that by assessing another person's motives accurately, we can build a life surrounded by kindness and protected from meanness. This is simply untrue.

Though we are attentive to both the positive and negative intentions of others, we are more concerned with the negative. We are constantly looking for how much "meanness" or "disrespect" was involved. With this preoccupation we tend to overlook loving intentions. Many a person's positive intentions are interpreted to be simply a cover up for some seedy darkness, ready to strike you with your defenses down. So we remain guarded ready to defend and attack at all times. We are on alert — with attack, manipulation and coercion on stand-by. This leaves our body in a constant state of stress. Stress is a biochemistry that wears down the body. It is a main source of many degenerative diseases. In essence, we are destroying ourselves in our attempts to discern the motives of others.

Accurately assessing the intentions of others is impossible. Before reading this, you probably weren't aware of your efforts to uncover people's motivations. Most of us aren't even totally aware of what is motivating us to take certain actions. Yet, we demand children as young as three years old tell us, "Why did you hit him? Why did you take the puppet? Why are you feeling angry?" The truth is that we make up motivations. How we choose to make them up effects both the person we attribute the motives to and ourselves. If you make up negative motives you will be guarded, ready for defense or attack. If you make up positive motives, you will be relaxed and calm.

With children, you have the opportunity to make up the intentions behind their behavior. You can assume the children are trying to make your day difficult, they are mean or they like being disrespectful. Alternatively, you could assume a child is hurting on the inside, needs some love or is misbehaving because she lacks better skills for getting what she wants. Again, the choice is yours. Your choice in attributing negative or positive motives directs your handling of each situation. If you choose to attribute a positive intent, you will feel peaceful inside. If you choose to attribute a negative intent, you will feel inadequate yourself and bring less patience to your handling of the conflict. When you choose to be unforgiving, you will see intentional acts of meanness instead of innocent mistakes.

Years ago a boy and his dog, a black labrador, got lost in Florida's Ocala National Forest. Fortunately, both were found the next day. Television news reporters announced that the dog had stayed with the boy to keep him warm. I wondered, "Who interviewed that dog?" Soon after, sales of black labrador puppies in Florida soared as parents bought dogs to protect their children. If we are going to attribute intentions to others, why not attribute noble ones? We did it for the dog.

Love sees the best in people, including children. Being determined to find fault in others simply means that we are unwilling to change. We want the world to go according to our plan. When that doesn't happen, life feels out of control and scary. We then believe that if someone was to blame for this inconvenience, these "yucky" feelings could be dumped on someone else. Therefore, we attempt to give away our anger, fear, condemnation and judgments to return to a state of peace. It does not work this way because what you offer to others you experience within yourself. When you offer condemnation, you feel condemned. When you give people credit for having good intentions, you have far more "good days" and you keep your self-esteem high. You also highlight for your children the best aspects of themselves and others. Your interpretation of your children's actions defines both them and you. That is powerful!

> **Love sees the best in people—including children.**

Principle # 3: Children are either extending love or calling for love (help).

The Power of Love simplifies the search for other people's motivations. Love says that there are only two intentions that a person may have. The first intention is to extend love. This is demonstrated in behaviors that are kind, respectful and helpful. The second intent is a call for love. In this instance the behavior is hurtful to themselves and others, showing a need for love to be extended.

Children utilize the skills they have been taught to meet their needs. A college student of mine shared an interesting experience. She was taught in grade school to put her head down on her desk when she was "bad." This practice remained dormant in her subconscious until one day in high school a group of friends were talking during the teacher's lecture. The teacher stopped the lesson and screamed at the girls, chastising them for being rude and inconsiderate. Ginger, my student, immediately put her head down as the feelings of being "bad" cycled through her body. The teacher then began to shout, "Well, Miss Ginger, if you don't find my words interesting or worth staying awake to listen to, you can march yourself down to the principal's office. I don't take to students who deliberately act disrespectful to me." The teacher had interpreted Ginger's head down position as one of disrespect. Ginger, in her mind, had put her head down in respect for the teacher. This was the skill that Ginger learned. Many children are taught, mostly through modeling, to scream when they are angry, to hit when they are frustrated, to manipulate when they want something and to appease others to avoid conflict. The Power of Love perceives these behaviors as calls for help.

Skill #1: Reframing

One of the brain's many tasks is to discern patterns. It tends to repeat past behaviors. Commiting yourself to view the world through a different set of lenses doesn't mean you will be automatically successful. Our brains have been trained to attribute negative intentions to others and ourselves. We have also been trained to focus our attention on what is *wrong*. Attention follows intention and vice versa. If you focus on what's wrong you have attributed negative intention. If you attribute negative motives to others, you will focus on behaviors that were not good enough. How do you know if you need to reframe a situation? Notice if you are upset. When you are upset, you are focused on what you don't want in your life. Thus, you have attributed negative intention. The solution is to reframe the situation and the people in it. You must shift your beliefs about the other person's motives from negative to positive. Remember, when the behavior is hurtful, the child's intent is to call for help. Ask yourself, "What help does the child need?" The answer could easily be that the child needs physical restraint, needs to learn anger management skills or needs to learn new social skills to get what he wants.

Activity to move from negative to positive intent

Reframe the negative intent attributed to children on the left to a positive intent. I did the first one as an example.

Negative intent	Positive reframing
Children are just mean.	Children need social skills.
They are just trying to get my attention.	_____
They sure know how to push my buttons.	_____
He's just hurtful for no reason.	_____
He keeps others from learning.	_____
She is disrupting this class.	_____
She is just plain lazy.	_____

If you feel unsure of your responses, remember there are no wrong answers, as long as you have answered with the Power of Love and Positive Intent. Notice in your answers that negative intent assumes the child's behavior is about *you*, while positive intent let's the child's behavior be about *the child*. Below are some sample answers.

Negative intent	Positive reframing
Children are just mean.	Children need social skills.
They are just trying to get my attention.	This child needs help in learning to focus.
They sure know how to push my buttons.	I must learn to stay calm.
He's just hurtful for no reason.	He needs help managing his frustration.
He keeps others from learning.	He needs work he can be successful at.
She is disrupting the class.	She is having trouble with this work.
She is just plain lazy.	She must feel hopelessly unsuccessful.

> **Being determined to find fault in others simply means that we are unwilling to change ourselves.**

164

Principle # 4: Attributing positive intent creates teaching moments by transforming resistance into cooperation.

Imagine you are a 5-year-old child sitting at a table with four other 5-year-olds. The kindergarten teacher walks by and places a tub full of toys in front of you. The teacher thinks she is placing down counting bears for a math lesson. You know differently! These are toys! You instantly grab the bucket of toys and lock your arms securely around it. Your eyes dart out to the other children daring them to even touch your toys.

Suddenly, events unfold that make little or no sense to you. The child beside you starts to cry and another calls out for the teacher. The child opposite you folds her arms across her chest and glares at you saying, "You're not my friend any more." The remaining child simply leaves the table to go to another area. The teacher approaches and you sense an atmosphere of increasing fear. You hold tighter to the bucket to safeguard your bears.

The teacher then says, "Mark, the counting bears are for all the children. How would you feel if someone had all the bears and wouldn't give you any? Don't you want to share with your friends?" If you could talk to yourself in your head you would probably say, "No, I want them all. Does it look like I want to share?" At age five, however, you have not developed inner speech and communicate mostly through actions. So, you turn your back on your teacher and hold the bucket tighter than ever.

Your teacher then says with increasing irritation, "Mark, should you have all the bears? What should you be doing with the bears? What is our rule about sharing in this classroom?" Since you are well aware of the rule, you respond with "take turns" as your answer. Of course, knowing the answer to the question and giving up the bears are two different issues, so you put the bucket in your lap for safe keeping.

Completely frustrated, the teacher shouts, "Mark, give me the bucket." You ignore her. She becomes even more agitated and screams, "Mark do you want your name on the board? Do you want to sit by yourself?" You don't care where you go as long as the bears go with you, so you stand up and walk off with the bucket. Your teacher, totally frustrated, tries to grab the counting bears from your hands. You try to hold on and in the struggle end up hitting the teacher. The next thing you know you are at the principal's office and your mother is coming to get you. You are not sure what happened, but a sense of doom prevails.

©1999 Loving Guidance, Inc.

Children call for help in many different ways.

In this story, the teacher began each attempt to persuade Mark to share by unconsciously assuming his intent was negative. When you attribute negative intentions to other people, you subtly attack them. Your attempt to make them feel bad about themselves and their choices is a form of assault. You create a feeling of danger in others every time you try to make them feel bad, wrong or responsible for your upset. This sense of danger usually creates conflict as the other person becomes defensive, not cooperative. The conflict mounts if you proceed with your own agenda, without having first inspired the other person to cooperate. When you learn to attribute positive motives to other people, you possess a powerful skill. Attributing positive intent is the skill you need to transform opposition into cooperation.

> **Willingness comes from attributing positive intent.**

Why children must say "no"

Children will oppose you. Their ongoing development dictates that they will violate the rules and limits at certain times and in certain situations. Children need to say *no* sometimes to test the limits of themselves and the social rules that prevail. Passive and aggressive teachers unconsciously invite children to test limits more often than teachers who are assertive. At each stage of life right through adulthood, people need to resist and oppose to further clarify who they are and what they believe.

The nature of your response to children's negative behavior is critical. Many teachers respond in a way that actually encourages children to be more oppositional. If you usually assume that children's motives are negative, you unconsciously make matters worse. By attributing negative motives to children, you do the following:

- ☑ You attempt to make the child feel bad for his actions.
- ☑ You focus him on what is wrong or not good enough.
- ☑ You imply that he is deliberately making your life more difficult.
- ☑ You highlight character flaws that he will incorporate into his self-concept.

Mark's teacher was unconsciously instructing him to fight instead of cooperate to get his needs met. She *began* her exchange with Mark by assuming he had selfish motives. When the children's actions are outside the limits of acceptability, your first task is to inspire them to cooperate. Only then can you teach them what to do to bring their behavior back within acceptable limits. The manner in which you *begin* your interaction when a conflict looms is critical. Let's look at how Mark's teacher innocently encouraged Mark to dig in. Pay close attention. The intent of the message is somewhat subtle.

When Mark's teacher first realized she had a problem, she said, "Mark, the counting bears are for all the children. How would you feel if someone had all the bears and wouldn't give you any? Don't you want to share with your friends?" Her statement tells Mark his view of the situation is wrong. The bears are not his. They are for everyone. The teacher implies that Mark is selfish. A kind child would willingly share. Mark faces two choices. He can submit to her attack by admitting that he is wrong and give up the counting bears, or he can defend his honor by resisting. Whether Mark submits or resists depends on his temperament, age and mood. He might have submitted by grumpily pushing the bucket towards the middle of the table. He might have submitted by relinquishing the tub and staring at his feet while the counting bears were distributed. In either case, his joy in the learning process would be diminished. In the example, Mark chose to resist the perceived attack by holding *his* bucket of bears tightly.

> **Even if you refrain from a direct attack on your child, your implication and tone can hurt him deeply.**

Mark probably did not hear his teacher's attack message, but he felt it. You might think, "Doesn't he need to know his behavior was wrong?" Yes, he does. However, your goal is to communicate this information in a fashion the child can hear and to create an environment in which the child can maintain his dignity while choosing to be cooperative. If Mark hears repeatedly that he just wants things for himself and doesn't care about others, he will come to view himself as selfish. He will act in a way that confirms this self-image. This is called a self-fulfilling prophecy. Remember, what you focus on, you get more of.

When her first attempts to influence Mark fail, the teacher steps up her unconscious attack. She says, "Mark, should you have all the bears? What should you be doing with the bears? What is our rule about sharing in this classroom?" Her hurtful messages have become more direct. On a deep level, Mark hears, "What's wrong with you? Are you a stupid kid? Don't you know anything?" She is attributing negative motives rendering him powerless. Mark is left with two choices—submit or defend.

If Mark submits, he unconsciously accepts the hurtful labels (wrong, bad, stupid) and incorporates them into his self-concept. Mark again defends his position.

The teacher, now very frustrated shouts threats, "Mark do you want your name on the board? Do you want to sit by yourself?" Her message is, "You are guilty and deserve punishment." Again, she is attributing negative intentions to Mark. You may ponder, "Well, wasn't he wrong? Didn't he deserve to be punished?" I would say no. He is only five years old, still learning how to share. He was trying to influence others and make the world go his way. He was learning that the world does not necessarily follow his rules.

> **When the attack-defend process gets rolling, communication and connection break down.**

The saddest part of the whole attack-defend process is that, when it happens, you lose the ability to reach the person you love. It is also sad that this process leads us to the belief we must punish ourselves when we make a mistake. We grow up attributing negative motives to ourselves when we make innocent human errors. The blame we heap on ourselves keeps our self-esteem low and robs us of the strength we need to make lasting changes in our thinking and behavior. We often feel bad about ourselves, but seem paralyzed when it comes to acting to resolve our problems. If you are overweight, you can diet and exercise or you can feel rotten about being heavy. The catch is you cannot simultaneously feel guilty about your situation and focus on what you *must do* to change it. The choice, to bask in guilt or improve your life, is yours.

> **You cannot simultaneously feel bad about what you have done and focus on what you must do differently.**

Becoming brain smart

Science has recently verified what many people have felt for years. You do not have to be conscious of something for it to effect your learning. All of us have had gut feelings. Researchers who study the brain estimate that we unconsciously process close to one trillion bits of information per second. However, our *conscious* mind can only process about 50 bits per second. An enormous amount of information reaches us on an unconscious gut level. Ninety-nine percent of all learning is unconscious (Jensen, 1997). Intent is something we unconsciously feel that greatly effects our response to others.

Both psychology and physics have documented the impact of our image of a person on themselves. Psychology speaks of the self-fulfilling prophecy. Our labels of others eventually become their labels of themselves. However, in my example the teacher did not come right out and call the child stupid, lazy or disrespectful. The adult's words and tone implied were much more subtle. Research led by Larry Dossey (1993) demonstrates bacteria isolated in a petri dish can be killed by negative human thoughts. We have been taught that if you can't *say* something nice, don't say anything at all. The key to success is much deeper than this. We must monitor our *thoughts* and our *intentions* in addition to our words.

Quantum physics, as explained by David Bohm (1981), proposes the universe consists of matter floating in a vast ocean of interrelated and connected energy. On the energy level, we are all connected. Current research on plant and human interaction has revealed that house plants can feel their owners thinking about them over distances as great as seven hundred miles. If a scientist used measuring devices in my house in Florida while I was in Denver thinking, "You cute little plant, keep growing," the plant would respond to my tender thoughts. Research on tomatoes shows the energy field surrounding the vegetable changes as the knife approaches to slice it. This energy field in which we all seem to operate is called the morphogenetic field (Brennan, 1987). Children sense the emotional state of the teacher, impacting their cognition (Mills, 1987).

Clearly, our intentions are conveyed across the morphogenetic field to one another. We have all experienced a conversation that felt like something was not right. The words a person says may sound plausible, yet still we may feel uncomfortable. On some level we sensed a dishonesty, an attack of some sort. In these instances, the person's intentions are being communicated subconsciously. We can say the same words with the intent of being open or with the intent to manipulate. We can say the same words to children with the intent to punish or with the intent to teach. The intention is more powerful than the words spoken.

We make it up!

There is a better way to help ourselves and our children handle conflict. Since conflicts arise when you proceed without first winning the child's cooperation, you must do something to confirm you are allies at the start of an exchange. You must start out by assuming that the child's motives are positive. Instead of assuming the child is bad or trying to make your life difficult, you can shift your perception. You can assume instead that the child is simply trying to achieve a goal, but lacks the appropriate skills to do so.

Activity to determine Mark's true intent

When Mark grabbed the bears, what do you think was his intention? Check one:

_____ He wanted to keep the other children from learning math.

_____ He wanted to irritate his teacher to get more of her attention.

_____ He wanted to humiliate the teacher in front of the other children.

_____ He wanted to make sure he got enough counting bears.

Answer: The truth is we don't know Mark's intention. We make it up. If we are going to make it up, we might as well make it positive. When we define children positively, we hold them in high esteem. Since we get what we give, we hold ourselves in high esteem also. The first three choices attributed negative intent, while the last response attributed positive motives to Mark.

If we are going to make it up,
we might as well make it positive.

We make up other people's intention.

When you attribute positive motives to a child's behavior, you position yourself to teach and the child to learn. You also model respect and loving kindness. Picture yourself again as little Mark. You have just grabbed all the counting bears. Your teacher approaches and says, "Mark, you wanted to be sure you have enough counting bears. I want you to have enough, too. Count out ten bears for each person at the table and ten for yourself." Can you feel that *beginning* the interaction from this frame of reference is more likely to elicit cooperation? To further illustrate the contrast between attributing negative and positive intentions to children, review the following examples.

Negative intention:

Adam:	"I don't want to hold your hand."
Dylan:	"You're my partner and I need to hold your hand," as Dylan reaches one more time for Adam's hand.
Adam:	Pushes Dylan's hand away and punches him in the stomach.
Teacher:	"Adam, what are you doing? Was that nice to hit your partner? How do you think he feels when you hit him and refuse to hold his hand? Would you want someone to treat you like that? That is rude. Go to the end of the line. You will not have a partner."
Adam:	Screams, "No," and runs down the hall.

Teacher:	Sends two children to the office for help in covering the class and catching Adam.

Positive intention:

Adam:	"I don't want to hold your hand."
Dylan:	"You're my partner and I need to hold your hand."
Adam:	Punches Dylan in the stomach and says, "I don't want to hold your hand."
Teacher:	"Oh Dylan, Adam punched you in your stomach, that must have hurt. Tell Adam: *I don't like it when you hit me, it hurts!*"
Teacher:	"Adam, you wanted to walk without holding hands today and you wanted Dylan to understand this. When he didn't listen to you, you got mad and hit him. You may not hit. Hitting hurts. If someone does not listen to your words come and get me. I will help you."
Teacher:	Says to both boys, "Today you two will walk beside each other with your hands beside you. You will be a different kind of partner."
Boys:	Both boys walk quietly down the hall side by side.

In the first example, the teacher both implied and stated Adam's "badness." Adam's reaction to this was predictable. In the second scenario, she attributed a positive motive to Adam. She stayed calm, helped the children be calm and taught them important new skills. Dylan learned to be assertive when he had been wronged. Adam learned to ask for help instead of hitting when he feels frustrated. The teacher learned to be flexible and open to new ways of being partners.

When we attribute positive intention to a child's behavior we are able to stay calm and help calm our children. We send the children the message that their inner core and their essence are good. We also send the message that their choices of behavior are not helpful. With this frame as the backdrop, most children are more willing and motivated to learn a new skill, comply with adult commands or choose a more appropriate behavioral response.

Principle # 5: Attributing negative intent to children teaches "gang readiness" skills.

When we attribute negative intention to a child's behavior we tend to get upset. When we are upset, we focus on what we don't want and have a tendency to escalate our punitive stance with words, tone or actions. When we escalate, we invite children to escalate their behavior. They may run from the pain inflicted on them, hide to protect their self esteem or strike out to retaliate. They are seeking an escape from their powerless state.

Attributing negative intent also defines children for each other. We are unconsciously labeling and defining children as bad, mean, selfish, inconsiderate, etc. Other children quickly learn who these "bad" children are, selecting not to play with them or become their friends. The only ones who choose to become friends with the bad kids are other bad kids. Unknowingly, we are helping the bad kids find each other and bond. A gang is forming in front of our eyes. Attributing negative intention to children's behaviors builds "gang readiness" skills.

Bully prevention program—start young

Research (Olweus 1987) has shown that 8-year-olds identified as bullies are six times more likely to be convicted of a crime by age 25, and five times more likely to end up with serious criminal records by age 30. Aggressive behavior that is learned early becomes resistant to change if it persists beyond eight years of age (Walker, 1993). Aggression is a learned skill.

Even though bullying appears to be worst in the middle school years, its origin is in early childhood. Bullies are disconnected children. It is of no surprise that the families of bullies are also disconnected and their members live in an emotionally cold environment. It is important to remember when we reach out to children to also reach out to their families. Most bullies say, "My parents don't like me." Research indicates four factors in the home environment are related to the development of aggressive behavior. These factors are (from Hoover & Oliver, 1996):

1. Negativism, particularly by the mom
2. Indifference, neglect and rejection by primary caregivers
3. Harsh, punitive child rearing strategies
4. Permissiveness regarding the use of aggression to solve problems

Bully prevention must start in the early childhood years. It begins by using positive intent to teach bullies different ways of getting their needs met. Look back at the four home factors that contribute to aggressive behavior in children. Think now of a chronically aggressive child you have experienced in your teaching career. Did that child end up receiving tremendous amounts of negativity from peers and teachers year after year? Did teachers dread the possibility that this child would be assigned to their classrooms? Did that child end up experiencing indifference and rejection by his or her peers? Did the child's constant disruptions and hurtful attitudes and behaviors receive harsh punishments? Did many people lose control and deal aggressively with this child?

Did the school come up with a plan to "fight" defiance? Unless the children are *seen* differently and then *treated* differently, they will not *act* differently. Every time you are calm enough to attribute positive intent to a young bully's behavior, you will have planted a seed of peace on earth and goodwill for all.

Principle # 6: Children cannot behave differently until they are seen differently.

When do you need the most encouragement? For myself, it's when I'm feeling unsure, undeserving or not good enough. I've noticed that I make terrible choices at these times. I often choose to be short-tempered and critical towards myself and others. I also may choose to overeat and find other ways to indulge my feelings of failure. At these times I need encouragement, not lectures that provoke more guilt within me. The same idea applies to children.

Most teachers accept the premise that when a child makes a decision an adult likes, the child has earned encouragement. This is demonstrated by teachers praising children for "good" behavior. The underlying message is, "When you do what I want, you earn my love. When you ignore what I want you to do, I will withhold my love." Many adults have internalized this kind of thinking. Many of us desperately seek approval and try so hard to please for this very reason. We act appropriately not because we love others, but because we fear they won't love us.

The question is, how can we encourage children who have made a mistake or are choosing to be hurtful? How do we set limits and be loving at the same time? How can we give unconditional love to children without being permissive or supporting inappropriate behavior? The answer lies in attributing positive intention to all behavior, whether we judge the actions good or bad. Reflecting an admirable motive back to your child helps her feel worthy, owning both her intention and her action. This will define both of you in the highest possible light. Helping children own responsibility for both their motives and their acts makes them more likely to choose to change their behavior and accept new strategies.

The power of positive intent

When you attribute positive intentions to yourself and to others, you accomplish the following:

☑ You uphold the highest image of yourself and others. By upholding an admirable image of others, you focus their attention on their best qualities. With children, your continual focus on their best selves strengthens their self esteem.

☑ You foster cooperation by joining with someone to solve a problem. The children will view you as an ally.

☑ You foster a sense of security. Children who feel secure are more likely to share feelings with you about their problems. We are never upset for the reasons we think we are. When we feel secure, we can explore the real upset that is hiding behind our hostility or anger. When children feel secure, they are better able to move from a disorganized internal state (tantrums, fits) to an organized one (level-headedness).

☑ You foster responsibility. The child is willing to own his intentions and actions because they do not mean he is bad. When he is able to own his motives and actions, he is able to accept responsibility. This empowers children to make conscious choices about continuing their current course of action or changing it.

☑ You set the child up for a teaching moment. The child becomes conscious of her current actions and of her freedom to choose another course. You can help the child feel safe even while you help her realize the hurtfulness of her actions. She is then more likely to be ready to learn another way of behaving than she would be if she felt threatened.

☑ You plant healthy seeds within the child that will help her handle and embrace diversity. People can look, think and act differently than you, and you can still be accepting of them for who they are.

☑ You encourage the child to develop her own will. You do this by acknowledging she need not obey you to keep your love. You allow the child to discover her own true self, instead of steering her towards becoming a person who constantly scrambles for the approval of others.

☑ You model unconditional love.

©1999 Loving Guidance, Inc.

**You cannot seek approval
and set a limit at the same time.**

Skill #2: Positive intent, hurtful actions

Children convey their wants and needs through their actions. They hit and grab to get what they want. You must teach them to communicate with words. First attribute positive intent, then set the limit and teach. The following demonstrates this process:

Part 1: Attribute positive intent

Step 1: State the child's positive motive. You can usually do this by completing the sentence, "You wanted _____." This builds security and cooperation. For example, if one student hits another on the head with a pencil you might say, "You wanted Cameron to look at you."

Step 2: State for the child the skill she used to achieve her goal. Make no judgments, simply *describe* your child's actions. It usually works to use a phrase like, "So you _____." This builds consciousness. In our current example, you would say, "You wanted Cameron to look at you, so you thumped her on the head with a pencil." Consciousness builds the frontal lobes of the brain and supports reasoning over reacting.

Step 3: Give the benefit of the doubt to the child. More than likely you will say, "You didn't know the words to use to _____." or "You didn't know how to _____ without being hurtful." This defines the child as good person who made a mistake. You might say, "You didn't know what else to do to get Cameron's attention." This builds self-esteem.

Part 2: Set the limit and teach assertiveness

Step 4: State the limit and why it is needed. This gives the child a clear boundary of what is not acceptable. Do this by completing the sentence, "You may not _____! _____ hurts." You would say, "You may not hit Cameron with the pencil. It hurts."

Step 5: Teach the child what you want her to do in the situation. Then ask her to do that action or say those words. With this, your child will start to immediately practice the appropriate way to fulfill her needs. To teach your child a new course of action, use the following words: "When you want _____, say (or do) _____. Say (or do) it now." In the example with Cameron, you would say to the aggressive child, "When you want Cameron to look at you, say: *Hey Cameron look here.* Try it now."

Step 6: Encourage the child for being willing to try a different approach. If possible, point out how the new approach proved successful. You might say, "You did it! Cameron is looking right at you." This begins the process of cementing the actions into the child's neural brain networks.

**What we say to children becomes their inner speech
for the rest of their lives.**

Activity to practice attributing positive intention

It is important to teach children who rely on nonverbal communication strategies to use language skills appropriate for their developmental age. It is also important to teach children to use appropriate language when hurtful situations arise. For this to happen, we must attribute positive intention. Practice in the following situations:

Situation 1:   **Child pulls on a teacher's dress and waves frantically in her face.**

Intent: You wanted _____ so you

_____ .

Benefit: You didn't know _____ .

Limit: You may not _____ . _____ hurts.

Teach: When you want _____

                  Say (or do) _____.

Practice: Say it now (child repeats words or actions).

Situation 2:   **Child pushes another child away from the water fountain.**

Intent: You wanted _____ so you

                  _____.

Benefit: You didn't know _____.

Limit: You may not _____. _____hurts.

Teach: When you want _____

                  Say (or do) _____.

Practice: Say it now (child repeats words or actions).

Situation 3:   **Child goes up and hits Angie for seemingly no reason.**

Intent: You wanted _____so you

                  _____.

Benefit: You didn't know _____.

Limit: You may not _____. _____hurts.

Teach: When you want _____

                  Say (or do) _____.

Practice: Say it now (child repeats words or actions).

Possible answers: There are no right answers. Remember the goal is to see the best in each moment and in each child. The following are some dialogue examples:

Situation 1:   "You wanted my attention so you pulled on my dress and waved your hands like this." (Demonstrates hand movements)
"You didn't know what else to do to get my attention."
"You may not pull on my dress. Pulling hurts."
"When you want my attention raise your hand like this." (Shows how to hold hand high and not directly in the teacher's face)
"Show me you know what I mean." (Child raises hand appropriately)
"You did it. Your hand is up like this." (Shows how it is done)

Situation 2:   "You wanted a drink of water so you pushed your classmate out of the way."

"You didn't know the words to use to get a turn."

"You may not push. Pushing hurts."

"When you want a drink of water, say: *May I have a turn? I am very thirsty.* Say that now." (Child repeats the words to her classmate)

Situation 3: "You wanted to let Angie know that you felt angry with her so you hit her."

"You didn't know how else to let her know how angry you were."

"You may not hit. Hitting hurts."

"When you want Angie to know you feel angry, say: *I feel angry because _____.* Say that now and tell her what is upsetting you."

When you don't know what the child wanted

Sometimes we really don't have a clue as to what the child wanted. All we see is the child using nonverbal strategy to achieve a goal. In this case, describe the child's nonverbal actions to build consciousness within the child. Then with an inquiring tone state, "Your body is telling me you might feel _____." Fill in the blank with the emotion you think is being displayed. Generally when this mirroring is done, children are more likely to begin talking and expressing what happened. The following is an example:

Situation: Child slams his math book shut and slumps back down in his chair with arms crossed.

Intention: "You slammed your book and slumped back in your chair with your arms folded like this (imitate the child). Your body is telling me you might feel frustrated."

Child: "I can't do math. It's stupid."

Now you can attribute positive intent.

Teacher: "You wanted to let me know you needed help with math, so you slammed your book. You didn't know what else to do. When you feel frustrated, come to me and say: *I need help.*"

 ## Activity to practice "when you don't know what they want"

Practice the following scenarios using the technique just described.

Situation: Child is kicking chairs and stomping his feet.

Intention:_____

Situation: Child is curled up under her desk with her head tucked between her knees.

Intention:_____

_____

_____

Skill # 3: Positive intent, hurtful words

Older children are more likely to be hurtful with words. They can exclude others. "Bug off, we don't like you!" They may attack through name calling. "Beat it, lard bucket!" This verbal form of bullying is extremely destructive to the educational process. The same process of attributing positive intent can be used to transform these moments of negativity into positive interactions. Remember, the skill of positive intent is used to *begin* the interaction with the attacking child. It does not mean it is the only skill you use. You may start the interaction with attributing positive intent and then conclude with giving consequences. Remember, the "victim" is addressed first and empowered with assertiveness. The following is an example:

"Beat it, you fat slob!"

In this situation, Monica is standing with some friends and Sandra approaches the group. Monica turns to Sandra and says, "Beat it, you fat slob." The teacher sees this scene occur. The teacher approaches Sandra. Since Sandra's upset is great, the teacher uses the skill of empathy by saying, "Sandra, your face is red. I can imagine you must feel totally embarrassed and deeply hurt by what was said." Sandra continues to look down. The teacher continues with empathy, "I heard Monica say some very hurtful things to you. I can tell by the look on your face how painful those comments were." At this point Sandra looks up and makes eye contact. The teacher then empowers Sandra to assertively speak to her attacker by telling her the exact words to use. Sandra says, "I don't appreciate being called names." Then the teacher turns to Monica and uses the steps in delivering positive intent.

Step 1: "Monica, you wanted to let Sandra know that you were busy talking to your friends . . ."

Step 2: "So you called her hurtful names.'

Step 3: "It seems you didn't know any other way to get your point across.'

Step 4: "You may not call people names, it is very hurtful."

Step 5: "When you want to let a classmate know you want privacy with your friends, say: *Sandra, this is personal. I would like to talk to my friends alone. We can talk later.* Say that now, so you can remember the next time what to say that is helpful and not hurtful."

Step 6: "It's hard to do things differently when feelings have been hurt. Both of you gave it a try. Many kids would not have bothered. Good for you both."

Notice in the above example that the steps are the same, but the language changes to address the developmental level of older students.

Activity to put it all together

Role play the following scenes. Address the victim first to teach assertiveness, then address the attacker with a positive intent to create a teaching moment.

Scene 1: James pushes Kareem to sit on the red carpet square.
Scene 2: Melissa calls Sheila "stupid face" when she answers a math problem incorrectly.
Scene 3: Several boys are chanting, "Girls are prissy heads."

Assessment to be conscious while putting it all together

1. Did you go to the victim first? Did you ask, "Did you like it?" or did you forget and say, "How did that make you feel?"

2. Did you empower the victim by giving them words to say or did you ask, "What could you say?"

3. Did you offer positive intent to the attacker by starting your sentence with, "You wanted ____?" or did you start off with, "Why did you ____?"

4. Did you give the attacker specific words to use for their new skills or did you ask, "What could you have done?"

5. Did you ask the attacker to practice the skill right now by saying it?

6. Did you encourage both students at the end? How did you do this? What words did you say?

The teaching moment

Positive intent is a skill used to create teaching moments. It is especially powerful for teaching bullies. During conflict, at least one party is upset. When a person is upset they are using the reactive centers of the brain, not the area of higher thinking skills. Positive intent diffuses the situation, allowing the child to shift from reacting and defending to listening and learning. Positive intent does not see children as bad guys to be punished. It sees them as calling for help. The child is unconsciously saying, "Help me! I know no way to interact without hurting others."

Teaching children how to behave in a socially acceptable manner is no different than teaching children to read or do addition. Imagine the following scene: "It is math time. Who can tell me what 2 + 2 equals?" Several children raise their hands. The teacher calls on Jerome. He says five. The teacher raises her voice and says, "Why are you doing this Jerome? How many times do I have to speak to you about this? Do you want your name on the board? You know five is not correct! Was it nice to say five?"

This sounds ridiculous. Of course, we can see that no matter how long we talked to Jerome this way, he would never learn to add 2 + 2 = 4. Yet, we forget to teach when it comes to discipline. We focus instead on what the child has done wrong and how *bad* they are for acting that way. It is time to start *teaching* the children how to behave.

And I didn't know the words to say to stop her!

The phrases, "You didn't know the words to say," and, " You didn't know what else to do," are extremely valuable and powerful. I suggest you memorize them, put them on a banner and hang them in your room until they become second nature. This is a helpful statement to use with children when they are using hurtful strategies with each other. The underlying message is, "You did the best you could with the skills you had." This sets the child up to be more likely to want to learn new helpful strategies. By entering interactions attributing positive intent and using the current strategies instead of judging the situation as bad, we are preparing the child for a teaching moment. We are preparing them to learn a helpful verbal strategy they can use to achieve their desired goals. This promotes cooperation in the classroom.

Physical structures that support the Skill of Positive Intent

Each of the classroom structures necessary to build the school family were discussed in chapter 2. The physical structures that support the Skill of Positive Intent are the celebration center and the class meeting or circle time.

Celebration center

The purpose of the celebration center is to celebrate children. You can celebrate events of change such as losing a tooth, welcoming a new sibling to the family, graduation of an older sibling or a great grandmother's birthday. You could celebrate children's efforts in academics and efforts to be helpful. The center is a way for children to honor children. It is not place where rewards are given for special events or behavior.

The celebration center for young children could consist of a special celebration chair. I suggest using an old chair that the children have painted and decorated. Next to the chair could be a prop box of items that support the celebration. One teacher had a large wooden tooth necklace that she used to help celebrate children who had lost a tooth. The child who had lost a tooth sat in the celebration chair wearing the tooth necklace as the class sang the *Tooth Song* to the tune of *The Farmer in the Dell.*

First verse	Second verse
"You lost a tooth.	"New ones will grow.
You lost a tooth.	New ones will grow.
You're growing day by day.	You lost a tooth today.
You lost a tooth."	And new ones will grow."

Children in older grades can decide what will constitute their celebration center, what they would like to celebrate and how they will go about celebrating. One fourth grade classroom decided their celebration center would be on the computer. They had a program that made certificates. During designated times, students could go to the computer and make certificates for someone else in the classroom. Students completed the certificate, shared what they had done with the teacher and discussed their plan to present the certificate during the start of the day routine. If the teacher approved the plan, the event occurred. On the morning I visited this classroom, Douglas received a celebration certificate from the class in honor of spelling successes. He received a certificate for improvement and the following poem:

> You couldn't spell,
> On the test you would fail!
> You could have given up! And you did a time or two,
> But you dug deep and worked harder, until you knew-
> How to spell a word or two!
> So good for you! Good for you!

The poem and the certificate were handed to Douglas during a class meeting. His response was charming. He said, "Thanks for caring, spelled: K-A-R-I-N-G." The class laughed and the teacher looked nervous. Then he said, "Just kidding! Spelled: C-I-D-D-I-N-G." The laughter increased and this time the teacher joined in.

Class meeting or circle time

The purpose of the circle (for young children) and class meetings (for older children) is to provide a gathering space for the class to unite for the brain smart start of the day, to solve daily problems and also to connect with, support and celebrate one another. Through solving daily problems, the teacher demonstrates the skill of positive intent. Positive intent is a way of framing problems for children so the world is not divided into "good guys" and "bad guys." By assuming positive intent, we frame problems in terms of missing skills. With this intent, the problem solving procedure will run smoothly. It avoids evoking the need children sometimes feel to punish those they perceive as the creators of the problem. Children are able to spend their time thinking about solutions instead of blame, revenge and punishment. Below is an example:

Mrs. Lott, a third grade teacher, has gathered her class for their usual class meeting. She begins the session with a song that signals the children that they will be solving a problem. The song is sung to the tune of *Have you ever seen a Lassie?*

> Time to solve some problems, some problems, some problems
>> Time to solve some problems so gather round here

I'm willing to solve some problems, some problems, some problems
I'm willing to solve some problems and think clear.

Mrs. Lott begins the discussion by saying, "Kevin, you had a problem you wanted to bring to the class so we can come up with a solution." Kevin finally says, "Yea. Mark, Cindy and Heather are mean. They hog the balls on the playground." Mrs. Lott uses the Skill of Positive Intent to reframe Kevin's comments. She says, "So Kevin, you've noticed that several classmates are playing with the balls during recess and others are not able to get a turn."

She then turns to the class and asks, "Has anyone else experienced the problem of wanting a turn with something at recess and not knowing how to make that happen." Many hands shoot up in the air. Heather snaps back, "Yea, I can never get a rope. Some people won't share." The teacher rephrases Heather's remark with positive intent. "So, Heather, you wanted to play with jump ropes, but didn't know what to say to get a turn."

The teacher is now ready to present the problem to the class. She says, "So it seems we have a problem. Our problem is that many students would like turns with different items on the playground. We need some solutions for taking turns. What are your ideas?" The children begin coming up with ideas to solve the problem. The ultimate solution is for those who want an item to say, "May I play with the ball, please?" Those who are playing with a ball have the choice of asking the child to join them in play or to set a timer for five minutes at which time the object will be given to the child who asked for it. They called this procedure "join or timer" and practiced what it would look like during recess with a couple of role plays.

The class meeting above was successful for a number of reasons. One key to its success was the teacher's ability to rephrase the children's statements and offer positive intent to the situation and students involved.

 ## No time like the present!

This month vigilantly practice the following with yourself:

☑ Wish people well. Do this silently from your heart while you are driving, standing in lines or passing people on foot. Notice how you feel when you do this.

☑ When you or others make a mistake, attribute a positive intention. Instead of chiding yourself, "I can't believe I forgot to go to the store," reframe it. Say, "I wanted to get home in time to greet the children when they got off the school bus, so I will spend time with the children and go to the store later."

☑ When a car pulls out in front of you, resist yelling, "You stupid idiot!" Reframe it. Say, "Boy, is he in a hurry."

☑ Notice how often you try to figure out others' intentions. How much energy does this occupy? Pay attention to how often you are inclined to attribute negative intention to yourself, your spouse, your colleagues and the children you teach. Who do you tend to give the benefit of the doubt and who are you hardest in judging?

☑ When you are upset reframe your thinking. Take a deep breath and say to yourself, "I am willing to see this differently." Then ask yourself, "Am I extending love or calling for help?" Obtain the help you need.

☑ Practice giving positive intent to the children in the classroom. Focus on children who chronically misbehave.

☑ Use positive intent in class meetings to facilitate problem solving.

☑ Create a celebration center.

 ## Look for these teaching moments

Look for times when children are hurtful to each other with words or actions. Do not wait for the victim to come to you. Proactively use these conflicts as teaching opportunities in your classroom. The behaviors you are looking for are the same ones you were looking for when you were working on the skill of assertiveness. The difference is the idea that you are going to work vigilantly on offering positive intent to the aggressor. Do not forget to go to the *victim first*.

When in class meetings, reframe children's statements about problems from negative intent to positive intent. Two examples of this follow:

Negative intent	**Reframed with positive intent**
"Marsha is a jerk."	"You are having some conflict with Marsha?"
"Jeremy is mean."	"You didn't know the words to use to tell Jeremy acceptable ways to treat you?"

 ## Behaviors to use as teaching moments are:

Physical hurtfulness
Pushing
Shoving
Poking
Hitting, etc.

Social/emotional hurtfulness
Name calling
Exclusion
Racism
Sexism
Intolerance of physical differences

185

Chapter 6

Empathy

Handling the fussing and fits

Power of Acceptance

The moment is as it is

Empathy

Handling the Fussing and the Fits

Power: Power of Acceptance
The moment is as it is

Value: Compassion

Purpose: To help children accept and process their feelings so as to see the world from others' perspectives

Brain Development: Empathy wires the brain for self-control, allowing children access to higher cognitive processes

Emotional Development: Empathy is the heart of all emotional intelligence and the key to intellectual development

Empathy Principles:
1. The moment is as it is.
2. Resisting the moment as it is creates upset. Upset prevents you from giving empathy to others.
3. Empathy is the heart of emotional intelligence.
4. Empathy is about understanding and joining with others, not taking on the pain of others as your own.
5. Until you feel your feelings, you will not allow children to feel theirs.

Principle #1: The moment is as it is.

The motto to promote this month is, "The moment is as it is." As you reflect on this motto, think how often you believe things *should* have gone differently. You may fight against what is happening by saying, "This should never have happened," "What should you be doing," or "I can't believe you are acting this way." You may negate and deny what is happening by saying, "We don't run in the halls," or "That is not the way we treat each other in this school." This, of course, is said shortly after a child has run or a student has behaved inappropriately. The icon for this skill is a man holding a series of four balloons. Each balloon represents one of four feelings: sad, mad, glad and scared. Balloons are generally associated with celebrations, especially birthdays. This icon reminds us that when we accept the moment as it is, we will also accept our feelings as they are. Once this occurs, life will be a celebration with each moment as beautiful as the next. To experience this current moment, take a deep breath and say to yourself as you inhale, "This moment is as it is." As you exhale, relax and say, "I am safe even if the world does not go my way."

The Power of Acceptance gives you the frame of mind that promotes change. Resisting "what is" facilitates conflict and firmly entrenches old behavior patterns into your brain. When you passionately struggle saying, "This shouldn't be," you program your brain to be resistant. The passion of anger and disappointment generated by resisting "what is" becomes the glue cementing judgments in your mind. These judgements, generated from your resistance, prevent your mind from considering other viewpoints. They become thoughts you refuse to question, even though they may not be true. With frantic action, these judgments seek to prove they are right. Pursuing this goal, your judgements distort reality and attack anything that would contradict their point of view. Resistance to "what is" prevents empathy because it prevents us from being able to see another's point of view. Acceptance is quietly observing what is. From this position you can see how each person perceives the situation from different perspectives. Truth becomes relative and compassion becomes real.

Resisting what is—The prerequisite to attack

I adore the Olympics. During the 1998 Winter Olympics, my assistant and I were driving back to our neighborhood in Florida after conducting an out-of-town workshop. I was determined to be home by 8:00 pm to watch every minute of the Olympics. Traffic scratched my plans. I refused to accept the fact that I was missing the games. I asked my assistant to find the Olympics on the radio. When she said, "I don't think they're on the radio," I exploded. I negated the situation. "They have to be on the radio!" Then I attacked with, "What kind of country is this? We go to the moon, but don't broadcast the world's greatest sports event on the radio?" I was ranting because the world hadn't gone my way. We can't negate the moment without attacking ourselves or someone else.

This wasn't my first adult fit, nor was it my last. Over the years, I have become aware of how many fits adults have. I estimate adults are throwing fits over 50% of the time. Adult fits range from mild (complaining, whining) to moderate (verbally attacking through criticism, name-calling and judging) to severe (physically hurting one another).

"Fussing and fits" is my general term for the emotional upset people display when the world does not go their way. A toddler scribbling on the walls cries when you take away the crayon. A 4-year-old who wants crackers ignores the fact that you have none. A 9-year-old slams doors when you deny a request to sleep at a friend's house. A 30-year-old teacher gets upset when children forget to raise their hands during class. A 62-year-old grandpa curses when a car in front of him has its blinker on unnecessarily.

Disappointment is tough. We all need to learn how to handle frustration. We have ample opportunities to do this ourselves and to teach our children, too. Every time a child whines, stomps her feet, screams, name calls or attacks in any fashion, you receive such an opportunity. To teach children to cope with upset, you will need the skill called empathy.

> ## You must teach your child how to handle disappointment and frustration.

Teachers often ask me, "How can I get the children to happily do what I want when I want it?" I surely do not have the answer. (I'm still working through the absence of the Olympics on the radio.) However, I do know of some helpful approaches. First, use the Power of Acceptance: "This moment is as it is." Only when you accept the moment that exists can you offer empathy to others, staying relaxed enough to take the other person's perspective. When you resist what is, you become so enmeshed in your own perspective that no other perspective seems to matter. Second, let go of your expectation that children can give up what they want in order to follow your wishes and still be happy about it. Third, stop trying to control children's feelings in hopes this will control their behavior. Children have a right to all of their feelings. Without them, they would be lost. Feelings serve us as our core system for discerning right from wrong. Feelings are our moral navigators. We do not need to stop having them. We need to become acutely aware of them and then learn how to express them more appropriately.

Principle # 2: Resisting the moment as it is creates upset. Upset prevents you from giving empathy to others.

Upset —fear, anger, sadness, disappointment, irritation and so on—is an inside job created when the world fails to run as we planned. Feelings are not caused by events, but by our perception of events. A person who enjoys a roller coaster ride strengthens her immune system with every twist and turn. A person who perceives the ride to be a suicide attempt stresses her immune system. The roller coaster itself does not create joy or upset, it is just the trigger for the feelings. When a child becomes upset he is resisting the moment as it is. For example, a child wants to finish writing in his journal and you want him to put away the notebook to prepare for a class visitor. Our hope is that the child will *accept* the situation and be cooperative. To help the child we must offer acceptance. This acceptance comes in the form of empathy. If we were to resist the moment we might think, "He *should* listen the first time I tell him to put away his journal." By focusing on what *should be* as opposed to *what is* we are negating the moment just like the child who wants to continue journal writing. If we offer resistance to the moment, we increase the possibility the child will offer resistance in return. If we offer acceptance we are increasing the likelihood of obtaining acceptance in return.

The only way for you to process your upset is to reframe your perception of the situation. If you think a child *should* know better than to question your authority, you will not be able to calm yourself down. If you are willing to change your perception, to see differently, you will be able to remain calm or re-establish your inner peace. You could see that the child is simply resisting the moment as it is, not acting disrespectfully toward you personally. With this change in perception, you are now empowered to offer empathy; without it you cannot.

Principle # 3: Empathy is the heart of emotional intelligence.

The desire to be understood is a powerful human motivator. It is one of our basic survival needs. Most people would not expect empathy to be as essential as food or water. Yet think about this: Violence (every war that has ever been and every fight in every home) has its roots in lack of empathy. Without empathy we will destroy one another. With empathy we create a oneness where attack is impossible. In *The Lost Art of Listening,* Dr. Nichols states, "The yearning to be listened to and understood is a yearning to escape our separateness and bridge the space that divides us. We reach out and try to overcome that separateness by revealing what's on our minds and in our hearts, hoping for understanding." Empathy has the power to transform relationships. It reminds us of our connectedness with each other and strengthens our sense of self. We feel connected, can clarify our thoughts and discover what we feel when we're with someone who offers empathy. When others understand us, we can understand ourselves.

As children, the response we received from adults about our feelings, actions and intentions coauthored us. We create the image of who we are from the understanding we receive from others. Claudia remembers growing up and constantly hearing her father say, "You should have thought about that before." Now as a 45-year-old woman she finds herself unable to feel disappointment and is therefore unable to relate to those feelings in others. She avoids this feeling by blaming others for the consequences of her actions. In essence, she finds herself treating others like her father treated her, thinking, "you should have thought about that before." She thinks herself selfish, impatient and uncaring. Her father's emotional clumsiness has found its way into another generation.

Empathy is understanding what another person feels and having insight into their thoughts and actions. When you empathize with children, they realize you care about their ideas and feelings. Your empathetic response to your child's emotions helps her to feel validated and to gain insight into herself. True empathy demands that you listen to children's feelings and thoughts *without needing to change them*. When you empathize with children, you teach them the following:

- ☑ Self-awareness
- ☑ Self-control
- ☑ Recognition and acceptance of emotions
- ☑ The knowledge that emotions can be expressed to others
- ☑ The ability to label feelings with appropriate words

☑ The understanding that feelings influence behavior

☑ The realization that relationships are based on mutual esteem and communication

Your empathy builds a foundation for your children's sound emotional development. You can give yourself and the children in your care no greater gift than an empathetic environment.

You realize how vital empathy is when you see what becomes of people who never develop it. Heinous criminals—rapists, child molesters and perpetrators of family violence—lack empathy. Only when empathy is absent can people willfully hurt others.

> **How you respond to your child's upset teaches her how to respond to the upset of others.**

Principle # 4: Empathy is understanding and joining with others, not taking the pain of others as our own.

We have been taught that to care about others is to join with them. However, we have misperceived joining as taking on the feelings of others and/or agreeing with their judgement. Have you ever been in a good mood when a friend calls to share her most recent upset? Your mood changes as the conversation continues. If she talks about how she perceives herself to be unfairly treated, you also feel irritated. If the story involves sadness or loss, you may feel sad as the story unfolds. The same seems to be true when a friend calls to share delight and happiness related to uplifting events. We were taught that to be empathetic, we *should* feel what the other person is feeling. However, if we take on the feelings of others, those feelings trigger pain within ourselves. To alleviate our discomfort, we then tend to offer some form of false empathy to others. We want to *fix* them in some way. We may implement this "fixing" by giving advice, telling a joke, distracting or reassuring. The underlying message that all false empathy offers is, "Don't feel how you are feeling." To truly empathize with another you must see from their perspective. You must understand and *accept* how they feel based on how *they* perceive the situation. This can only be done by listening carefully and suspending our judgements of how people should think, feel or act in a given situation.

We were also taught that friends who care join with others by agreeing with them. We have been taught to see upset people as victims and, as such, support the position that they have been unfairly treated. In essence, we have been taught that to see from another person's perspective involves agreeing with the person as to the "badness" of their situation. This supports that age-old saying, "misery loves company."

193

As time goes on, other people's stories, pain and struggles become *old*. Our inner voice may lament, "Why don't they do something about their lives." We separate ourselves from these people who "bring us down." We get tired of their negativity. You can see why we may begin to avoid certain people if we operate from the beliefs expressed in the previous paragraphs: **1)** that to care is to feel what the other feels and **2)** that to care is to join them in their victimization

True empathy has a cognitive and emotional component. We *do* need to understand another's perspective, but this does not equate to agreeing or disagreeing with their judgments of themselves, the world or others. The cognitive component of empathy requires suspending our judgments. It demands that we neither agree nor disagree; we just accept the story through careful active listening. The emotional component of empathy requires us to glean the feelings the person is most likely experiencing from her perception of the situation. This feeling is then reflected back to her so she feels validated, sane and loved. The feelings of others are not captured as our own, triggering within us our own memories, judgments and desires. We do not feel as they do; we understand that their perceptions of a situation are uniquely theirs and that their perceptions created their feelings.

How did our understanding of empathy get so distorted? The answer comes from understanding how empathy is developed in childhood.

Developmental levels of empathy

Empathy is developed in increments. Ten-month-old Erin sees another baby fall. Tears well up in her eyes as she crawls to her mom as if *she* were the one who was hurt. Michael, a 16-month-old, goes to get a teddy bear to give to a friend who is crying. The development of empathy starts in infancy (Radke-Yarrow & Zahn-Waxler, 1984).

Stage 1: Empathic distress (0-12 months) Infants begin by experiencing "empathic distress," which is defined as experiencing another's painful emotional state (Hoffman, 1982). Being born without the ability to differentiate self from others, infants are totally attuned to the emotional states of others. Even a few months after birth, infants react to disturbances in those around them as if it were their own distress. Caregivers can attest to the fact that when one baby in the center begins to cry, all others join in like a chorus. Some children begin their life journey with less options to exercise empathic distress. These infants are in greatly distressed states for significant periods of time. A few possible sources of discomfort to these infants are being medically fragile, premature and/or drug exposed.

Watch children in your classroom. Are some of them in stage one empathy—do some children seem to cry when others do? Notice yourself. Do you tend to take on the feelings of others as your own? If so, you too are at Stage 1 in your development.

194

Stage 2: Egocentric empathy (1-6 years) Once babies cognitively differentiate themselves from others, their empathic distress can begin to transform into reciprocal concern for others. By about one year of age, infants begin to realize that the misery of others is not their own. As this dawning realization settles into the awareness of the toddler, the task becomes "what to do about the distress of others." Toddlers see the world primarily from their own perspective. In doing so, they may use inappropriate means to attempt to comfort others. For example, Caroline (30 months old) approaches a distressed baby (13 months old) and offers him some cookies. The screaming infant is not interested in the cookies and attempts to get away. Caroline follows him around and strokes his hair, but he pulls away. Caroline continues to shove the cookies in the child's face and pat his head and shoulders. The upset toddler frantically tries to escape. Caroline demonstrates an understanding of the young boy's distress and seeks to comfort him in ways that have been used with her (food and touching). However, she is unaware that her own behavior is causing the child more stress. As children mature from ages one to six years, the ability to discern whether their expressions of compassion were helpful or unappreciated increases.

Pay attention to the students in your classroom. How do they offer empathy to others in distress? Do they offer hugs, food and words of comfort, or do they withdraw, make fun of and try to distract the child from his feelings? This observation will tell you a lot about the types of empathy they have received from their significant others. Notice also, how perceptive your children are at discerning whether their empathic gestures were helpful or not. Did the child take into account the other person's perspective or were they focused totally on their own giving? Notice these same things about yourself. How many times have you attempted to be empathic with a friend and find yourself offering advice? Were you able to discern if your empathy and advice were helpful or not? Did you continue with your admonitions just like the toddler despite your friend's continued cry to be heard? When we listen to our friends and take their feelings as our own (Stage 1), and then offer them advice, whether it's wanted or not, we have moved from Stage 1 to Stage 2 in our development.

Stage 3: Reciprocal empathy (6-9 years) Between the ages of six and nine, children's growing cognitive maturity and awareness allows for a more reciprocal nature to evolve in empathy. A child will be able not only to be empathetic, but also to discern if the form of empathy offered is helpful to the recipient. They can now fully appreciate situations from another's perspective (Selman, 1980). They have the capacity to understand that no one person's perspective is absolutely right.

Stage 4: Global empathy (9-11 years of age) As the child moves closer in age toward adolescence, another cognitive shift in perspective-taking is noted. The pre-adolescent is able to react to the global distresses of categories of people. Children age nine and ten become concerned about oppression, poverty and illness. Before this time, empathy was limited to the specific immediate distresses within their own lives.

Projects such as world hunger, the rainforest and homelessness now become meaningful to these children and are important channels for their developing energy.

Stage 5: Conscious empathy (11 years of age and up) Conscious empathy is mature empathy. It is based on love. Love always does the following five things:

- ☑ Increases security (reduces the fear of loss)
- ☑ Goes from the worthy to the worthy (to give love you must feel lovable)
- ☑ Acknowledges free will (people choose their perceptions, thoughts, feelings and actions)
- ☑ Holds an image of others as "good enough"
- ☑ Relies on faith (all is well) instead of worry

Conscious empathy involves listening while holding an image of the "upset person" as capable and competent to handle the emotions and the situation in which they are involved. To be truly empathetic we must see that conflict is not a bad thing, but an opportunity to learn. We must refuse to judge the situation as bad even though our friend is invested in that perception.

Resist the temptation to see others as victims.

One summer I taught school in Montana. It was a week-long course on *Conscious Discipline*. We were discussing empathy. I asked a person to share a story with me so that I could demonstrate the difference between the lower stages (immature/false empathy) and Stage 5 (conscious/true empathy). Marilyn volunteered. I listened to the story two times. The first time I demonstrated using immature empathy (Stages 1 and 2). I felt her misery and joined in her judgments of the situation as bad.

Marilyn began her story, "During the past year I had noticed that children attending my church school needed after-school care due to their parents' work schedules. After noticing this need, I began to study the situation and went to Minneapolis to visit an excellent after-school program. From my research, I spent another six months writing up a proposal and creating a workable budget to fund the program. It took me about a year and I did it on my own time with a sense of helping my community. When I presented the proposal to the Board of Directors of the church, they rejected the proposal. They quickly dismissed me and the needs of the children."

At this point I said, "I can't believe they would do such a thing." Marilyn responded, "I couldn't either. I felt like I wasted my time on nothing, to be shot down in less than thirty minutes." I said, "This all happened in under thirty minutes! They hardly listened!" Marilyn agreed, "I know! I've never been so angry and hurt at the same time."

"I would be too," I stated in an empathetic tone of voice. Marilyn now showed signs of tears and anger. She continued with her story, sharing that the congregation would not support her, even close friends sided with the church Board of Directors and no one cared about the children. Continuing with my demonstration, I too became upset and we both agreed the world does not care about its young.

I then stopped the demonstration. We repeated the discussion, but this time I utilized conscious empathy. My goal was to listen, holding an active image in my mind that all was well and that Marilyn was capable of handling whatever emotions this event triggered within her. I will begin the dialogue when Marilyn stated, "When I presented the proposal to the Board of Directors of the church, they rejected the proposal. They quickly dismissed me and the needs of the children." This time we progressed like this:

With conscious empathy, I said, "You are so dedicated to children and your profession (she is a teacher). You spent all that time researching what is best for your community with the goal of being helpful." Marilyn lightened in her posture and tone of voice and said, "Yes, I learned a great deal, some of which I have used in my own classroom working with fourth grade students, but I can't help but be angry with the church for turning down my proposal. The vote was five to four (this was new information not shared in the first conversation)."

"You were able to convince four powerful people in your community about the needs of children. Few professional lobbyists have been that successful with the U.S. Congress! I am impressed that you took the time to assess the needs of your community and act on your desire to help. Few people I know have the ability to follow through on what is important to them and actually do something about it. You saw a need and carried out a plan to address it. It didn't happen as you planned and I hear your disappointment. I also hear your persistence and vigilance to make a difference," I said.

Marilyn said, "I have always been like that. I see a problem and I go for answers." At this point Marilyn was at peace with the situation. We stopped the role play and she said that this began as a role play but after a year of anger and resentment toward her church she felt the issue was over. She had peace within herself. She thanked me and we hugged. We admitted that though it was role play, we bonded on some level. The level was one of love.

Assessment #1: What type of empathy did you receive from your parents?

Using the stages of empathy mentioned above answer the following questions:

1. What level of empathy do/did your mother, father and significant others operate from?

Assessment #2: Becoming self-aware

Below are some common ways empathy is offered to children. Each form of empathy is usually an attempt to offer empathy without first accepting the moment as it is. Read each one and reflect upon yourself. Decide if you have fallen into the trap of trying to listen and offer empathy without accepting the moment as it is first. Decide which type(s) of immature empathy you tend to offer.

Immature empathy #1: Sharing similar experiences from your own life

Michael approaches the teacher and shares, "Last night we had to put our dog, Murphy, to sleep." The teacher responds, "I know how awful you must feel. Two years ago we had to put our dog, Bo, to sleep. It is really, really, sad."

Why we do this? Our intention is to be understanding. Of course, talking about our lives and our experiences removes children from their experiences and their feelings. We do this not to be mean, but because when a person shares a story with us, it triggers a resonance in our brain. This resonance fires neurons that recall similar experiences. It takes conscious effort to override this natural physiological reaction and set aside our need to talk about our experiences in order to truly listen to the children.

Immature empathy #2: Gushing with sympathy

Vanessa had just returned from school from a bad car wreck she and her family had experienced. Her mother and younger brother were still in the hospital. Vanessa began to share her experience with the class when Mrs. McClean began stating, "Oh, how awful! That was just dreadful! You poor child and your family — how devastating! You must be worried about your mom and your brother!" Mrs. McClean's exaggerated concern for Vanessa and her family was not related to Vanessa's experience. In fact, Mrs. McClean did not even hear what Vanessa had to say because she was too busy offering her concern. The message being sent to Vanessa was, "You poor helpless thing!"

Why do we do this? We have caught the feelings of others instead of listening to them. We also believe that gushing with sympathy is empathy. We do this so show others we care and have "good manners."

©1999 Loving Guidance, Inc.

Immature empathy # 3: Giving "fix-it" advice

Carlos was upset. He had lost his lunch money on the bus. As he explained this situation to his teacher, she began immediately solving his problem and offering him advice. In doing so she missed Carlos's main concern. It was not about lunch but about his grandmother's response to his carelessness.

When we offer unsolicited advice to others the subtle message we are sending to them is, "stop bothering me with your complaints and do something about it."

Why we do this? Some people want advice. They think other people should have an answer for their distress and should try to alleviate it. Giving advice is equated with a person who "cares." The problem is the person is in front of us: Is it a person expecting others to relieve pain or is it a person that knows happiness is an inside job? For young children, responding to distress with advice trains them that it's other people's jobs to keep them happy. It's possible that the real reason people give advice is that they can't tolerate their own anxiety. People who tend to deal with their own feelings by staying busy and distracting themselves offer advice to others regularly. They send a message, "Do something constructive and the feelings will go away, it works for me."

Immature empathy # 4: Offering humor to lighten the situation

Mary Gayle had lost her homework. She was very upset and could not seem to retrace her steps or recall its location. As she explained her upset to the teacher, the response was, "I guess your middle name needs to be changed to Xerox," and chuckled. A jokester offers distraction instead of emotional engagement.

Why we do this? People with the need to constantly make light of or joke about a situation have a lot of nervous energy. Their humor is a defense against boredom and connecting.

Immature empathy # 5: Reassuring

Melissa was doing a cooperative group project with four other students. Melissa was meticulous about her personal work. Some of the group members, in her mind, were not doing their best work. She came to the teacher very upset and was sharing her fear of the quality of work being produced in her group. The teacher's response was, "Everything will be fine, just you wait and see." Reassuring someone is a subtle way of dismissing them. The underlying message is, "There is no need to feel this way." A significant part of failed attempts at empathy take the form of telling children not to feel the way they do.

Why we do this? Most attempts to reassure others and talk them out of their feelings is our need to calm down our own uneasiness. In essence the listener is saying, "Don't upset me with your upset." Most people are concerned about future events. They share this worry with you. If you could control the future, reassurance would be appropriate. However, since you cannot control the future, listening to the person and offering empathy for their current upset is much more effective.

Activity to determine your favorite empathy mode

In the spaces below, write the immature empathy techniques you use. Order them by rank. The most common one you use will go in space number 1, the second most common in number 2 and so on. Then read the statement to the right of your immature empathy technique and respond accordingly.

1. _____ **I will forgive myself and change**   yes   no

2. _____ **I will forgive myself and change**   yes   no

3. _____ **I will forgive myself and change**   yes   no

4. _____ **I will forgive myself and change**   yes   no

5. _____ **I will forgive myself and change**   yes   no

Commitment # 1: I am willing to become conscious of the immature ways I unconsciously offer empathy. I will also vigilantly work to see from the other person's perspective and discern their feelings instead of "catching" their upset with my judgements. In short I will accept the moment as it is.

Signature _____   Date _____

Activity to suspend judgments

With a partner you will practice suspending judgments while listening. To discern the difference between judging and accepting you will conduct a two-part experience.

Part 1: I agree, I disagree One person is the talker, the other is the listener. The talker shares a frustrating experience from his or her life. The listener consciously agrees (yes, this is awful) or disagrees (I don't think it is as bad as you think) with the person. The conscious agreement or disagreement happens in your inner speech. You do not need to verbalize your position. From these positions of agreeing or disagreeing, notice the types of immature empathy that emerge. Do this for two minutes.

Part 2: The moment is as it is Repeat the experience. This time the listener consciously refrains from judging the other person's situation. They accept that all is well. Again, this non-judgmental position occurs in one's inner speech. You may say to yourself, "All is well. This person can handle these feelings and this situation. I will just listen carefully." From this position of acceptance, pay conscious attention to feelings and words spoken. Do this for two minutes.

Once you have completed the exercise, discuss the differences between the two experiences from the talker's point of view and from the listener's point of view. What did you discover?

Activity to really listen (say what you hear)

Dr. Harville Hendrix (1988) developed a listening strategy guaranteed to be empathetic. This technique is called "intentional dialogue." It contains three parts — mirroring, validating and empathizing. In the following exercise, you will practice using the skill of intentional dialogue.

Use the same partner (if possible) used in activity #2. This time, reverse the roles. The listener in activity #2 becomes the talker in activity #3. The talker is to share some upsetting event in his or her life. The listener is to do the following:

1. Mirroring: This is the process of accurately reflecting back the content of the message. Listen carefully and repeat back to your partner what you heard. Begin the reflection by saying, "Let me see if I understand you correctly. You said . . ." After the listener reflects back the content, he or she ends the mirroring by checking for accuracy, saying, "Did I get that right?"

2. Validating: This is the process of indicating to the other person that what she is saying makes sense. You must set aside your own perceptions and frame of reference and appreciate the logic of the other person. Validating does not mean you agree or disagree with the other person's perceptions. It means that you surrender your place as the center and source of "truth" and allow space for the other person's interpretation of reality. You might use words such as, "What you are saying makes sense," or "Given your experience, it makes sense that (rephrase the message)."

3. Empathizing: This is the process of recognizing the feelings of another person while he or she is expressing a point of view or telling a story. You might say, "And I can imagine that you might be feeling. . ."

Summarized, the steps to intentional dialogue are:

1. Listen by saying, "Let me see if I understand you correctly. You said ____." Complete this part by saying, "Did I get that right?" Modify if needed.

2. As you understand the other person's perception of a situation, say, "What you are saying makes sense."

3. Knowing that the perception creates the feelings, complete the process by saying, "I can imagine that you might be feeling . . ."

Discuss how each person felt during the dialogue after completing the exercise.

Principle # 5: Until you feel your feelings, you will not allow children to feel theirs.

To understand the emotions of another person, you must first accept and acknowledge your own. This is a challenge because most of us have been programmed to deny our feelings. Many of our own parents taught us that if our feelings were hurt or if we didn't like something, we were to ignore our emotions. They said things such as, "It's not that bad," "Don't worry about it," or "Don't think about it." Also, many of our parents rescued us from the consequences of our choices. They would bring lunch money to school if we forgot and help out with projects we procrastinated starting. They would save us and then berate us. They commented, "What were you thinking? Did you even bother to think? If you had done what I said to, none of this would have happened." This angry response from parents to our disappointing choices demanded us to focus on their feelings of anger instead of our own feelings of remorse. It is impossible for us to teach children skills we have not mastered ourselves. Therefore, we must learn to *feel* our feelings and to *express* them in acceptable ways. Doing both requires skill.

Thinking about your feelings and feeling them are two different things. Many adults think about their emotions and confuse thoughts with feelings. If you ask a friend, "How do you feel?" and she responds, "I feel like nothing is going my way," she has expressed a thought, not a feeling. To get in touch with your thoughts and feel your feelings, you must know the difference between them. Practice discerning whether what you are focusing on is a thought or a feeling. The difference matters enormously.

You will experience confusion when you think one thing and feel another. When you align your thoughts with your feelings, you will become centered. From this position, you can communicate effectively with others. Just for practice, how do you feel right now? Did you answer with an emotional word such as happy, sad or scared? If you answered without using a feeling word, it probably was a thought.

Activity to discern thoughts from feelings

Sit quietly with your eyes closed. Closing your eyes reduces sensory stimuli from the outside, allowing greater success at focusing on your insides. Think of an upsetting conversation you had with someone recently. Play the conversation back in your head. Pay attention to the words as you replay the scene. Do this for 30 seconds. Then shift from focusing your attention on the thoughts/words to your body. Emotions are in your body. They are energy in motion. Can you discern some energy in motion? Focus on your stomach. Is it tight? Focus on your chest and on your throat. Feel the pulsating energies. These are feelings. Once you find one say, "Hello frustration," or "Hello anger." The first step to developing a relationship with anything is to say, "Hello."

> **Of all the world's languages, the most difficult one is the language of feelings.**

To empathize with children, you must first offer yourself empathy and compassion. You must accept your feelings instead of telling yourself, "I shouldn't feel like this." Out loud, tell yourself, "I feel frustrated and it's okay." If you don't verbalize your feelings, you will act them out like children. Catch yourself thinking about how others are feeling about your life choices. Stop yourself and refocus onto your own feelings. Of all the world's languages, the most difficult one is the language of feelings.

Margaret, a mother of three, was returning to teaching after staying home with her children for years. She felt scared about her job and her abilities. Usually she succeeded in hiding her terror at work, but at home it was a different story. She felt depressed, angry and anxious. Margaret tried to stay busy to avoid feeling her feelings, but she simply could not escape a deep sense of inadequacy.

Margaret's suffering manifested itself in her actions at home. She tried to silence her self-doubt by being positive and convincing her children they were splendid. As

Margaret struggled to feel better inside, she made comments like, "Jamie, you are wonderful," and "Mardell, you are such a good little girl." When her anxiety became too much, she attempted to control her children's feelings. When her children expressed anxiety about school, she'd say, "You are all right," "There's no need to be upset," or "I will not tolerate outbursts." She wouldn't let her own anxiety surface, so unconsciously she wouldn't allow it in her children either. A teacher cannot help children manage their emotions while denying his or her own emotions. As an adult, you can consciously choose to be egocentric or empathetic. What you choose is what you will teach children.

Practice feeling your feelings today, recognizing that feelings are like weather. Some days are sunny, others are cloudy and some bring storms. Weather simply comes and goes. Resisting it is insane. Use the Power of Acceptance—the moment is as it is— and relax. Feel your weather patterns come and go. You aren't bad if it rains today!

The more skilled you become at reading feelings of yours and others, the more caring you will be. Conversely, the less skilled you are at empathizing with others, the less caring you will be. In Western culture, people rarely verbalize emotions. You must read feelings through nonverbal cues like tone of voice and facial expression. In fact, 90% or more of an emotional message is nonverbal. Practice reading nonverbal cues from children. Do this by saying what you see. You might say, "Look at your face. You seem excited," or "Your body seems tense. Something on your mind?"

Notice that these comments are tentative inquiries. Use voice inflection to communicate this. You must never tell someone how to feel. When you make educated guesses, children will generally confirm your guesses or correct you. Confirmation can come in two forms, nonverbal and verbal. Nonverbal confirmation may come in an exaggeration of the feeling described. The child's face and body will say, "Yes, I do feel sad," by looking even sadder. Verbally, the child may tell you what is bothering her or she will correct you, saying something like, "No, I'm just tired."

Practice taking time to allow yourself to feel your feelings. Some of us allow ourselves to feel "positive" feelings of joy, happiness and excitement. Most of us run from feelings labeled "negative" like sadness, anger and fear. We believe if we allow ourselves to feel these feelings **1)** they will never go away **2)** we will become irrational and **3)** they will take over our minds and bodies like a demonic possession, forcing us to do evil things. We fear feeling. The irony of the situation is that as long as we refuse to feel, we resist ourselves. The more we resist, the more the feelings persist. If you stop to feel your feelings and accept them as part of you, they will dissipate and disappear.

Activity to help feelings dissipate

Bring into your mind a painful experience (or a physical pain in your body). As the feeling of upset surfaces within you, allow yourself to feel it. Close your eyes and *join* with the feeling. If thoughts enter into your head, just let them go by and refocus yourself on the feeling. When you are focused on the feeling, begin a conversation with it regarding acceptance. You might say, "It is okay that you are here. You don't have to go away. You can stay as long as you want to." You might even begin loving the feeling. Metaphorically you can wrap your arms around the upset, soothe it and rock it. You might even sing a lullaby. The ultimate message is that this feeling is acceptable and allowed to exist. What you will find is that as you do this the feeling and the pain begins to go away. An anxiety you could have carried around in your life for fifteen years could slowly dissipate in three minutes with acceptance and empathy.

> Before we can be empathetic with children
> we must start giving ourselves
> empathy and compassion.

Commitment 2: This month I will focus on feeling my feelings and offering empathy to myself instead of judgment. When I am upset and think that I have made a mistake by having inappropriate thoughts, actions or feelings, I will resist the temptation to punish myself and offer myself empathy instead.

Signature _____ Date _____

Becoming brain smart

Currently there are two camps in regard to brain function, the modular view and the holistic view. The modular viewpoint emphasizes that different parts of the brain are highly specialized for certain capacities. The holistic camp argues that the brain functions as a whole and that any one part can be recruited for multiple tasks. In essence everything is connected to everything else. My thoughts are that the two viewpoints are not mutually exclusive and that the brain probably operates in some degree from modules that are complexly interconnected.

The mid-brain area (limbic system) of the brain, composed of such structures as the amygdala, thalamus, hypothalamus, hippocampus and pineal gland, has been hypothesized to be the seat of emotions. Others suggest that our feelings are processed in other areas of the brain (Damasio, 1994). Candace Pert in her book, *Molecules of Emotion* (1997), suggests that our feeling are not restricted to the brain at all but dispersed throughout the body. Probably in the end, we will find that all of these great minds are correct to some degree.

More important than the source of emotions is the role of emotions in learning. It turns out that learning is an emotional experience. Even though we may be presented with information and evidence that something might be true, it is verified by the limbic system. In other words, something is deemed true or not, simply when it *feels* true.

Scientists have promoted the notion that the major source of irrational behavior and thinking is due to emotions. We now know that emotions are indispensable for rationality. There are far more neural fibers going from the mid-brain (the emotional part of the brain) into the neocortex (reasoning part of the brain) than fibers going from the neocortex into the mid-brain. What does this mean? It means that emotions are powerful motivators. Emotions chart the course for moment to moment choices as well as long-term goals. We are emotional beings. Unless we learn how to process emotions they can lead us into destructive patterns. Joseph LeDoux (1996) states, "When fear becomes anxiety, desire gives way to greed, or annoyance turns to anger, anger to hatred, friendship to envy, love to obsession, or pleasure to addiction, our emotions start working against us." Mental health requires good emotional hygiene. The source of emotional hygiene is empathy. Most emotions occur without our conscious awareness of them. Empathy provides the mirror for children to become aware of their feelings and in turn, aware of themselves. The more a child receives empathy the more "whole" they become and the more efficient is their brain organization. Research confirms this. Robert Rosenthal, a Harvard psychologist, studied the relationship of empathy to intelligence. Results indicated that the children with the highest empathy performed better on SAT, IQ and school achievement tests (Norwicki & Duke, 1989).

Offering empathy to children

Historically, emotions have received little, if any, attention in schools. Schools are there to educate and therefore are geared to attend to the cognitive realm, not the emotional arena. As the above mentioned brain research has crept into public awareness and educational circles, token attention to emotions has been given by some. Some schools have bought curriculum kits to teach children empathy and anger management. Usually, a teacher sets aside a specified time each week to "teach" empathy. This lesson is negated by the rest of the week when empathy may be lacking in her day-to-day dealings with children. The following assessment will help determine how much and what type of empathy (immature or mature) you are offering in your program.

Assessment #3: Do you offer empathy during conflict times?
Pre-test: Write how you would respond to the following situation. It is extremely important that you write down the exact words you would probably say.

Situation: Calvin arrives at school late and enters the classroom. You tell him he must go to the office and check in. This sets Calvin off. He stomps his feet and shouts, "I'm not going to the damn office." He pushes Rodney out of the way and kicks the wall.
Your likely response:

Your response is an indicator of your own teaching style in regard to empathy. Researchers have identified four styles. Here are brief descriptions of them. Which characterizes you?

Empathy style #1: Ignoring feelings, no empathy. Adults in this category ignore emotions and focus only on behaviors. They fail to use emotional moments as chance to connect with children or teach them how to express their feelings.

During "The Freeze" game in a kindergarten class, several children begin to go wild. Recess had been canceled for two days due to rain and the activity level has been rising like the humidity. During the frenzy, Ryan is trampled by a couple of runners. He begins to cry. At this point, Mrs. Graves turns off the record player and demands in a firm voice that all the children return to the rug and have a seat. Ryan continues to cry and refuses to move over to the rug area. Mrs. Graves states, "Cross your legs, put your hands in your lap and sit quietly." Several children look at where Ryan is crying. Noticing this, Mrs. Graves assures the children saying, "He is fine and will join the group soon." She turns to Ryan and says, "Please join us when you are ready."

Mrs. Graves typifies a teacher who ignores feelings and trains other children to ignore feelings also. Ryan's upset was not relevant to her agenda. This scenario may seem harmless, but when messages like these add up moment after moment, day after day, it becomes possible to understand how the New York incident reported in the news years ago could take place. It seems over thirty people heard or observed a woman being beaten to death and did nothing. Maybe they were programmed to ignore their own or another's distress.

Empathy style #2: Fixing feelings, immature empathy. Some adults notice children's feelings, but either expect them to handle their feelings independently or to get over them. The goal is to "happy up" children. If empathy is offered, it is of an immature form.

Michael did not complete his magnet experiment on time. When it is time to share he feels frustrated. When the teacher calls on him, he throws his paper down, stomps and has a full-blown temper tantrum. Mrs. Baker, the teacher, asks Michael to remove himself from the group until he can calm down. As he leaves the group he knocks all the papers off the top of a desk. Mrs. Baker says, "Calm down Michael, you can share tomorrow. Pull yourself together. It is not the end of the world." With this he turns and sticks his tongue out at the teacher. Mrs. Baker's response is, "That was not necessary, nor was it nice. Why are you acting this way?" Later that day, Mrs. Baker consults the behavior specialist and Michael is placed on a point system. Each time he accepts responsibility for his behavior without showing signs of irritation or anger, he receives points and "good day" notes to his parents. After so many points, Michael can go shopping in the classroom store for goodies.

Mrs. Baker exemplifies a person who attempts to fix feelings. She did nothing to help Michael process his emotions. She attempted to distract him by sending him to magically soothe himself. She bribed him with a point system. She did nothing to help him feel, accept and transform his emotions into healthy relationship skills.

Empathy style #3: Punishing feelings. These adults criticize children's feelings. They may forbid *any* display of anger or even punish irritability. Emotions, especially negative ones, are seen as disrespect. The hallmark statement of this style is, "I'll give you something to cry about!"

Children in Ms. Lem's classroom are on a card system. Each day children begin the day with three cards. Their goal is to end the day without losing a card. Each card removed from the child has a negative consequence attached to it. After doing an AIMS jelly bean sort and graph activity, two boys engage in a loud shouting match. Ms. Lem immediately turns her attention to the boys and takes a card from each. Jerod, already angry with Jason, is more outraged with the loss of the card. He screams, "This isn't fair, you stupid idiot," and pushes an empty chair in frustration. Ms. Lem immediately takes his remaining card, calls the principal and tells him in front of the class how "rude, disrespectful and hateful" he was acting. Jerod is informed that his parents will be called and he will not be allowed back into her classroom until after the conference.

Ms. Lem lashed out at Jerod's inappropriate expression of anger. She in essence called him names in response to being called one herself. Punitive approaches almost always model the exact behavior they try to eliminate.

> **Before you can empathize, you must stop equating disobedience with disrespect.**

Empathy style #4: Coaching feelings with empathy. Some teachers understand that misbehavior represents an intense feeling without an appropriate outlet. These teachers utilize moments of upset as opportunities to teach emotional good sense. Below is an example.

At the school breakfast, Arthur is not allowed to sit next to his friend, Sarah. He becomes angry and gets into a fight with the fifth grade cafeteria monitor. The fight ends when the school bell signals the end of breakfast and the beginning of the school day. When Arthur enters the classroom he says to his teacher, "I'm not going to do anything today. My mom is going to come in here and talk to you. You are going to be sued." Arthur pushes over a chair after these comments.

Mrs. Camden takes a deep breath to calm herself down and says, "Arthur, your face is red, your fists are balled tightly and you seem really angry. Something happened?" Arthur replies, "I don't have to talk to you. I hate this school." Mrs. Camden calmly responds, "You seem extremely angry with something that happened at school." Arthur grumps, "Just leave me alone."

Mrs. Camden reaches out to touch Arthur and he pulled away. With this she comments, "Arthur, you pulled your arm just like this (she demonstrated his actions for him). Arthur looks at his arm and then at Mrs. Camden's arm and finally makes eye contact. Mrs. Camden responds to this nonverbal connection by saying, "You are just not ready to talk about what happened." Arthur's body begins to relax. When Mrs. Camden notices Arthur relaxing she knows he is calming down and letting go of his resentment and anger. To help him further process his emotions in regard to his experience she then offers him a choice. "Arthur, you may write in your journal or draw. Which would you like to do before the day begins?" Arthur decides to draw. In his drawing he shows the fight in the cafeteria.

Mrs. Camden represents a teacher who helped Arthur process and express his emotions in a socially acceptable manner. She was a mirror for him so he could be conscious of his feelings. In doing so she helped him regain self-control.

Empathy style post-test. Look back at the words you used to handle the upset with Calvin in the pre-test assessment. From your response, what type of empathy style would characterize your teaching? To help you analyze yourself, count the number of feeling words you used. These words might be: scared, sad, disappointed, happy, angry, irritable, etc. If no feeling words appear, you are probably relying on style # 1.

As you reflect on your results, reflect also on your childhood. If your feelings were ignored growing up, you would naturally learn to ignore the feelings of others. If your feelings were fixed, you learned to be a fixer. Does this make you a bad person? Or, does this make you a person who is consciously aware of something you might want to work on changing? The choice is yours.

Handling the fits and fussing with children: See, feel, hear

When you empathize, you symbolically say, "I see you, I hear you and I feel you." Your task is to notice, describe and reflect. There is no place for judging in these reflective statements. When your child is upset, do the following to let her know you understand: Reflect back what you *see*. Reflect back what you *hear*. Reflect back what you *feel*.

Empathy helps organize the brain

An out-of-control, upset child needs empathy to become organized again. Anger is a secondary emotion originating from fear. Fear triggers an unconscious emotional hijacking in the brain that throws a child into a fight or flight mentality. Emotional responses can and do occur without the involvement of the higher processing systems of the brain believed to be involved in reasoning. The portion of the brain activated in fear (upsetting) situations is small. Empathy is critical to facilitate children's access to their whole brain in order to problem solve.

The brain works as a whole, but can be thought of as having three levels. The lower levels deal mainly with survival issues and avoiding pain. These lower levels are the *brain stem*. The middle levels deal mainly with feelings and seeking pleasure. These levels are called the *limbic system*. The upper levels are more able to see the big picture, can focus on problem solving and seek novelty. These upper levels make up the *cortex*.

Sometimes children physically express their upset by throwing their bodies on the floor or lashing out to hit and kick others. These children are unconsciously using their bodies to express their conflicted inner states. These children are operating from the lower levels of their brains, in their brain stems. To help these children become conscious and move from this level, say what you see. You might say, "Your arms are swinging like this (demonstrate). Your eyebrows are furrowed and your face is very red."

When children become upset, they also can express themselves verbally through name calling, complaining or whining. Inappropriate verbal expressions signal that a child is operating from the middle levels of the brain, in the limbic system. To help children become conscious of themselves and more organized, you can say what you sense the child is *feeling*. Saying, "You seem angry," or "You seem very disappointed," will help a child become more organized.

A child who is able to accept what is happening and is ready to problem solve is generally operating from the upper levels of the brain, in the cortex. To facilitate problem solving with this child, it is helpful to say what you *hear*. By mirroring back what the child says to you, you enable the child to organize her thoughts enough to begin solving the problem. If a child says, "It is not fair that some children get more time to work on their projects," you might respond, "You are concerned that others are getting more time to finish their projects than you?"

Our job is like that of an elevator operator. We are to assist children to move from the lower levels (brain stem - survival), to the middle levels (limbic system - feeling), to the upper levels (cortex - problem solving) of the brain. With each level children become more organized, calm and in control of themselves. So if a child is out-of-control or flailing her body, describe what you see. "Your arms are going like this, your feet are stomping, your eyebrows are pulled tight (demonstrate for the child)." More than likely her body will organize and her mouth will take over, "Stop it. I hate you!" At this point you can reflect back what you think the child is feeling. "You seem very angry?" This will help the child organize her emotions enough to begin expressing the problem. "You won't let me do anything." It is important to reflect back what you thought you heard to help the child begin solving her problem. "You don't think I let you do what you want to do?" At this point the child is probably capable of sharing with you the real issue. "I wanted to play with Carmen and you said I had to clean up." With the problem out in the open you can then sum up what happened and teach the child another way of expressing herself. "You were disappointed when you heard you couldn't play with Carmen. It's hard to not be able to do what we want to. You have a choice. You can clean the paint or the brushes in the sink. Which will you do?"

You do not always need to use all three statements (see, feel, hear) to build empathy, but the combination is powerful. Each type of reflection becomes a bit more abstract. When you reflect what you see, your words are concrete. When you reflect what you have heard, you must listen carefully and understand the child's meaning. When you reflect back your child's feelings, you are relying on a certain level of guesswork. If you are wrong, though, the child will usually correct you.

> **Understanding does not change the limits on behavior, it just helps children to become better able to accept them.**

The chart on the following page will help you assess what part of the brain a child might be operating from. Once you make this assessment, you can select a discipline skill that would be helpful.

Brain Smart Discipline

Hierarchical Organization of the Brain	Function	Sensitive Periods of Development	Emotional & Behavioral Indicators of Stress	Discipline Skill to Use	Words to Say	Possible Results of Persistant Stress on this Brain Level
Cortex (Frontal Lobes)	**REASON LOGIC** Analysis Language Compassion Empathy	Approximately 4 years to 8 years old	Annoyed Irritated Example: "He pushed me!"	**PROBLEM SOLVING** Reflect content (hear) Facilitate problem solving, conflict resolution or teach another way of handling the situation	"When she pushes you say: *Stop! I don't like to be pushed.*" "Be a S.T.A.R."	Underdeveloped empathy and problem solving skills
Limbic System	**EMOTION MEMORY** Feelings Motivation Affiliation	Approximately 15 months to 4 years old	Angry Blaming Judging Name calling Example: "Stupid idiot!"	**EMPATHY** Reflect feelings (feel) Give words to the child's experience Help label feelings	"That frown is telling me you may feel angry. Something must have happened. Go to the safe place and be a S.T.A.R., balloon, drain or pretzel."	Underdeveloped empathy Underdeveloped attachment and affiliation Overdeveloped emotional reactivity
Brain Stem	**SURVIVAL** Fight or flight Reactive and fast Motor skill regulation (doesn't talk)	Approximately birth to 15 months old	Furious Physically attacking Runs away Withdrawn Constantly anxious Example: hitting	**COMPOSURE** Actively calm yourself **NOTICING** Reflect behavior (see), describe the child's actions and behavior	"You knocked over your chair and are pounding your fists on the table." "You are safe. Breathe with me. I won't let you hurt yourself or others."	Overdeveloped anxiety and impulsivity Poor affect regulation Hyperactivity Sleep disturbances Increased muscle tone Hypervigilance

Activity to find where in the brain a person is acting from

Work with others to determine which level of the brain the person is operating from: the brain stem, limbic system, or cortex.

1. A mother refuses to buy her two-year old child candy at the grocery store checkout counter. The child begins screaming, crying and swatting at the mother.
What part of the brain is the child in? _____

2. While Joshua shared his views at a meeting, someone interrupted him and began to argue with his position. Joshua listened, restated the other person's point of view and then said, "I can see why you believe that. The reason why I differ in my opinion is..."
What part of the brain is Joshua in? _____

3. While Sandra is on the phone, her three-year old finds a pen and begins drawing on the walls. Sandra yells, "No," grabs the pen and sends the child to her room.
What part of the brain is Sandra in? _____

4. While driving home from work, a teenager runs a red light in front of an elderly woman, causing her to swerve her car. The old woman yells, "Jerk!" as she drives by.
What part of the brain is the woman in? _____

5. A seven-year-old finds out her best friend is moving. At dinner she won't participate in any conversation; she just sits there with her head down, moving her food around the plate with her fork but not eating anything.
What part of the brain is the child in? _____

6. A ten-year old boy is refusing to do his homework after school at the designated time. The father recognizes his son's attempt to feel powerful and refuses to get into a power struggle with the boy. The father says, "Could it be that you are trying to prove to me that I can't make you do your homework? If so, you're right. I only hope that you choose to follow the agreements we've set as a family."
What part of the brain is the father in? _____

Your intent is critical: Acceptance is the key

Your intent is critical to the use of empathy. If you intend to make children stop acting or feeling a certain way, you will try to use empathy to manipulate and your tone of voice will betray your motives. I once heard a frustrated teacher say, "I know it's hard to stop what you are doing. Now put your journal away." Her attempt at empathy was aimed at getting the child to be obedient, not helping the child to become organized and aware of herself. Often in workshops, teachers will say, " I tried that and it didn't work!" My question then is, "What do you mean *work*?" The answer is usually that the child did not "happy up" and become obedient. Empathy is bigger than obedience. It is wiring a brain that can process disappointment, frustration and anger without acting out these emotions in a hurtful manner. Like any skill it must be offered long before it is internalized. If we labeled "cup" for an infant one time, would you expect the child to learn the word? No. The same is true for empathy.

Skill #1: Reflecting back what you *see*

Jake stomped into the room and threw down his backpack so hard it knocked over a chair. The teacher reached out to touch him on the shoulder to get his attention and he immediately jerked away. Accepting the moment as it is instead of wishing it were different or saying to herself, "Jake shouldn't act like this," the teacher reflected back what she saw. "You pulled your arm back just like this (she demonstrated the action) when I reached to touch your shoulder." Jake looked up and for the first time made eye contact with his teacher. At that point she further reflected back what she saw. "You came in stomping your feet, your face looked strained and you threw your backpack so hard that the chair fell." Jake responded with, "I hate coming to school." The teacher had successfully moved Jake from the lower levels of his brain to the middle levels. She then responded, "You seem angry?" Jake then began to talk about his bus ride to school. By reflecting back what she saw, the teacher helped Jake become calm enough to begin talking about his upsetting experience. When reflecting back what you see, focus on the child's body. Pay close attention to facial expression and posture.

Activity to reflect back what you *see*

Role play the following situations. One person will be the teacher and one person will be the student. In the role play use the skill of reflecting back what you see. As you reflect back what you see notice the "student's" face. Did he or she become organized and make eye contact with you? If not, continue to reflect what you see.

Situation 1: Teacher touches child on the arm and she pulls away

Situation 2: Teacher says something to a student and the student covers her face with her hands

Situation 3: Teacher touches child's arm and the child pushes the teacher's arm away

Situation 4: Teacher smiles at the child and the child makes eye contact

Skill #2: Reflecting back what you *feel*

Fernando walked into the classroom screaming, "I hate Mrs. Ortiz. She's an idiot." Mr. Frankel heard Fernando, took a deep breath to calm himself and said, "Fernando, you seem really angry with Mrs. Ortiz." He stared at Mr. Frankel and announced, "I am never going to music class again. You can't make me. No one can." Mr. Frankel said, "Let me see if I understand. You are very angry with Mrs. Ortiz. So angry you feel it best not to return to class. Is there more I don't understand?" "Yeah," said Fernando, "You don't understand what an idiot she is." Since Fernando went back to name calling, Mr. Frankel went back to the feelings and said, "You seem really frustrated." At this point Fernando's body relaxed and he shared how he felt embarrassed when Mrs. Ortiz had him sing in front of the whole class. Once the problem was defined, Mr. Frankel could then proceed with problem solving. He summarized the problem for Fernando so he could begin to see his options. "So the problem is that Mrs. Ortiz had you sing in front of the class and you felt really embarrassed, so you have decided to solve the problem by never going back to music class." Fernando just stood there and said sadly, "Yeah." Mr. Frankel said, "How do think that will work for you?" "I don't know," said Fernando. "Do you think it would affect your music grade?" Fernando looked shocked with this new line of thinking. Noticing his face, Mr. Frankel continued by saying, "Would you like to explore other ways to solve the problem?" With this, both Mr. Frankel and Fernando discussed options.

To reflect back what you think a child might be *feeling*, focus on the body language to discern the emotion. Do not over-emphasize the child's words. They can be misleading ("I'm fine"). Listen for the feelings underneath the words. Reflect that back to your child. All expressions of hate and name calling are anger, which ultimately are fear put into action. So when a child resorts to name calling, you reflect back the feeling under the hurtful act. Deal with the hurtful act later.

Common mistakes when reflecting feelings

☑ **Reflect instead of question.** The purpose of questioning is to elicit information. The purpose of reflecting is to increase the child's self-awareness. If you are asking questions, you are *not* reflecting feelings. Questions ask children to think, not to feel. Avoid saying things like: "You seem pretty sad, don't you?" "Why are you angry?"

☑ **Sounding all-knowing.** Your reflections ought to be tentative and correctable. You want to leave room for your child's response and for possible correction. Statements that sound all-knowing are *not* reflections. Tentative inquiries like, "You seem angry?" are helpful. Avoid saying things like: "You must be feeling sad." "I know you are angry."

Skill #3: Reflecting back what you *hear*

To reflect back what you *hear*, listen closely to the children and then summarize the essence of their statements, paraphrasing in your own words what you think was communicated. Your reflections offer tangible evidence to the children that you have listened to them with empathy and have understood their perspective. This is basically the same process you practiced in the earlier exercise with intentional dialogue. A child might say, "You can't make me take a shower. It's my body." You could reflect back to the child the following, "You want me to know that it's important to you to be responsible for taking care of your own body." The child might respond, "Yeah." You then could say, "That makes sense, it is your body." From here you can begin the problem solving process. In this situation, you might say, "To take care of your body you must shower every day. When will you be taking care of your body today?"

With a nonverbal child, you must summarize the expressions of her body. If her face looks angry, say, "Your face is telling me you wanted to do it by yourself." If she kicks the door you could say, "Your foot is saying: *let's go*." Then prompt the child to say, "Go," or "Bye-bye."

Anger: The most difficult emotion to reflect

Sadness shows up in posture (curled over like a steamed shrimp). It may also show up as tears, pouting and withdrawal. Happiness announces itself with bouncing smiles, joyful shouts and hugs. Fear comes out in nail-biting, fidgeting and wide eyes. Many adults will tolerate these expression if they do not reach extremes. However, anger may make itself known through kicking, hitting, spitting and swearing, behaviors that tend to scare adults. Therefore, adult empathy for anger is rare. Paradoxically, empathy is the best skill you can use to help children gain control over angry emotions and behaviors. With the dangerous aggression many children display, teaching ourselves to reflect back children's emotions is extremely helpful to children and to society.

Sometimes when I am doing a workshop, I will have participants write down the Seven Basic Skills of Discipline on seven separate cards. I read scenarios and the teachers are asked to hold up the skill (written on a card) that is most effective in beginning the interaction with the child. We have discussed how important empathy is for an upset child. I give an example of a child who falls and hurts her knee. Most participants hold up the card that says "empathy." I then give a situation where a child is mad at a friend. Again, the empathy card is shown. Finally I say, "A child walks up to you and says: *You're stupid. I hate you.*" At this point no empathy cards appear and the consequences card is selected. Resisting the urge to attack those that attack is a huge task. Yet, for children to obtain self control we must learn it ourselves.

It is important to remember that anger is a secondary emotion. It is a cover for fear. Every angry situation is a resistance to "what is." This resistance is created because we believe we would be safer if the situation had gone as we had planned or expected. Therefore, we find the current situation threatening in some manner. When we help children process anger it is a two-step process. The first step is to mirror for them their anger by assisting in labeling the feeling. This is done by saying such things as, "You seem angry (frustrated, furious)." The second step is to help children get in touch with the fear underlying the anger. This might be done by then saying, "Something scary happened?" or "Something must be really worrying you (concerning you)?"

Listen for the underlying emotion in the children's words in the exclamations below. Note how a teacher can reflect those emotions with this two-part process.

Children's words	Teacher reflections
Part 1: "You're stupid"	"You seem frustrated with me."
Part 2: "You're always picking on me."	"You seem afraid that I don't like you?"
Part 1: "I hate you."	"You seem angry with me."
Part 2: "You are going to fail me."	"You seem worried that I am more in charge of your grade than you are."
Part 1: "You can't make me."	"You seem angry?"
Part 2: "I don't have to do anything that I don't want to."	"It's scary when things seem out of our control."

Activity to role play with anger

With a partner, role play the following scenarios. Upon completion of the exercises, discuss with your partner how it felt to offer empathy in response to upset as opposed to more traditional approaches of offering judgements, lectures and threats.

Scene 1: One of your students returns from physical education in an upset state of mind. As he enters the classroom he looks at you and says, "School is stupid. I hate it here." Then he stomps off.

Scene 2: A student has forgotten her permission slip to go on a field trip. In the morning you explain where she will spend the day while the class goes to the Pumpkin Patch Farm. The student responds, "This isn't fair. You could let me go if you wanted. You're an idiot. I hate you." Then the child gestures as if she were going to kick you.

Putting it all together: Dealing with tantrums

A temper tantrum is an uncontrolled outburst of anger that usually arises from a child's (or an adult's) thwarted efforts to control a situation. The tantrum says, "I have tried desperately to make the world go my way. Now I'm so frazzled I can barely stand it. I feel terrified, helpless and powerless."

Both children and adults have temper tantrums. Think of your last tantrum and how awful it was to think that you may have hurt someone during it. Think of the comfort you would feel if you knew that although you had spun out of control, someone else stayed calm to assure your safety and that of your loved ones.

Teachers need to understand temper tantrums and help children move through rage without feeling abandoned. Rejection, abandonment and shame create more rage, and increase the odds of more tantrums. A calm adult creates safety for the child and reduces the chance of future tantrums. If you can help children move *through* temper tantrums, you can then begin teaching them better ways to affect their world or cope with it. Tantrums occur in two modes: **1)** out-of-control with no physical threat to yourself or others and **2)** out-of-control with threats to yourself or others. When no threat is involved, empathy and time can restore the child to an organized state. When threat is involved, the child must be restrained. This restraint is supported by empathy.

Remember, only by staying in control yourself can you help your out-of-control child. (As the flight attendants say, "Put your own oxygen mask on first. Then put the mask on the child.") Shift your focus from stopping tantrums to helping children move through them by reflecting back what you *see, feel* and *hear*. Pay close attention to the next example. Be alert to the teacher's reflections of what she *sees, feels,* and *hears*.

Melissa, age six, hates when anyone gets in her very large personal space. One morning during opening circle, Cassandra sits on Melissa's carpet square. Melissa goes crazy. She throws herself on the floor kicking and screaming. Mrs. Brookes takes several deep breaths and tells herself, "This moment is as it is. Relax and solve the problem." She starts describing what she sees. "Melissa, your arms are going like this (demonstrates)." Melissa continues flailing her arms and hollering. Mrs. Brookes ignores the words and focuses on her body. "Your face is scrunched up." Mrs. Brookes makes her face as much like Melissa's as possible. Melissa looks up briefly and makes eye contact with her teacher. Mrs. Brookes continues to actively calm herself and says, "Your whole body is telling me you feel angry." Melissa looks at Cassandra and shakes her fist at her. Mrs. Brookes facilitates this communication because of Melissa's language delays by saying, "Cassandra, Melissa shook her fist to tell you she was angry when you sat on her carpet square." Mrs. Brookes continues to help Melissa move into problem solving. "You wanted Cassandra to move off you square. When you want her to move say: *Move, please.* Tell her now." Melissa is able to say, "Move, please."

In this story, Mrs. Brookes kept herself calm enough to help Melissa through her tantrum. She offered compassion to Melissa and taught the rest of the class how to offer compassion to people who are out-of-control.

Later that day, Cassandra once again sat on Melissa's carpet square. Melissa starts screaming and throws her body on the floor. Mrs. Brookes notices Melissa by saying, "Your arms are swinging and your heels are kicking the floor." As Mrs. Brookes demonstrates this for Melissa, she kicks Mrs. Brookes. Mrs. Brookes lets out a yelp of pain and grabs her shin. Melissa swings her fist attacking Mrs. Brookes. The teacher takes several deep breaths and restrains Melissa, making sure Melissa's arms are tucked tightly into her own chest. Mrs. Brookes states, "I will keep you safe. I will not let you hurt yourself or anyone else." After this statement of the limits, she begins to empathize with the child. "Your arms are pushing against my body, your feet are moving just like this (mirroring the movements if possible). Your whole body is saying: *I feel angry. It's scary to be out-of-control.*" At this point, Mrs. Brookes reiterates, "I will keep you safe. I will not let you hurt yourself or anyone else." Melissa proclaims, "Let me go. I'll be good. Just let me go." Mrs. Brookes says back what she heard: "You want me to let you go." With this, Melissa's nonverbal struggle becomes louder. Mrs. Brookes continues to notice her and then says, "I will be happy to let you go when your body is relaxed and you are breathing deep like me." As Melissa begins to breathe and relax she begins to sob. Mrs. Brookes holds her, rocks her and says, "It's okay to cry." She continues to hum *Let it be* by the Beatles until Melissa grows calm. As she organizes, she takes Melissa over to Cassandra and re-creates the teaching moment, going back in time to do the situation over. Below is a summary of the steps for dealing with temper tantrums:

☑ Offer empathy. Say what you see, hear, and feel.

☑ Restrain the child, if necessary for safety reasons.

☑ Say, "I will keep you safe. I will not let you hurt yourself or anyone else."

☑ Say, "I will be happy to let you go when your body is relaxed and you are breathing like me."

Activity to reflect and plan for change

Take some time and reflect on what you have learned about empathy, children and yourself. Answer the following questions as part of that process.

What I learned:

How I typically respond to upset children:

How I plan to change my response to upset children:

What I plan to do for myself when I am upset:

Physical structures that support the Skill of Empathy

The physical structures mentioned thus far in this book help build the school family, teach children to maintain self control and encourage problem solving. All of them also support the Skill of Empathy. These physical structures are centers in the classroom that are designed to help children move from their brain stem (lower brain levels) to their cortex (higher levels of the brain). This helps children to gain better control of themselves and to access the higher cognitive processes necessary to see a situation from another's perspective. Though all the centers mentioned in this book support the Skill of Empathy, we will focus on the *we care center*.

We care center

The we care center was first introduced in chapter 2. It is further explained in the following two classroom examples.

Mrs. Lee's kindergarten class had decided the we care center would be a tote bag. On the tote bag were several hearts and a quote written by Mrs. Lee in permanent marker. The quote read, "In our school family, we care about each other." One day Mrs. Lee was reading a book during center time. All of a sudden, Kasy begins to cry. Kareem, who was the we care person for that week, picked up the we care tote bag and walked over to Kasy. He said, "Would any of these help?" In the we care bag was a stuffed animal, several bandaids, a bottle of lotion and a small baby blanket. Without a word, Kasy reached in, pulled out the stuffed bear and held it. Her body began to relax.

In Mr. Carter's fifth grade class, Michelle had been suspended from school for a series of infractions. Several class members went to the classroom we care center which consisted of fancy stationary and envelopes. They wrote Michelle letters to keep in touch with her and wish her well. Each of the letters said she was missed in the school family and that the class is looking forward to her return.

 # No time like the present!

This month vigilantly practice the following with yourself:

☑ Feel your feelings. Where does anger arise in your body? What does it feel like? What thoughts are triggered by the feeling? Focus on the feeling and release the thoughts.

☑ Catch how often you deny your feelings or focus on how others are feeling, instead of yourself. Change statements such as, "I shouldn't feel _____" to "I feel _____ and all is well."

☑ Practice accepting the moment as it is. When life is not going your way, pay attention to your attack or defense thoughts. Attacking does not change "what is," it only changes your mind from peaceful to conflicted.

☑ Say to yourself, "The moment is as it is, *relax* (breathe) and solve the problem." Do this every time you feel upset.

☑ When a child is upset offer empathy as your first skill. Do this by saying what you *see, hear* or *feel.*

☑ Create a we care center for the classroom.

☑ Practice assessing whether a child is in the brain stem, limbic system or cortex. Use the appropriate empathy skill to facilitate problem solving.

Look for these teaching moments

Watch how the children express feelings. Watch how they verbally, nonverbally (facial expressions, body language) and physically (actions such as crossing arms, hitting others, stomping feet) express sadness and disappointment, anger and frustration, happiness and joy, anxiety and fear. The following list will help you focus on the emotional aspect of your classroom:

 ## Disappointment and Sadness

Verbal expressions	*Physical expressions*	*Nonverbal expressions*
"It's not fair."	Withdrawn behavior	Downcast eyes
"I wish we could ____."	Reluctance to be engaged	Steamed shrimp posture
"This sucks."	Crying, pouting	Droopy eyes and face
"Bummer, damn, etc."	Whining, complaining	Slow moving
"I don't care."		Shuffling feet

Frustration and Anger

Verbal expressions	*Physical expressions*	*Nonverbal expressions*
"This is stupid."	Screaming and shouting	Furrowed eyebrows
"I hate you" or "I hate __."	Throwing items	Constricted face
Curse words	Stomping	Folded arms
Name calling	Physically attacking (hitting,	Tense muscles
"You can't make me."	kicking, biting, etc.)	Hands in fists
"You said we could __."		Red in the face

Anxiety and fear

Verbal expressions	*Nonverbal expressions*	*Physical expressions*
"Do we have to?"	Wide eyes	Fidgeting and hyperactivity
Excuses and blame	Shallow breathing	Busy hands, sitting on hands
"I don't know."	Darting eyes	Nail biting
"I don't want to."	Lack of eye contact	Rubbing arms, legs, etc.
"I can't."		Withdrawal and hiding
		Non-conversational language (fine, okay)
		Physical complaints (headache, stomachache)

221

> When children are upset,
> offer empathy or positive intent first.
> Then ask questions and facilitate problem solving.

Commitment #3: I am willing to commit the next 21 days to learning to be a more empathetic person with myself and others. I will vigilantly work to be a mirror for others by reflecting back what I see, what I sense they feel and what I hear.

Signature _____ Date _____

Chapter 7

Consequences

Helping children learn from their mistakes

Mistakes are opportunities to learn

Consequences
Helping Children Learn from their Mistakes

Power:	Power of Intention Mistakes are opportunities to learn
Value:	Responsibility
Purpose:	Help children reflect on their choices and motivate them to make changes in their behavior

Brain Development: The brain thrives on feedback for growth, learning, intelligence and survival

Emotional Development: Consequences teach children cause and effect relationships

Consequence Principles:
1. Mistakes are opportunities to learn responsibility.
2. Punishment and rewards rely on judgement. Consequences rely on reflection.
3. Your intention in administering consequences will determine their effectiveness.
4. Consequences delivered with empathy allow children the opportunity to learn how to be responsible for their choices.

Principle #1: Mistakes are opportunities to learn responsibility.

This month, the motto to promote for yourself, your classroom or your program is, "Mistakes are opportunities to learn." As you reflect on this motto, think of mistakes you have made over your lifetime, last year, this week or even yesterday. Take time to think how these events shaped who you are today. We all make mistakes and we all have made choices that yielded painful outcomes. This is a given. What matters most is what we learned from these experiences. Did they motivate us to reflect, grow and change? Or did they pound us down with regret, shame and stagnation? Take a deep breath. While inhaling say to yourself, "Mistakes are opportunities for learning." While exhaling say to yourself, "I forgive myself for past errors." The icon representing the Power of Intention is a problem-solving maze. It represents learning by trial and error. A person seeking to solve a problem makes a choice (a turn in the maze) that is non-productive. Is this person "bad" or do they simply need to reflect and make another choice. Often we believe children's trial and error attempts at getting the world to do their bidding makes them "bad," deserving punishment.

Mistake is the term I use to define conflict situations. When we make "poor" choices, we create conflict for ourselves and others. Traditionally, classroom conflicts have been viewed as bad. They interrupt the teaching process and therefore are believed to ultimately destroy learning. Newspaper articles say teachers can no longer teach because children are so unruly. Teachers themselves proclaim, "Disciplining children takes all my time." When viewing mistakes (poor choices) made by children as *bad,* the teacher locates the *bad* guy and punishes him in an attempt to make him feel *bad* for his choices. We make the child feel bad in the hope that he or she will make better choices in the future. The goal is to get children to *feel bad* in order to *act better*. Delivering punishments for infractions is the usual approach to getting children to feel bad. This model of conflict and resolution is not effective. If we are honest with ourselves, we know we must feel good about ourselves in order to act better or change. When we feel poorly, we tend to act poorly. Viewing conflict as bad, as a disruption to the learning process, sets us up to unconsciously label some children "bad." Ask children who the bad children are; they know. These bad children are excluded from friendships and ultimately bond together.

Recently, I noticed that my favorite jeans were getting tight. I decided to exercise more and to diet. I kept up my new regimen for two weeks and then, feeling proud, I rewarded myself with a new pair of pants. Soon after this, business travel disrupted my healthy routine and the pants (both new and old) grew tighter again!

Immediately, I began beating myself up with fault-finding self-talk. I said to myself, "Why am I so stupid? I never finish anything I start. I deserve to be fat and ugly. No wonder no one loves me." I felt guilty for backsliding and considered myself a failure. Instead of viewing my mistake as a opportunity to learn, I saw myself as *bad* and then made myself feel *bad*. From this inner state of worthlessness, I sought comfort food (starting with chocolate ice cream and cake) instead of choosing to eat healthy.

> **It is not human nature to feel bad about mistakes and good about accomplishments. We learn this mind set.**

In those few weeks, I replayed the childhood lessons I learned from being raised with rewards and punishments. For following my plan, I rewarded myself (new pants). For failing, I punished myself (Becky-bashing self-talk). Neither the reward nor the punishment effectively motivated me to resume my healthful ways. Upon reflection, I realized that rewards and punishments had not really helped me to learn or to grow.

Most of us have not truly embraced the concept that mistakes are opportunities to learn. Think of the last mistake you thought yourself to have made. How did you handle your error? Did you tell yourself, "I have made a mistake. What can I learn from it? How can I improve?" Or did your mind work on the theme of worthlessness? "How could I have done this? I am horrible. This is all my fault." Perhaps your mind spun to the rottenness of others. "He should have told me. Some friend he is. I would never treat him like that." Punishment and blame don't facilitate the learning process, they stop it.

Conversely, when we feel we have done something right or "good," we tend to view ourselves as worthy. How do you think our minds learned to create these inner dialogues in which we bash ourselves over mistakes and build ourselves up over things viewed as accomplishments? You may think this is human nature, but it is actually a learned pattern.

©1999 Loving Guidance, Inc.

We have internalized a value system, setting ourselves up to feel "good" if we believe we are right and "bad" if we believe we are wrong. With this system in place, we get into regular power struggles in desperate attempts to be right so we can feel good about ourselves. Here's the mental pattern: pleasing others makes you good and disappointing others makes you bad. We pass this world view to our children.

There is another way. We must be willing to change our attitude about conflict. Instead of viewing conflict as disruptive to the teaching process, we can see it as an opportunity to teach. In each conflict situation practice saying to yourself, "Oh! An opportunity to teach." In perceiving conflict this way, we stop our tendency and unconscious intent to punish. We also prepare ourselves to help children learn from their mistakes and reflect on the consequences of their actions. Remember from this moment forward, when you experience conflict in the classroom, in your home or in your head, say to yourself, "Oh, an opportunity to teach or learn!"

Commitment #1: Take a deep breath and repeat silently the following oath in your mind. "I am willing to make mistakes. Mistakes don't mean I am 'bad.' Mistakes mean I have the courage to change. In removing my fear of making mistakes, I free myself to change."

Signature _____ Date _____

Principle # 2: Punishments and rewards rely on judgment. Consequences rely on reflection.

Punishment and reward systems of discipline are prevalent in education. Some programs rely on children drawing cards when rule infractions occur. Each card carries progressively worse results. The first card might say the child's name will go on the board, while the third card might mean a trip to the principal's office. Some programs have visual displays of children's "mistakes." A child who misbehaves may see his apple fall from a tree or a clown's smile become a frown. Other programs offer rewards for "good" behavior. Children receive stickers, points, tokens and opportunities to visit the treasure box. Parents and teachers sometimes equate punishment and reward with discipline, but these systems do not teach or create self-control in children.

A reward or a punishment is chosen when an adult *judges* a child's behavior to be good or bad, then delivers something good or bad to express that judgment. When adults rely regularly on rewards and punishments, children come to depend on the judgment of others as the basis for their own moral decisions. Reward and punishment create "other control." Children grow up focusing on what others demand of them and what they demand from others. The focus for change becomes external. The ultimate side effect is the devastating desire for others to change so that we can be happy.

Consequences have a different mode of operation than punishment and rewards. Consequences help children think about the effects of their choices, then draw conclusions about the wisdom of their actions. Teachers need to help children behave *like scientists studying their own behavior*. Did the child achieve the desired outcome? If not, how does it feel and what other strategies could the child try in a similar situation the next time? Children can learn to examine their own behavior and make changes until their true goals are reached. Children who learn to *reflect* on their choices and the outcomes that result become conscious of their own actions. With this consciousness they feel empowered, increase their emotional intelligence, learn from their mistakes and become responsible citizens. Children who are allowed and facilitated to experience the consequences of their choices develop their own inner compass for moral living. The focus for change becomes internal. The ultimate outcome is the empowering belief that happiness is an inside job and therefore available to everyone.

> **When children see the connection between their behavior and the result of that behavior, learning has occurred.**

Becoming brain smart

Classroom environments designed on a reward and punishment system are relying on judgment and threat to create order. The work by Hart (1983), Lozanov (1991) and Nadel (1984) has confirmed the brain operates differently when a threat is perceived. Under threat (of either getting the punishment or not obtaining the reward) the brain reacts with increased blood flow and electrical activity in the brain stem (survival centers) and decreased blood flow to the neocortex (higher thought centers). When the brain goes into a survival mode it becomes less capable of planning, pattern-detection,

228

receiving information, creativity, classifying data, problem solving and other higher order skills (Jensen, 1997). Most of us experienced this restricted blood flow to the neocortex during high school or college exams. Do you remember feeling pressure on an exam and searching your mind hopelessly for an answer you *knew* that you knew? As soon as you turned in the test, went outside and relaxed, the answer came back to you!

A threat is any stimulus that causes the brain to trigger a defensive reaction or a sense of helplessness. They can be physical, "Do you want a spanking?" They can be intellectual, "You have 30 seconds to finish that work." They can be emotional, "Go put your name on the board." At-risk children can be easily threatened by discipline programs based on reward and punishment. They are the ones most likely *not* to receive the reward and most likely *to* receive the punishment. Because the classroom is a constant threat to them, they are often making choices that are biologically-driven. Their decisions are short-sighted and survival-oriented. They are not "unmotivated" as many would like to think. Instead, the part of the brain that must be engaged for long-term planning (neocortex) is receiving less blood flow and is less efficient.

In an attempt to create more positive classroom environments, educators have switched from relying on negative consequences to offering rewards. A reward is defined as a consequence which is both predictable and has market value (Jensen, 1997). If it is only predictable and has no market value such as a hug, smile or a rub on the back, then it is an acknowledgement, not a reward. If it has a market value, but no predictability such as a spontaneous gift certificate, cookie or pizza party, then it is a celebration, not a reward. However, if a child is told that if they behave a certain way they will get a treasure from the treasure chest, then that is a reward.

Reward systems carry the overt and covert messages of threat. Basically this message is, "if you don't meet the standard of behavior set for the reward, some opportunities will be withdrawn from you." Children fear they will not get the sticker, the popcorn party on Friday or whatever is being offered. Reward systems have side effects for children. These side effects include the following:

1. Loss of optimal brain functioning due to threat
2. Reduction in long-term quality performance
3. Reduced ability to develop values of caring, respect and friendliness
4. Reduced ability for creative and higher-order thinking skills
5. Reduced self-confidence
6. Reduction in inner drive and intrinsic motivation (Jensen, 1997)

Many teachers of young at-risk children resist paying attention to this research. What they see in their classrooms does not fit with the research findings. They say, "The children love the rewards. Work, effort, compliance and productivity have improved."

This can be explained if you understand the research completely. Research indicates that rewards are effective in motivating children for low-level skills such as memorizing facts or completing a meaningless, repetitive task. In the skill-and-drill early childhood programs that focus on the basics of numbers, colors and letters, external rewards are welcomed by the children. Rewards reduce higher-order thinking skills, but will not be noticeable in classrooms focused on low-level skills. Research (Jensen, 1996) also indicates that rewards lower anxiety levels in complex environments by offering predictability. At-risk children experience more stress and anxiety than children with less risk factors. Their brains may have more trouble picking up patterns due to the threats they face on a daily basis. Rewards become a salient pattern for them. They seek the reward to lower their stress levels. This is why teachers see excited young learners in reward environments and subsequently ignore the research. The illusion is seductive.

The same results can be achieved by creating classrooms that are meaningful, fun and creative. Stress can be reduced by deep breathing, music, movement and relaxation. Predictability can be built into the classroom by accentuating routines and rituals. We gain order, rote learning, memorization and obedience governed by external means when we use rewards. By using problem-solving classrooms, we gain creativity, critical thinking skills, risk taking, optimal brain functioning and responsible, caring children who are intrinsically motivated. The choice is ours.

Further discouraging the use of reward systems is the fact that the brain operates differently when the motivation to act is external from when the motivation comes from within the child. Over time, external motivation programs inhibit problem solving,

230

hinder the ability to delay gratification and inhibit change (Caine, Caine, & Crowell, 1994). In short, the result is the creation of impulsive children who can be defiant and aggressive, and whose behavior does not improve over time.

The part of the brain needed to make changes is located in the frontal lobes. The frontal lobes do not engage when a child perceives that others have control or when they feel pressured to perform. It is time for all of us to change—to let go of our fears and engage our own frontal lobes.

Principle #3: Your intention when administering consequences will determine their effectiveness.

The skill of using consequences with children emerges from the Power of Intention. Your intention in giving consequences will determine their effectiveness or worthlessness. Your intentions will dictate whether children grow to view mistakes as learning opportunities or as failures. For children to learn from the consequences of their actions, they must reflect upon their choices, acknowledge the impact of those choices on others and be willing to choose to change.

> **At any given moment, you are either being responsible or offering blame. The choice is yours!**

All of us have experienced the consequences of our behavior. Everyone has over-eaten or had too much to drink. The consequences may have been uncomfortable, yet we repeated the behavior. At other times, we have learned from an experience, saying, "I will never do that again," and keeping that commitment. What determines whether we change or repeat our mistakes? The answer is in our intentions. When we impose consequences on ourselves in a punitive or permissive state of mind, we block our ability to reflect. These intentions cut short the learning process and initiate an orgy of blame. The blame may be aimed at yourself or at others. Blaming blocks future change from improvement because it focuses you on finding fault instead of finding solutions. Consequences can be delivered by teachers with the following three intentions:

1. **The intent is to punish:** The goal is to make children feel guilty, wrong or bad about themselves or their behavior.

2. **The intent is to save:** The goal is to save children from intense feelings of discomfort, generally because they are uncomfortable for us.

3. **The intent is to teach:** The goal is to help children to feel, reflect and be responsible for their choices.

Getting someone to feel guilty or bad attempts to control how he or she will respond to a situation. The feelings of the child are dictated through lectures such as,

231

©1999 Loving Guidance, Inc.

Getting children to feel bad prevents them from thinking.

"You should have known better. What got into you? Can't you listen! If you had listened to me, none of this would have happened." The punitive position clearly states that the child should feel rotten, miserable and unworthy because of what you have done. It teaches children to focus their attention on you, rather than to think about the consequences of their own behavior.

Trying to rescue children from the feelings created by their choices is also a means of control. Parents run to school with forgotten lunches, permission slips and homework. This rescuing says that feelings of disappointment are bad, that they will overwhelm you. It sends the message, "You are inadequate," and that the adult knows best how to run the child's life. Children learn to focus their intelligence and energy into manipulating adults to rescue and protect them from consequences of their behavior.

Allowing children to feel and reflect on their choices gives them the opportunity to be responsible for past actions and gives them the freedom to choose healthier options in the future. The examples below demonstrate how each intent might look in response to the same situation.

Situation: In Mrs. Hawthorne's class, children are to finish their work on time and place it in the work folder to be collected. The work is collected and Ellen's work is not in the folder.

1. **The intent to punish—Meant to inspire guilt:** "Ellen did you complete your work today?" Ellen nods her head yes. "Well, it is not in the folder. Do you want to fail? You know better than this. We do the same procedure in this class every day. We have been in school six months. I expect you to know what our procedures are by now. The work is not in here. As far as I am concerned, it is not done. You need to learn to think and be responsible for your work. Maybe you will remember now." Notice how the teacher began the interaction asking a question to which she already knew the answer.

232

2. **The intent to save—Meant to rescue the child:** "Ellen, honey, did you forget to turn in your work today?" Ellen nods her head yes. "Well, go get it now so I can make sure and look it over to see how your skills are progressing. Remember in the future to file your work in your folder, okay?"

3. **The intent to teach—Meant to promote responsibility:** Mrs. Hawthorne says nothing to Ellen. She collects the work, reviews it and hands it back to the other children. When Ellen sees the work being returned she says, "Mrs. Hawthorne, here is my work from yesterday. I forgot to hand it in." In a compassionate voice, Mrs. Hawthorne says, "Oh Ellen, you forgot to hand in your work. You must have just remembered when you saw the papers being returned. I only look at work that is put in the folders." "It's not fair," shouts Ellen, "I did the work!" With an open heart and empathetic tone, Mrs. Hawthorne responds, "Yes, you did. That must be very disappointing. You put in all that work, then missed the credit. That must be terribly frustrating. I will be happy to look at any work that you put in the folder."

Teaching right from wrong: The seeds of responsibility

When your intentions are punitive or rescuing, your ultimate goal is really control. You are dictating the feelings children should have or shielding them from feelings they would have had. The child who was made to feel miserable over forgetting to put her work in the folder and the one who was shielded from the result of that action both missed the opportunity to experience their own emotions. As Jim Fey (1995), founder of *Love and Logic Discipline* says, "The child was robbed of a real world experience." He says for children to learn from their mistakes, they need equal doses of empathy and consequences. That is what Mrs. Hawthorne provided Ellen in the last example. She empathically helped Ellen feel her own disappointment and frustration.

Children cut off from their feelings lack the essential emotional equipment needed to decide whether they are on or off course. Without this equipment, children cannot decide to change courses and generally persist in making the same or similar mistakes. Children can learn right from wrong by monitoring others' judgments of them or they can learn it through awareness of their own emotions. The choice is ours.

> **Being conscious of your intent when delivering consequences is the key to their effectiveness.**

Activity to discern intentions

On the next page are four consequences a teacher might deliver to a child for the same situation. Read each scenario and write **P** for punitive intent, **S** for the intent to save or **T** for the intent to teach.

Situation: Carl's classroom job is to feed Murphy the hamster and to change his water. Toward the end of the day, Mrs. Cline notices that Murphy's water is filthy.

1. "Carl, come over here. Look at this water. Poor Murphy is going to die because you don't care. I gave you this job because I thought you could handle it. I must have been wrong. You will not be allowed to have this job again." _____

2. "Carl, remember it's your job to feed and get fresh water for Murphy. I reminded you this morning. Don't forget." At the end of the day Mrs. Cline notices Murphy's water is still dirty. She cleans it and mumbles about "kids these days."_____

3. "Mrs. Cline announces to all children that classroom jobs are to be finished by 10:00 a.m. At 10:15 she notices Murphy's water is not cleaned. She asks the class for a volunteer. At this point Carl shouts, "Hey, that's my job!" Mrs. Cline responds, "Yes, it was your job up until 10:00. Now it will be someone else's job." Carl pushes some papers and sulks. Mrs. Cline notices this and says, "It is hard to lose your job. I know how much you care about Murphy." _____

4. Mrs. Cline punishes Carl by taking away his opportunity for class jobs for three days. She says, "Until you can act responsibly you will not have any responsibilities. The class was counting on you and you let them all down." _____

Answers: Teaching intent: # 3, punitive intent: # 1 and 4, rescue intent: # 2

Consequences delivered with the intent to punish or rescue are ultimately ineffective. If you use them regularly, children are likely to engage in the following types of defensive/attacking thinking or acting:

☑ **Resentment/blame:** Children compare their behavior to others'. They focus on why they got caught and others didn't. "This isn't fair. You always pick on me."

☑ **Revenge:** Children focus on getting back at the person they blame for the problem or the one punishing them. "I'll show her. I'll fail fourth grade, then she'll be sorry."

☑ **Rebellion:** Children focus on not being caught. "I'll do what I want and just be more careful next time."

☑ **Reduced self esteem:** Children may focus on pleasing others. "I am bad and deserve to be punished. This is for my own good. I must try harder to be good."

☑ **Apathy:** Children may focus on feelings of helplessness and hopelessness. "I give up. I don't care. I can't win, so why try? I just want to be left alone."

How often do you engage in these types of thinking patterns? Can you see the relationship between the discipline you received as a child and your current thoughts?

Recently I was in an airplane heading to a workshop in Montana. I sat in front of a family of three. Directly behind me was a boy (around age four) who had two action figures to play with for the four hour flight. To amuse himself, he began banging the tray table on the back of my seat up and down, jarring me.

Being a discipline expert, you might imagine I could handle this one easily. My first decision was to remain silent in hopes he would stop. During my silent period, I seethed and blamed his mother. The more critically I judged her, the madder I got. I was just about to speak to the boy when I asked myself, "Becky, do you want to have this child pay for the discomfort you think he is causing or do you want to teach him?" My answer to myself was, "He must pay!" With that, I spun around and addressed the family in a cold, hurtful way. The child did stop flapping the tray table, but that whole family was on edge. The baby started fussing. The mother became hypercritical of the boy, slapped him and he cried.

> **You must consciously choose to maintain self control and focus on teaching in every conflict situation.**

After this experience I had several choices. I could punish myself with critical self-talk like, "Look what you have done now. You are supposed to know better. You don't know what you are doing. You are such a fake." I could justify my actions (rescuing myself) by saying, "That mother should have known than to bring a child on to a plane with nothing to do." Or I could offer myself empathy and feel the consequences of my actions in order to take full responsibility for the experience. I chose the latter. With this responsibility, I deepened my resolve to change my old patterns and committed myself to doing it differently the next time. Living in Orlando with all the families coming to Disney World, I would surely be given another opportunity! I initially imagined that when I became more conscious of how I was handling children, I would be a steadily loving, yet firm disciplinarian. I discovered that this is simply not the case. You must consciously choose how to conduct yourself *in every interaction.*

Principle # 4: Consequences delivered with empathy allow children the opportunity to learn how to be responsible for their choices.

Pain is our body's signal something is out of balance. It says, "pay attention to this area and make some different choices." People who ignore the pain put themselves at risk for possible disasters. We have all heard of people who knew something was wrong, but put off seeing the doctor until it was too late. One summer, my family vacationed in Alaska. I was determined to climb this particular mountain. It was a steep hike of 14,000 feet up to the Harding Icefield. After about three hours of hiking, I felt pain in my right knee. At around five hours a similar pain was felt in my left knee. Both times I ignored the signal and kept on hiking. As a result of this event, I damaged both knees and required therapy and surgery to restore health and balance to my system.

Psychological pain works in the same manner. Upset, disappointment, sadness and frustration are signals. These signals say, "Pay attention to this and make different choices." If we ignore the pain or project the pain on to others (look what you are doing *to me*, how you are *making* me feel, etc.) we will repeat the same choices.

Helping children learn responsibility is a four step process according to Jim Fay and David Funk (1995). They suggest the following:

1. Give children tasks and guidelines they can handle

2. Hope they blow it by making "poor" choices

3. Stand back with liberal dosages of empathy and allow the consequences to do the teaching

4. Give the same task again

To help children learn responsibility we can use three types of consequences: natural, imposed and problem solving. With natural consequences, nothing is prearranged. The consequences a child experiences are directly related to the child's choice of behavior. A child touches the stove, the hand is burned. Imposed consequences are created by adults in response to children's choices. Problem-solving consequences are co-created with children as a result of their choices.

Skill # 1: Natural consequences

Natural consequences arise without any prearranged adult intervention. If a child does not tie his shoes, he may trip over them. If a child repeatedly treats his friends poorly, he may find himself friendless. These consequences are possible and sometimes probable results of personal choices. Remember though, interactions with our environment yield a wide range of possible results. A child with untied shoes may not fall. Adults tend to overdo the prediction of harm: "If you run, you *will* fall." "If you don't eat vegetables, you *will* be unhealthy." These dire warnings send two messages: **1)** Adults are all-knowing and can read the future and **2)** You have no control over the events of your life. Children who internalize these beliefs grow into adults who give their power away to others and end up feeling victimized by life.

The role of the adult in natural consequences

The following five steps will help you teach children to learn from the natural consequences of their choices. Children aided with these steps play fewer blame games. To help remember these steps for natural consequences, use the acronym **G.A.M.E.S.**

236

G = give **G**uidance and possible outcomes
A = **A**llow the consequences
M = **M**odel self control
E = offer **E**mpathy
S = new **S**trategies

Step 1: Offer children **Guidance** and instruction about expected behavior as well as possible outcomes of "poor" choices. For example, you might say, "Friends like it when you take turns playing like this (demonstrate). If you treat your friends poorly they may not want to spend time with you."

Step 2: **Allow** children to experience the consequences of their choices.

Step 3: **Model** self control. When a child makes a "poor" choice, resist the temptation to lecture. "I told you so. If you had only listened." Resist the temptation to get angry. "What were you thinking?" Don't moralize. "Was that nice?" Use your mouth for deep breathing instead.

Step 4: Offer **Empathy** to children who make choices with disappointing outcomes. "You seem upset. It's hard to play alone and not be with friends." Empathy allows children to own their problems. This is the key to learning responsibility.

Step 5: Assist children in learning new **Strategies**. Example: "Would you be interested in learning ways to make new friends?"

Activity to find the "G.A.M.E.S."

In the situation described below, see if you can locate the 5-step **G.A.M.E.S.** process administered by the teacher. The letters are provided to help you along.

Show and tell situation: Etta has brought an especially delicate model of a butterfly to school for show and tell. To keep their items safe while in the classroom, the children are instructed to put them in their cubbies until circle time. Mr. Evans always models putting his things in a safe place each morning. Etta is so pleased with her butterfly that she wants to play with it and show it to her friends during center time. She decides to walk around the room carrying her butterfly.

Mr. Evans sees this and says, "Etta, I see you are carrying your special butterfly. You seem excited to share it. If you continue to carry your butterfly around it may get broken. Put your butterfly in your cubby so it will be safe until show and tell." **(G)** Etta pretends to put her butterfly away, but secretly keeps it in her pocket. Eventually the butterfly breaks as two children try to look at it at the same time. Etta begins to cry hysterically. The butterfly is on the floor in a million little pieces. **(A)**

When we train children to listen to others, one day the "other" is not us!

Mr. Evans approaches the scene, takes a deep breath, resisting the urge to lecture her **(M)** and says, "Oh, Etta, how tragic! Your precious butterfly is broken. You seem terribly sad and upset." **(E)** Etta responds, "They broke it, I hate them," as she points to the two children standing near by. "You sound angry. You chose to keep the butterfly out instead of putting it away and now its broken and you feel so mad." Mr. Evans helps Etta find a plastic bag to store the butterfly pieces.**(S)**

Can you remember times in your life when you made a decision that caused you great pain? Which type of person would you prefer to be around? One who predicts your future (and does it negatively)? One who blames you for not listening, constantly proving how wise they are through your misfortune ("I told you so")? Or one who is supportive, reflective and empathic?

Skill # 2: Imposed consequences

At times, of course, adults cannot allow a child to experience natural consequences. The natural consequence of playing in the street may be to get run over! The natural consequence of playing with guns may be to kill someone. Imposed consequences are prearranged. The adult (or society) creates a set of behavioral expectations. The consequences of not paying one's taxes are prearranged—there are penalties. The consequences of not handing in one's homework on time are prearranged by the teacher or the class.

Consequences do not teach children how to behave. They *motivate* children to use skills they already have or motivate them to learn new strategies. If you have taught children how to clean the room after center time and they fail to do it or the job is done poorly, then you may choose to impose a logical consequence. If you have taught the children to say, "May I have a turn," instead of grabbing objects and grabbing persists, you may need an imposed consequence. Imposed consequences can be developed at the spur of the moment by the teacher or developed in class meetings with children.

Steps in delivering imposed consequences

☑ **Present the child with the choice of skills to use or the rule.**
"You have a choice to hit your friend and get the toy or to ask your friend for the toy by saying: *May I have a turn?*" *or*
"The rule in the classroom is to paint only in the art area."

☑ **Present the child with the imposed consequence of choosing the old hurtful skill or breaking the rule.**
"If you choose to hit, you will play in the hula hoop on the floor with the toys I provide you during center time." *or*
"If the paint is removed from the art area, you will not be allowed to use it for the rest of the day."

OR

OR

The choice is ours to be empathetic or negative.

Which doctor would you prefer?

©1999 Loving Guidance, Inc.

☑ **State why this consequence is being imposed and relate it to safety (young children) and/or logic (older children).**

"Hitting hurts. It is not safe. My job is to keep the classroom safe. By playing in your own area, you will be safe and so will your friends." *or*

"The paint can get on the rug and make stains. You may paint only by the sink or over the tile."

☑ **Ask the child what she has heard and understood.**

"Do you understand what will happen to you if you hit again? Tell me." *or*

"Do you understand what I will do if I see the paint on the rug? Tell me."

☑ **Listen carefully to the child and clarify any miscommunications.**

"I will play in the hula hoop by myself." Your clarifying response might be, "For how long?" *or*

"I'll never get to paint." Your clarifying response might be, "Will you never be able to paint again or just for the rest of the day?"

☑ **If the child repeats the behavior, deliver the designated consequence with empathy and choices.**

"How disappointing to lose the opportunity to play with others. You can play in the hoop with this basket of toys or these books. Which will you choose?" *or*

"How disappointing for you, I know how much you like to paint. Feel free to play in other areas."

Imposed consequences are most often used when *safety* is an issue. Safety is vital for trust. The steps in imposed consequences can be remembered using a **C.I.R.C.L.E.**

241

C = **C**hoice of skills (old and new)

I = **I**mposed consequences for using old skill

R = **R**elated to safety or logic

C = **C**hild states back what was heard

L = **L**isten and clarify if needed

E = **E**mpathy with consequences

Activity to practice imposed consequences

Apply an imposed consequence in the following situation: Katrina did not come in from the playground when the teacher blew her whistle. Another child was sent out to get her. The whistle is the signal that recess is over. The children had been taught this signal for a number of weeks.

C • Step 1: "Katrina, you have a choice _____
_____."

I • Step 2: "If you choose again to _____
then _____."

R • Step 3: "Not lining up with the others _____
_____."

C • Step 4: "Tell me _____."
"Now I want you to _____."

L • Step 5 (Clarify if needed) "_____."

E • Step 6 (She does it again) "_____
_____."

Remember that there is no one right way to respond to children. The answers below are just suggestions to compare to your responses.

C • Step 1: "Katrina, you have a choice to come and line up when the whistle is blown, or to continue playing."

I • Step 2: "If you choose again to ignore the whistle then you will play next to me during recess."

R • Step 3: "When you are away from the group something could happen to you. You must stay together so I can do my job of keeping everyone safe."

C • Step 4: "Tell me what will happen to you if you choose not to line up again when the whistle blows."

L • Step 5 (if needed): "I will play next to you during recess," says Katrina. "That is exactly right, I don't want anything to happen to you," I would reply.

E • Step 6: "Katrina, how sad. I know you like to run everywhere. I have drawn a circle in the dirt. Feel free to play alone or with friends inside the circle."

Selecting imposed consequences

Use the following guidelines to help you create imposed consequences:

☑ The imposed consequence should logically relate to the event or be structured around safety. An effective imposed consequence for a child who runs in the class with scissors in his hand would be to lose the opportunity of using scissors without direct adult supervision. An ineffective consequence would be to have him miss recess, call his parents or lose points that contribute to some prize.

☑ When possible, create imposed consequences with the input from the children. You can do this through the process of class meetings.

Skill #3: Class meetings

The following five steps will guide you through a class meeting process. By using these steps you involve the children in the co-creation of imposed consequences. Creating consequences in class meetings is similar to the problem solving in Skill #4.

Step 1: "I've noticed ___." State what you have seen occurring in the classroom without bias or judgment. You might say, "I've noticed some children are talking while I am reading a story."

Step 2: "This is a problem for me because___. Does it bother anyone else?" This step allows the children the opportunity to own part of the problem. You might say, "This is a problem for me because I can't hear myself read and I lose my place in the story. Do children talking during story time bother any of you?"

Step 3: "So, a class problem is ___." Summarize the class problem. "So a class problem we seem to be having is children talking during story time distracting the teacher and other children."

Step 4: "What could we do to solve the problem?" Generally the children will respond (stop talking). At this point encourage them to focus on what *to do*. "Stop talking" would turn into "be quiet and start listening."

Step 5: "What happens if children fail to ___." This step allows you to create a class consequence. Remind children the consequence must be fair and safe for everyone.

Skill #4: Problem solving

"Poor" choices create conflict and problems for children and others. The logical consequence of creating a problem is solving the problem. The logical consequence of fighting with other children is to learn to solve problems without fighting. Problem solving, sadly, is not thought of as a consequence. This is because in the old paradigm, consequences (punishments) were used in an attempt to get the child to feel bad. Remember, our goal is different. It is to help children reflect on their actions, to change and then to make choices that bring successful outcomes.

Many teachers say, "I can't think of an imposed consequence that make sense and isn't a punishment." Often if the imposed consequence isn't obvious, problem solving is the technique to use. Imposed consequences are most effective in issues that involve safety.

The following steps are helpful in assisting children to solve their own problems. When children are actively engaged in solving their own problems, peaceful classrooms are a reality. For that reason the acronym to help you remember the steps is **P.E.A.C.E.**

244

P = discern who owns the **P**roblem

E = offer **E**mpathy to the child who made the "poor" choice.

A = **A**sk the child to think, "What do you think you are going to do?"

C = offer **C**hoices and suggestions.

E = **E**ncourage the child to come up with his own solution.

P • Step 1: Discern who owns the Problem. This step is critical. All too often teachers make the child's problem their own. Once the teacher believes it is his problem, he spends all his energy and critical thinking skills attempting to solve it. Imagine that your friend smokes. You decide for some reason that this is your problem. You spend years trying to come up with solutions to your friend's smoking. Nothing seems successful and you end up frustrated and angry with your friend. This happens every day at school. Children create problems for themselves and teachers take on the problems as their own. Some common child problems are pushing and shoving in line, talking during teaching, conflicts with peers, not completing homework and dawdling instead of working.

Start the interaction with, "You seem to be having a problem." After this, state what you have observed without any judgments. You might continue by saying, "I've noticed (describe the actions the child is taking)." For example: "You seem to be having a problem. I've noticed you visiting with your friends instead of working on math."

E • Step 2: Offer Empathy to children who make "poor" choices. Many times when you draw children's attention to the fact that they have a problem, their first tendency is to blame others. Mistakes threaten us. When we are threatened, our brains shift into a defense mode and we attempt to transfer the responsibility of a "poor" choice to something outside of ourselves. Such comments as, "My mom didn't put my homework in my backpack," "He started it," and "She was asking me a question," are common deflective statements. Empathy calms the brain, removes the threat and allows a person to take responsibility for his or her own behavior.

Once you tell children they have a problem, they will respond with emotion, perhaps an excuse or blame. Your job is to reflect back the feeling they express and offer understanding in the form of positive intent. You may also express sadness for them.

> **Teacher:** "Hey hold up! You seem to be having a problem. I noticed you pushing and shoving while lining up."
> **Student:** "I was here first. He started pushing me."
> **Teacher:** "You seem really upset. You didn't know what to say or do to stop others from crowding you. That's really sad because I won't leave until everyone is safe."

A • Step 3: Ask the child to think: "What do you think you are going to do?" It is important to ask children to solve their own problems. This comes from asking thinking questions. Jim Fay and David Funk (1995) suggest saying, "What do you think you are going to do," or "I'd like to hear you ideas." You could also ask, "How could you solve this problem," or "What could you do now that is helpful?" Continuing with the above example you might say, "What could you do to solve your problem?"

C • Step 4: Offer Choices and suggestions. Children, especially young ones, often have not developed a repertoire of solutions. They simply respond, "I don't know," when asked to think. You could reply, "Are you interested in some ideas," or "Would you like some ideas other children have tried?" These questions conjure willingness in children. The energy of being willing to learn a new approach is critical to change.

Offer children ideas, starting with some poor choices and moving up to more helpful choices. Jim Fay (1996) suggests that by proceeding in this manner you can engage the child's thinking processes. After each suggestion you offer, ask children (five years and up), "How do you think that would work?" This allows them to start thinking in terms of how their choices influence their lives and the lives of others. For younger children you could say, "So, do you think that would be helpful or hurtful?" The dialogue below gives examples of this step by continuing with the "lining up" situation.

> **Student**: "I don't know."
> **Teacher:** "That is hard not to know. Would you be interested in some ideas?"
> **Student:** "Yes."
> **Teacher:** "Some students have ignored the teacher and continued pushing and shoving. How do you think that would work?"
> **Student:** "That wouldn't be fun."
> **Teacher:** "Some students have requested a line-up chart so you know exactly where to stand. How do you think that would work?"
> **Student**: "You wouldn't be by your friends or you might always be in the back."
> **Teacher:** "Some students have chosen to be careful when they line up and if they bump each other they apologize. How do you think that would work?"
> **Student:** "I like that."

E • Encourage the child to come up with his own solution. End the interaction with encouraging the student. You might say, "I know you will come up with a solution for your problem. You can do this. Let me know what you decide and if you need help."

Similar steps can be used in class meetings to help children problem solve. Be sure to check back with children to make sure the solution is working for everyone. You could arrange a time for this or let it evolve naturally in the classroom. If the solution is not working, the children still have a problem. Your goal is to start the process over by asking them to think about solutions or come up with related, reasonable consequences.

Activity to P.E.A.C.E. role play

In a small group select one of the common child problems listed on page 251, or a chronic problem you are having in your classroom. Role play a problem solving session with the children. Use each step of the P.E.A.C.E. plan to guide you.

> **Chronic problems will not be solved with imposed consequences. They require problem solving.**

Principle #5: Reflect on your school-wide discipline programs and consequences.

Betsy Geddes, an educational consultant, often talks about creating consistent school discipline. She says, "There are two basic ways to set up a school discipline plan. One is widely used and seldom effective. The other is seldom used and very effective." The two approaches are the systems approach and the principle approach.

The systems approach is based on the goal of obtaining school-wide consistency. At the first of the year, rules are established as are the rewards or punishments that will occur when the rules are followed or broken. Some schools involve students in the rule and consequence discussion and some have standard rules for the school such as, "No running in the halls," "Be prepared," "Show respect," "Keep your hands and feet to yourself," and "No chewing gum." In addition to standard procedures for handling the rule, punishments are created. The child may receive a warning, a second warning and then a pink slip for detention (or some equivalent). Each infraction receives specified teacher interventions, whether negative (put your name on the board) or positive (receive a sticker). Programs that rely on the systems approach yield the following outcomes:

1. Teachers and administrators do all the planning, problem solving and record keeping. The work is so intense that more staff is sometimes hired to spearhead the system.

2. The same children show up for detention, suspension and loss of privileges.

3. Disharmony is created with teachers throughout the school. Some teachers adhere more rigidly to the system than others. These teachers comment, "I can't discipline if everyone is not doing their part." Teachers who want more flexibility to handle children's behaviors tend to hide what they are doing. They comment, "Oh, just do the system when the administration is looking and do what you want when they are not." The systems approach is designed for standardizing human behavior to create consistency and efficiency. It results in inconsistency, disharmony and ineffectiveness.

The principle approach to school-wide discipline builds consistency, not by trying to force everyone to do the same thing in the same way, but by operating from a set of core beliefs. Teachers are free to interact and discipline children any way they choose, as long as it doesn't violate the core beliefs and principles established by the school. Teachers work together to reflect on their approaches to make sure they are consistent with the principles established by the school. The focus of the principle approach is consistency in action and consistency with school mission statements.

247

Below are principles (guidelines) to use as a springboard discussion for your school.

1. The motivation to behave comes from being in a relationship with others. Creating positive school climates and nurturing school families supports the development of social skills.

    ☑ Does the school policy build relationships among *everyone*? Does it bring people together or does it separate into "haves" and "have nots?"

    ☑ Does the school discipline plan include efforts to build community?

2. The brain functions optimally when it feels safe. Safety comes from accepting and embracing diversity, allowing children to have their own thoughts and feelings, and from feeling a sense of belonging.

    ☑ Does the school policy promote a feeling of safety for *all*? Are excluded children actively helped to be part of the school? Are children's voices heard and represented in solving problems?

    ☑ Does the program build its policy on safety of rules?

3. Classroom conflicts are opportunities to teach, not disruptions of learning.

    ☑ Do teachers actively use conflict as teaching moments? Do conflicts in the classroom/school springboard problem solving and drive the social skills curriculum of the school?

4. Self-esteem is built by how we see others. Seeing the best in every situation promotes personal self-esteem. Treating others with respect promotes respect for all.

    ☑ Is respect shown for everyone during moments of conflict?

5. Contributing in meaningful ways to the school, the classroom and each other builds self worth.

    ☑ Do children have meaningful jobs within the classroom and school? Do older children reach out to the community to serve others?

6. Responsibility comes from owning and solving one's own problems with guidance. Children need to do more thinking than adults to solve their own problems.

    ☑ If a packaged discipline program is implemented who does the thinking, teachers or students? Who does the record keeping, teachers or students? Who does more work, teachers or students?

7. People who make mistakes in behavior deserve compassion and guidance as well as accountability for their actions.

    ☑ Does the policy or practice see the problem from all sides? Is empathy integral to the accountability process?

8. Families are part of the learning community.

    ☑ Are families considered team members with contributing voices?

Once you agree on a set of principles, everyone is free to create their own discipline plans as long as they adhere to the principles. These principles are used to check practices. If a school sets up a plan to address a problem, the plan must not violate any school principles. An example problem might be to reduce lunchroom noise. The solution proposed is to give children who "behave" the best fine-dining experiences. They will eat in a separate location with tablecloths and classmates as servers. Children who misbehave will not receive this privilege. Using the principles and the sample questions above, ask yourself, "Does this practice meet the goals of the program?" The answer is no. The practice would create "haves" and "have nots."

Each school and classroom begins the year focusing on safety, not rules. From safety comes principles that are used to guide teachers and student actions. These principles are taught daily by the actions of teachers and administrators. These principles bring about the guidelines for human interaction in school. Teachers are then taught strategies to deal with and resolve conflict instead of learning specified punishments and rewards to dole out for infractions. Children are taught specific problem solving and anger management skills. Children are held accountable to these teachings through consequences. The result of this approach to school-wide discipline yields the following:

☑ Children who change and grow as their individual needs are met.

☑ Consistency in what is preached is also practiced. Respect, integrity, compassion, composure, responsibility, commitment and interdependence are modeled and applied in daily interactions, not conducted at seperate programs or times.

☑ A family of teachers who work together, reflect, discover and change as needed.

Support from the school administration

Discuss with your staff the difference between the systems approach and the principle approach to school discipline. Lead the school in the following:

1. Determine the way you want your school to be. This discussion is the same at a school level as when led by a teacher in a class. The bottom line is, "How do you want your school to be?" This discussion leads to a set of guidelines for school interactions.

2. Create staff development plans that facilitate learning diverse strategies for dealing with conflict resolution, building school climate and fostering assertiveness.

3. Draw up procedures and/or guidelines to assist the school in reflecting upon interactions. This insures school policies and teachers' discipline plans are adhering to the school mission and guidelines for human interaction in school.

We can provide our children with a school where they reflect on choices and hopefully choose to change their behaviors, or we can provide one where children obsess about the wrongness of their actions and actions of others. The choice is ours.

Physical structure that support the Skill of Consequences

Most classroom management systems rely on consequences to guide children. *Conscious Discipline* believes consequences are one of many skills needed to help children become socially and emotionally competent. Consequences are the final skills in this book for a reason. The other skills are prerequisites to successful consequences.

In the beginning of the year (as in beginning of the book) the focus is on safety. "My job is to keep you safe. Your job is to help keep it that way." Starting the year with a focus on rules and consequences can trigger some children to downshift their brains away from learning from the beginning of the year. By starting the year focused on safety instead, we upshift children's brains, beginning the day and the year with each child having access to higher cognitive functioning (increasing learning effectiveness).

The next step is to teach the children the meaning of "help" in their job description. This begins with self-control and extends to helping others establish and maintain a feeling of belonging. Self-control is embedded in the school family. Caring is more important than control and giving to others is more natural than getting attention. To achieve this, we create class principles and procedures that children feel are "the way they want their class to be." Children decide if they want a class where they help each other be successful or where there is a climate of competition and put-downs. Procedures are taught through instruction about class routines. We demonstrate the principles through class rituals. Kindness, being prepared for class and respecting each other aren't rules, they are principles. Principles are taught, lived and modeled. Rules are enforced.

As teachers live and teach the principles the class deem important, rules will emerge. Rules are successful only when *connected* children already *know* how to behave, but choose to be hurtful instead of helpful. Rules carry consequences. These consequences involve loss of opportunities, use of problem solving and restitution. Class meetings and circle time support consequences. When consequences are experienced, empathy is provided so responsibility for one's choices is made conscious.

Class meetings and circle time

The physical structures that support the Skill of Consequences are class meetings and circle time. These structures provide time for discussions about consequences. Most schools require consequences be posted in the classroom. Consequences can be written and displayed as the rules of the school family emerge from class discussions throughout the year. As you display consequences, remember problem solving is part of the process. The first consequence may be problem solving (teacher assists student in learning new behaviors). The second consequence may be a willingness to choose again (child may do an instant replay using skills taught in the classroom). The third consequence could be a loss of opportunities related to the infraction or restitution of goods/services.

No time like the present!

This month, vigilantly practice the following with yourself and your students:

☑ The next time you make a mistake, stop your punitive self-talk. Focus instead on these questions: What choice did I make? What happened as a result? How did it feel to me? Did my choice achieve what I wanted? What new strategies might serve me better?

☑ Pay attention to your inner speech when you perceive that you have made a mistake. Do you bash yourself with punitive self-talk or do you offer yourself empathy, reflect and commit to change?

☑ Ask yourself, "Do I want my students to feel bad and pay for their *crimes*?" or "Do I want to teach my students to reflect on their choices, to change them and develop self-control?" Focus on your intent in delivering consequences.

☑ Ask yourself, "Have I relied too heavily on consequences in my classroom, school or program?" If so, do more problem solving.

☑ Use class meetings and problem solving as consequences especially for chronic problems.

☑ Allow children the opportunity to experience the consequences of their choices by avoiding lecturing and rescuing.

☑ Use the **G.A.M.E.S.** model to deliver natural consequences, the **C.I.R.C.L.E.** model for imposed consequences and the **P.E.A.C.E.** model for problem solving.

Look for these teaching moments

Chronic problems with individuals or with the class are teaching moments. Remember chronic problems do not respond to imposed consequences, they respond to problem solving. Look for safety situations for imposed consequences. If you teach children (through the use of positive intent and assertiveness) to get their needs met without hurting others and they continue to be hurtful, use imposed consequences. Imposed consequences motivate children to use the new skills you are teaching them.

Look for these specific behaviors

Shoving	Failure to complete work
Teasing	Name calling
Off-task behaviors	Excessive talking
Chronic problems	Rule infractions

References

Anderson, R. C., Shirley, L.L., Wilson, P.T. & Fielding, L.G. (1987). "Interestingness of children's reading material." In *Aptitude, Learning, and Instruction,* in R.E. Snow and M. J. Farr. (Eds.). Cognitive and Affective Process Analyses, Vol, 3, Hillsdale, NJ: Erlbaum.

Bailey, B. A. (1997). Motivating Children: Rewards and Relationships. *FOCUS, Journal of the West Virginia Association for Young Children,* Vol, 16, 22-24.

Bailey, B. (1994). *There's Gotta to be a Better Way: Discipline that works.* Oviedo, Florida: Loving Guidance, Inc.

Bailey, B. (1996). *I Love You Rituals: Activities to build bonds and strengthen relationships.* Oviedo, Florida: Loving Guidance, Inc.

Bailey, B. (1996). *Preventing Power Struggles* (audio tape). Oviedo, Florida: Loving Guidance, Inc.

Belknap, M. (1997). *Mind Body Magic: Creative Activities For Any Audience.* Duluth, MN: Whole Person Associates.

Bennett, M. (1993). *The Development of Social Cognition: The child as psychologist.* New York: The Guilford Press.Caine, G., Caine, R. N., & Crowell, S. (1994). Mindshifts. Tuscon, AZ: Zepher Press.

Bohm, D. (1981). *The Implicate Order.* London: Routledge & Kegan Paul.

Bohr, N. (1958). *Atomic Physics and Human Knowledge.* New York, NY: John Wiley and Sons.

Brennan, B. A. (1987) *Hands of Light: A guide to healing through the human energy field.* New York, NY: Bantam Books.

Caine, G., Gaine, R.N. & Crowell, S. (1994). *Mindshifts.* Tucson, AZ: Zephyr Press.

Canter, L., & Canter, M. (1976). Assertive Discipline: A take-charge approach for today's educator. Los Angeles: Lee Canter & Associates.

Capra, F. (1991) *The Tao of Physics.* Boston, MA: Shambhala Publications, Inc.

Colvin, G. (1993). *Managing Acting-Out Behavior.* Eugene, OR: Behavior Associates.

Damasio, A. (1994). *Descartes' Error.* New York, NY: Putnam & Sons.

Dennison, P. & Dennison, G.E. (1989). *Brain Gym: Teacher's Edition Revised.* Ventura, CA: Edu-Kinesthetics, Inc.

Dinkmeyer, D., McKay, G.D. (1989). *STEP: The parent's handbook.* MN: American Guidance Services.

Dossey, L. (1993). *Healing Words.* San Fransisco, CA: Harper Collins Publishers.

Elias, M. J., Zins, J. E., Weissberg, R., Frey, K. S., Greenberg, M.T., Haynes, N. M.

Elias, M. J., Bruene-Butler, L. Blum, and T. Schuyler. (1997). "How to Launch a Social and Emotional Learning Program." *Educational Leadership 54,* 8:15-19.

Fay, J., Funk, D. (1995). *Teaching with Love & Logic: Taking Control of the Classroom* (audiotape). Golden, Co: The Love and Logic Press, Inc.

Fay, J., & Cline, F. W. (1996). *The Life Saver Kit* (audio tape). Golden, CO: The Love and Logic Press, Inc.

Geddes, B. (1996). *Creating Consistent School Discipline: Two approaches to school discipline* (audio tape). Welches, OR: Geddes Consulting.

Glasser, W. (1985) *Control Theory*. New York, NY: Harper Collins.

Glenn, H. S. & Nelson, J. (1988). *Raising Self-Reliant children in a self-indulgent world: Seven building blocks for developing capable young people*. Prima Publishing & Communications: Rocklin, CA.

Gordon, T. (1974). *Teacher Effectiveness Training*. New York, NY: Peter H. Wyden Publisher.

Guerney, L. (1983). "Client Centered (nondirective) Play Therapy." In C.E. Schaefer & K.L. O'Conner, eds., *Handbook of play therapy*. New York, NY: John Wiley & Sons.

Hamilton, M. (1989). *Mood Disorders: Clinical features in comprehensive textbook of Psychiatry*, ed. H.I. Kaplan and B.J. Sadock. Baltimore, MD: Williams and Wilkins.

Harms, A.B., & Bailey, B. A., (1992). "Appropriate disciplinary techniques for use with kindergarten students." (unpublished manuscript). University of Central Florida, Orlando, FL.

Hart, L. (1983). *Human Brain and Human Learning*. White Plains, NY: Longman publishing.

Harter, S. (1982). "A Developmental Perspective on Some Parameters of Self Regulation in Children." *Self-Management and Behavior Change: From Theory to Practice*. (Karoly, P., & Kanfer, F. H., Eds.) New York, NY: Pergammon Press.

Heimer, L. (1983). *The Human Brain & Spinal Cord*. (New York: Springer-Verlog, 1983). NA=norepinephrine.

Hendrix, H. (1988) *Getting the Love You Want: A guide for couples*. New York, NY: Henry Holt and Co.

Hoffman, M. L. (1982). "Development of Prosocial Motivation: Empathy and guilt." In N. Eisenberg (Eds.), *Social cognition: Studies of the development of understanding*. Chicago: University of Chicago Press.

Hoover, J. H. & Oliver, R. (1996). *The Bullying Prevention Handbook: A guide for principals, teachers, and counselors*. Bloomington, IN: National Education Service.

Jensen, E. (1997). *Completing the Puzzle: The Brain-Compatible Approach to Learning*. Del Mar, CA: The Brain Store, Inc.

Kessler, R., Schwab-Stone, M.E., Shriver, T. P. (1997). *Promoting Social and Emotional Learning: Guidelines for Educators*. Alexandria, VA: Association for Supervision and Curriculum Development.

Kohn, A. (1992). *No Contest: The case against competition*. New York, NY: Houghton Mifflin Company.

Kohn, A. (1993). *Punished by Rewards: The trouble with gold stars, incentive plans, A's, praise, and other bribes*. Boston, MA: Houghton Mifflin Company.

Langdon, C. A. (1996). "The Third Annual Phi Delta Kappan Poll of Teachers: Attitudes Toward the Public Schools." *Phi Delta Kappan* 78, (30):244-250.

LeDoux, J. (1996). *The Emotional Brain: The mysterious underpinnings of emotional life*. New York, NY: Simon & Schuster.

Lewis, B. A. (1995). *The Kid's Guide to Service Projects: Over 500 service ideas for young people who want to make a difference*. Minneapolis, MN: Free Spirit Publishing Inc.

Lozanov, G. (1991). "On some problems of the Anatomy, Physiology, and Biochemistry of Cerebral

Activities in the Global-Artistic Approach in modern Suggestopedagogic Training." *The Journal of the Society for Accelerated Learning and Teaching.* 16(2), 101116.

Mager, R. F., & McCann, J. (1963). *Learner-Controlled Instruction.* Palo Alto, CA: Varian Press.

McKay, M., Davis, M., & Fanning, P. (1983). *Messages: The communication book.* Oakland, CA: New Harbinger Publications.

McKay, M., Fanning, P., Paleg, K. & Landis (1996). *When Anger Hurts Your Kids: A parent's guide.* Oakland, CA: New Harbinger Publications, Inc.

Middleton-Moz, J. (1999). *Boiling Point: The high cost of unhealthy anger to individuals and society.* Deerfield Beach, FL: Health Communications, Inc.

Millman, D. (1993). *The Life You Were Born to Live: A guide to finding your life purpose.* Tiburon, CA: H. J. Kramer, Inc.

Mills, R.C. (1987, April). "Relationship between school motivational climate, teacher attitudes, student mental health, school failure and health damaging behavior." (Paper at Annual Conference of the American Educational Research Association). Washington, D.C.

Morris, L. R. & Schultz, L. (1989). *Creative Play Activities for Children With Disabilities: A resource book for teachers and parents.* Champaign, Il: HumanKinetic Books.

Nadel, L. (1990) "Varieties of Spatial Cognition, Psychobiological Considerations." *Annal of the New York Academy of Sciences*, 608, 613-626.

Newby, T. J. (1991). "Classroom Motivation: Strategies of first year teachers." Journal of Educational Psychology, 83,165-200.

Niehoff, D. (1999). *The Biology of Violence: How understanding the brain, behavior, and environment can break the viscious cycle of aggression.* New York, NY: The Free Press.

Nowicki, S., & Duke, M. (1989). "A measure of nonverbal processing ability in children between the ages of 6 and 10." Paper presented at the American Psychological Society meeting.

O'Keefe, J., & Nadel, L. (1978). *The Hippocampus as a Cognitive Map.* Oxford, England; Clarendon press.

Olweus, D. (1991). "Bully/Victim problems among schoolchildren: Basic facts and effects of a school based intervention program." In D.J. Pepler & K. H. Rubin (Eds.), *The Development and Treatment of Childhood Aggression* (pp. 107-132). Cambridge, MA: Cambridge University Press.

Ornstein, R. (1991). *The Evolution of Consciousness.* New York, NY: Simon & Schuster.

Parens, H. (1987). *Aggression In Our Children: Coping with it constructively.* North Vale, NJ: Jason Aronson, Inc.

Perry, B. D. (1996). *Maltreated Children: Experience, Brain Development, and the Next Generation.* New York, NY: Norton.

Pert, C. (1997). *Molecules of Emotion.* New York, N. Y.: Simon & Schuster.

Piaget, J. (1963). *The Psychology of Intelligence.* Patterson, NJ: Little-Adams.

Pittman, T.S., Emery, J., & Boggiano, A.K. (Psychology General, 111, 23-59.1982). "Intrinsic and extrinsic motivational orientations: Reward-induced changes in preference for complexity." *Journal of Personality and Social Psychology*, 42, 789-797.

Polter-Efron, R., & Potter-Efron, P. (1995). *Letting Go of Anger: The 10 most common anger styles and what to do about them*. Oakland, CA: New Harbinger Publications, Inc.

Rogers, C.R. and Frieberg, H.J. (1994). *Freedom to Learn*, 3rd ed., Columbus: Merrill

Ruden, R.A. (1997). *The Craving Brain: The biobalance approach to controlling addictions*. New York, NY: HarperCollins Publishers.

Ryan, R,.M. & Stiller, J. (1991). "The social contest of internalization: Parent and teacher influences on autonomy, motivation, and learning." *Advances in Motivation and Achievement,* 7, 115-149.

Schwartz, B. (1982). "Reinforcement-induced behavioral stereotype: How not to teach people to discover rules." *Journal of Experimental Psychology*.

Seligman, M.E.P. (1987). "Learned Helplessness in Children: A Longitudinal Study of Depression, Achievement and Explanatory Style." *Journal of Personality and Social Psychology* 51, 435-42.

Selman, R. L. (1980). *The Growth of Interpersonal Understanding*. New York: Academic Press.

Snyder, C.R. (1991). "The Will and the Ways: development and Validation of an Individual - Differences Measure Hope." *Journal of Personality and Social Psychology* 60, 4, 597.

Sullivan, E. (1991) "The Study of Mood Transfer." *Personality and social Psychology Bulletin*.

Sylwester, R. (1995). *A Celebration of Neurons: An Educator's Guide to the Human Brain*. Alexandria, VA: ASCD.

Turecki, S. With Tonner, L. (1985). *The Difficult Child*. New York, NY: Bantam Books.

Turiel, E. (1983). *The Development of Social Knowledge: Morality and convention. Cambridge*: Cambridge University Press.

Walker, H.W., Colvin, G., & Ramsey, E. (1995). *Antisocial Behavior in Public School: Strategies and best practices*. Pacific Grove, CA: Brooks/Cole Publishing Company.

Walker, H.M. (1993). "Anti-social Behavior in School." *Journal of Emotional and Behavioral Problems,* 2(1), 20-24.

Wang, M.C., Haertel, G.D. and Walberg, H.J. (1997). 'Learning Influences' in Walberg, H.J. and Haertel, G.D. (eds) *Psychology and Educational Practice,* McCuthan: Berkley, CA, pp. 199-211

Wolfgang, C.H., & Wolfgang, M.E. (1995). *The Three Faces of Discipline for Early Childhood: Empowering teachers and students*. Boston, MA: Allyn and Bacon.

Suppliers

Able Data
National Rehabilitation Information Center
8455 Colesville Rd., Suite 935
Silver Springs, MD 20910
(301) 588-9284
> A computerized data base of commercially available rehabilitation aids, toys and equipment.

Toys for Special Children
c/o Stephen Kanor, Medical Engineer
Hastings-on-Hudson, NY 10706
> A selection of battery-operated toys, specially engineered for children with severe motor impairments.

Other works by Dr. Becky Bailey

Books Published by Loving Guidance, Inc.
- ❤ *There's Gotta Be A Better Way: Discipline That Works!*
- ❤ *Shubert's BIG Voice*
- ❤ *Shubert's Helpful Day*

Books Published by HarperCollins
- ❤ *Easy to Love, Difficult to Discipline: The Seven Basic Skills for Turning Conflict into Cooperation (To order call 1-800-331-3761)*
- ❤ *I Love You Rituals: (A Parent's Guide Children's Media Award Winner!)*

Audio Cassettes and CD's
- ❤ *Songs for I Love You Rituals (Cassette and CD available)*
- ❤ *Loving Guidance: Setting Limits Without Guilt*
- ❤ *Brain SMART: What you can do to boost children's brain power*
- ❤ *Transforming Aggression into Healthy Self-Esteem (Parent's Guide Children's Media Award Winner!)*
- ❤ *Conflict Resolution (Parent's Choice Award Winner!)*
- ❤ *10 Principles of Positive Discipline (Parent's Choice & Parent's Guide Children's Media Awards Winner!)*
- ❤ *Preventing Power Struggles (Parent's Choice & Parent's Guide Children's Media Awards Winner!)*
- ❤ *A Great Attitude*
- ❤ *It Starts in the Heart*

Instructional Materials
- ❤ *Picture Rule Cards*
- ❤ *Routine & Responsibility Cards*

Video
- ❤ *Touch a Heart, Teach a Mind: The Brain Smart Way to Build Bonds*
- ❤ *Creating the School Family: Building Social Foundations for Academic Success*

Ordering Information
To order, call **1-800-842-2846**

Or order online from our website at: **http://www.beckybailey.com**

Dr. Bailey is available for workshops and keynote addresses.
Her dynamic presentation style lightens and enlightens audiences.
Loving Guidance, Inc. also offers Loving Guidance Associates,
who are available for workshops, keynotes and presentations in your area.
To schedule a presentor for your next event, call **1-800-842-2846**.